The Elderly
Must Endure

The **ISEAS – Yusof Ishak Institute** (formerly Institute of Southeast Asian Studies) is an autonomous organization established in 1968. It is a regional centre dedicated to the study of socio-political, security, and economic trends and developments in Southeast Asia and its wider geostrategic and economic environment. The Institute's research programmes are grouped under Regional Economic Studies (RES), Regional Strategic and Political Studies (RSPS), and Regional Social and Cultural Studies (RSCS). The Institute is also home to the ASEAN Studies Centre (ASC), the Nalanda-Sriwijaya Centre (NSC) and the Singapore APEC Study Centre.

ISEAS Publishing, an established academic press, has issued more than 2,000 books and journals. It is the largest scholarly publisher of research about Southeast Asia from within the region. ISEAS Publishing works with many other academic and trade publishers and distributors to disseminate important research and analyses from and about Southeast Asia to the rest of the world.

The Elderly Must Endure

Ageing in the
Minangkabau Community
in Modern Indonesia

———

**Rebecca Fanany
and Ismet Fanany**

ISEAS YUSOF ISHAK
INSTITUTE

First published in Singapore in 2019 by
ISEAS Publishing
30 Heng Mui Keng Terrace
Singapore 119614
E-mail: publish@iseas.edu.sg
Website: <http://bookshop.iseas.edu.sg>

The responsibility for facts and opinions in this publication rests exclusively with the authors and their interpretations do not necessarily reflect the views or the policy of the publisher or its supporters.

ISEAS Library Cataloguing-in-Publication Data

Fanany, Rebecca.
The Elderly Must Endure : Ageing in the Minangkabau Community in Modern Indonesia / Rebecca Fanany and Ismet Fanany.
1. Ageing—Indonesia—Sumatera Barat.
2. Ageing—Indonesia.
3. Older people—Indonesia—Sumatera Barat—Social conditions.
4. Older people—Indonesia—Social conditions.
5. Minangkabau (Indonesian people)—Social life and customs.
I. Fanany, Ismet, 1952–
II. Title: Ageing in the Minangkabau Community in Modern Indonesia
HQ1064 I5F19   2019

ISBN 978-981-4818-46-9 (soft cover)
ISBN 978-981-4818-47-6 (ebook, PDF)

Cover photo: Market scene at Pasar Raya, Padang, February 2018.
Photo by Ismet Fanany.

Typeset by Superskill Graphics Pte Ltd
Printed in Singapore by Mainland Press Pte Ltd

Contents

ACKNOWLEDGEMENTS

The authors wish to acknowledge the contributions and support of everyone who took part in the research that allowed this book to be written. We specifically wish to mention the directors and staff of PSTW Sabai nan Aluih in Sicincin, West Sumatra, and PSTW Kasih Sayang Ibu in Batusangkar, West Sumatra, who generously allowed us to visit their institutions and discussed the context in which they work. They also facilitated us in talking with residents and understanding their situations.

Of course, we wish to thank the large number of Minangkabau of all ages who talked to us about their experiences and shared with us the details of their lives and the lives of their older relatives. In particular, we are grateful to the members of the Valley family who are profiled in this book as well as the younger individuals, who discussed their views and told us about their recollections and hopes for the future. Without their contributions, this book would be a much lesser work. While their names and the name of their village have been changed to protect their privacy, the details of their lives emphasize the themes of this book and bring them to life.

Finally, we wish to acknowledge the support of the School of Humanities and Social Sciences at Deakin University in Melbourne for the continued support required to complete the research contained in this book, as well as the Center for Research on Healthy Aging at Universitas Baiturrahmah in Padang, West Sumatra, which is working to understand the nature of Indonesia's older population and contribute to making their lives healthier and more satisfying.

Rebecca Fanany
Ismet Fanany

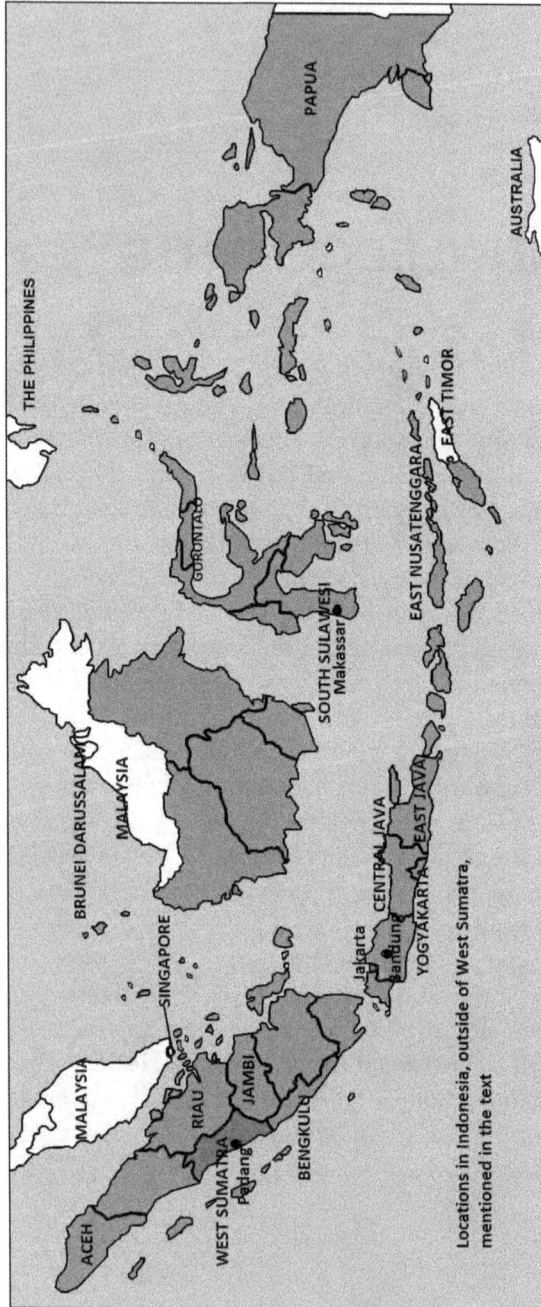

Map of Indonesia

Locations in Indonesia, outside of West Sumatra, mentioned in the text

Map of West Sumatra

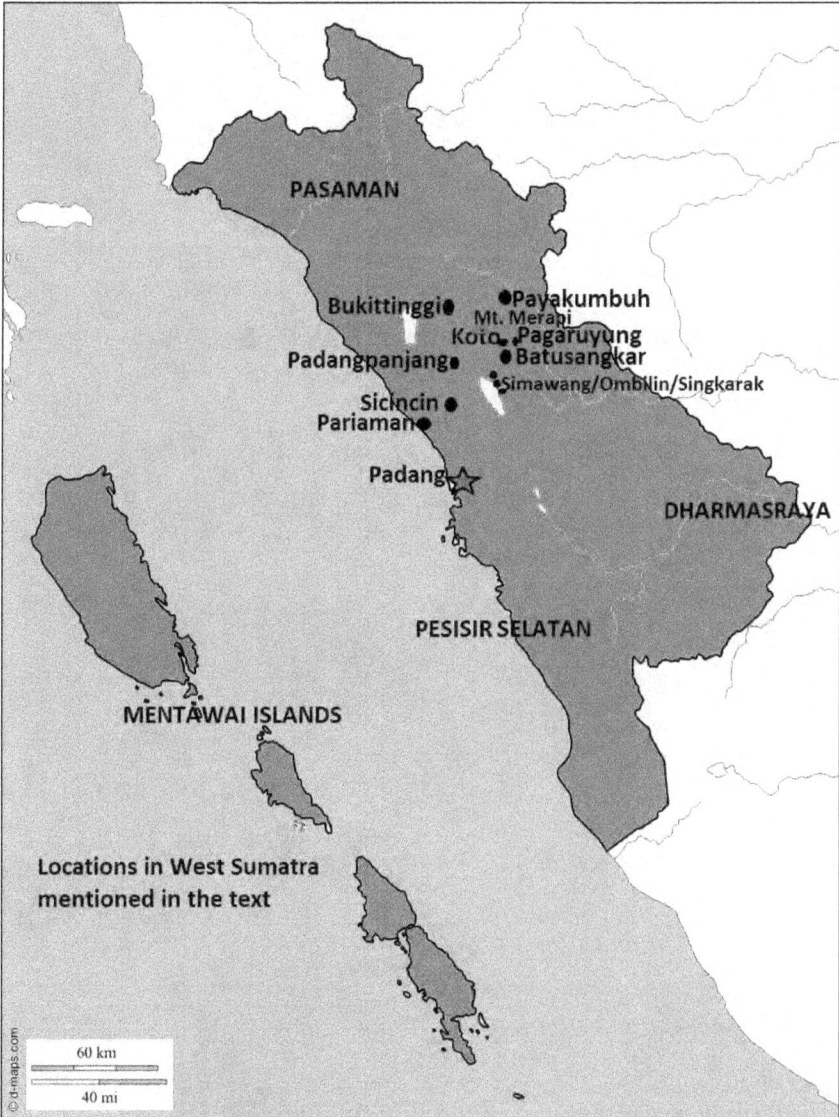

Locations in West Sumatra mentioned in the text

Map of the Village of Koto

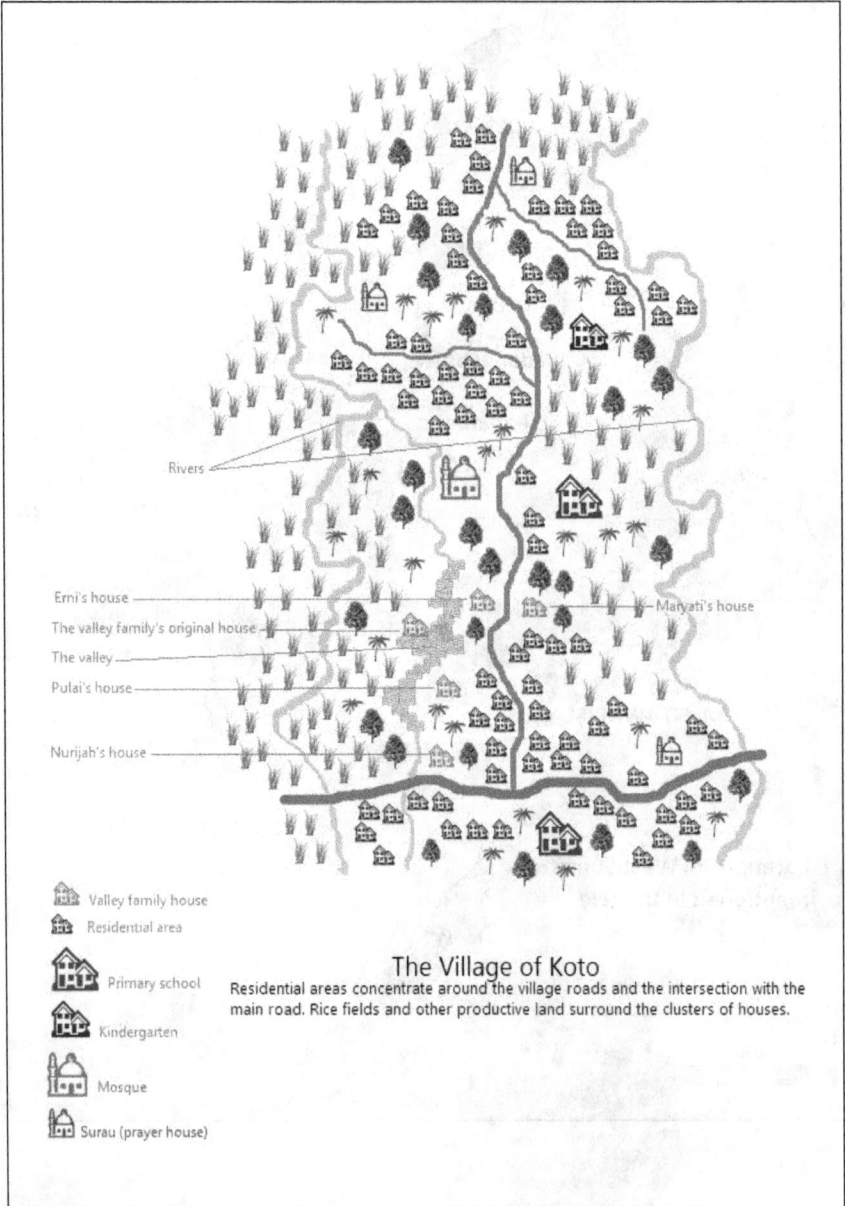

Rivers

Erni's house

The valley family's original house

The valley

Pulai's house

Nurijah's house

Maryati's house

Valley family house

Residential area

Primary school

Kindergarten

Mosque

Surau (prayer house)

The Village of Koto
Residential areas concentrate around the village roads and the intersection with the main road. Rice fields and other productive land surround the clusters of houses.

Aminah's Family Tree

Members of Aminah's family who appear in the text and their spouses where relevant

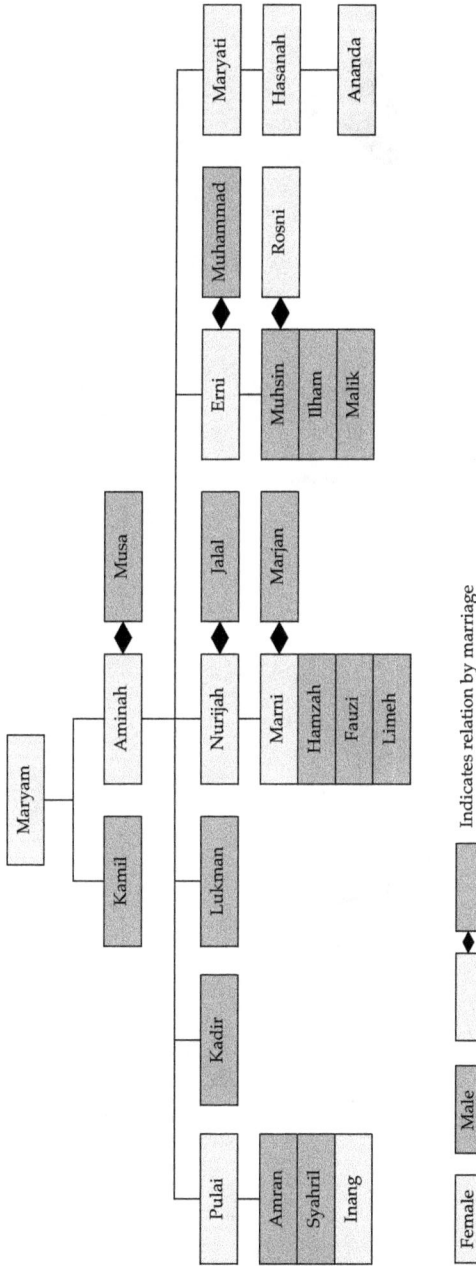

Female [ ]   Male [ ]   ◆ Indicates relation by marriage

It should be noted that children of the female members of the family will also be part of Aminah's line. Children of the male members, however, will be members of their mother's family.

1

Introduction

THE VALLEY FAMILY

On a hot night in Jakarta, a dozen members of a large extended family met at a restaurant in one of the many residential neighbourhoods on the outskirts of the city. They thought of themselves as the Valley family because their traditional, multifamily home had been located in a hollow in their native village of Koto in West Sumatra. Some of the diners were siblings; others were first cousins. A few of their children, who had been born in Jakarta and were married themselves, also attended. Some of their spouses came from other parts of Indonesia and sat a short distance away from the older family members. Except for these younger relations by marriage, everyone present was a descendant of a single Minangkabau woman, the grandmother of the older diners named Aminah, who represented the founding generation of this matrilineal family. As it happened, she had had no living sisters so the family had contracted at her generation but had expanded again as her four daughters and two sons married and had children. This generation was the parents of the older people present, and those who remained alive on this date were around ninety years of age. Most of the diners were over sixty, the age at which Indonesia labels a person "elderly" (*lansia*), but a few were in their fifties and were approaching the time of life when they would have to make decisions about their future. Many of those present were already retired; all were middle class; and most had had a college education. As they ate, conversation turned towards a usual topic that invariably came up any time any of them met — their life in the village before they moved away. For most of them, that moment had occurred when they were in their early twenties, had finished their education, and decided to move to Jakarta to seek better opportunities than were available locally in West Sumatra, their province of origin. One of them had left the village much longer ago and, through a combination of circumstances, had grown up in the city of Makassar, in South Sulawesi, a province on another island in the eastern part of Indonesia. Eventually, everyone present married and had children. A number of them had married other Minangkabau like themselves, even if they had met their partner in Jakarta, while several had married people from other Indonesian ethnic origins. The subsequent generation, their children, were now adults and were beginning to have children of their own. These family members had been born in the *rantau*, the Minangkabau term for regions outside the traditional settlement areas of the ethnic group, and had grown up under very different circumstances from their parents and grandparents. The conversation on this night took place in Minang, the first language of this and previous generations of the family. The younger Jakarta generation did not understand much of what was discussed and spent the time talking to each other in Indonesian and dealing with their young children. All of the older people spoke Indonesian well, some extremely so, to the point where their Minang was no longer fluent, but talking to each other about the family and things they had done in their youth required that they speak in the language of the village. The use of Minang, and the specific dialect of their region, indicated their ethnic identity generally, but, to other Minangkabau, placed them as coming from the *darek*, the highland region at the centre of West Sumatra that was the original home of their ethnic group. By the end of the evening, the stories and reminisces had demonstrated that the diners shared a very strong cultural memory that was likely at odds with what they had experienced first-hand and certainly very different from their daily life in the years since they had left the village. Now, as older people living in modern-day Indonesia, they were experiencing a life that would have been unimaginable to them as young people. What they saw of their older relatives' experiences was completely unlike their own situation and was, in fact, almost unrecognizable compared to what they might have expected if they had ever thought consciously about it.

OLDER INDONESIANS TODAY

The people having dinner and talking about their family and childhood on that night in Jakarta are part of a growing population of older people in Indonesia. Like many countries around the world, the Indonesian population is ageing. Like other developing countries, several decades ago life expectancy in Indonesia was low, balancing a high birth rate. However, considerable improvements in the standard of living and health status of the population have meant that people are now living longer. The World Health Organization (WHO) (2014) reports that average life expectancy for Indonesians of both sexes has reached seventy-one years. More notably, individuals currently aged sixty can expect to live on average eighteen more years. These figures have increased from sixty-two years of average life expectancy and an additional expected sixteen years of life at age sixty as recently as 1990 (WHO 2013). In 1950, shortly after Indonesia achieved independence from the Netherlands, life expectancy for both sexes was only 37.5 years (UN 2011).

The government of Indonesia calculates that, by 2020, 11.34 per cent of its population will be elderly. Indonesia is currently the fourth largest country in the world in terms of population, and this proportion will amount to some 29 million people. In 2000, there were about 14.4 million elderly Indonesians who made up 7.18 per cent of the population (Kementerian Kesehatan 2013). The rapid increase in this demographic group led the Indonesian government to form a national commission in 2004 to address the needs of the older population, which was a direct result of this observed population change. Historically, many of Indonesia's public health initiatives centred on maternal and child health, which reflects another pressing issue, namely high birth rates associated with continuing population increase (WHO 2008).

For this reason, Indonesia has had coordinated family planning activities in place since the 1950s. In 1969, the agency responsible for population management, Badan Koordinasi Keluarga Berencana Nasional (BKKBN, or National Coordinating Family Planning Agency) was founded with the responsibility for providing family planning information and support across the country (BKKBN 2011b). During the thirty-two-year

New Order government of President Soeharto, which ended with his resignation in 1998, BKKBN ran a series of campaigns through their regional branches involving the use of health promotion, clinical support, and social marketing to encourage Indonesians to have smaller families, ideally with no more than two children per couple. Indonesia's family planning activities during this period were very successful and were recognized with a United Nations Family Planning Award in 1989 (United National Population Fund 2014). In 2001, Indonesia implemented a system of regional autonomy that gave an unprecedented level of authority and responsibility to municipal and regency level governments. At this time, some of BKKBN's functions were devolved to these lower levels of government. These changes took effect in 2003, and, in 2009, BKKBN was given a new focus that expanded its primary function of supporting family planning. Its name was changed by national law to become Badan Kependudukan dan Keluarga Berencana Nasional (National Agency for Population and Family Planning), retaining its original acronym (Republic of Indonesia 2009). BKKBN's current vision is called "Balanced Population Growth 2015" (Penduduk Tumbuh Seimbang 2015) (BKKBN 2011). This reflects Indonesia's continuing concern with its fertility rate which is now 2.4 per woman of childbearing age (World Bank 2018), but also with its expanding population of older people who require facilities, health care, and social support at levels the nation has not experienced in the past.

For Indonesia, the rapid increase in the size of its elderly population was unanticipated. As a developing country, the government had tended to focus on issues that had historically been significant and that are associated with the achievement of its Millennium Development Goals (MDG). While health concerns such as infectious disease and immunization, maternal and neonatal health, nutrition (especially for children under the age of five), and accidents remain significant, Indonesia is now at a tipping point and is experiencing a risk transition from its past status to a situation that parallels that already being experienced in many countries of the world, namely a growing burden of chronic disease, much of which can be associated with the ageing population (WHO 2009). In 2010, the proportion of the population that was over sixty was the same as that aged under five (BPS 2011), suggesting that Indonesia's transition to a situation more closely replicating that now observed in the West is well underway.

In addition to being much larger than in the past, the Indonesian population aged over sixty is not evenly distributed around the country.

In rural areas, approximately 9.19 per cent of the population is considered elderly (aged over sixty). In cities, the comparable figure is 7.49 per cent (Adioetomo and Mujahid 2014). The age dependency ratio for older people has reached 13.3, meaning that for every 100 people of working age there are about thirteen older adults. This figure represents an average of rural and urban areas. When these are considered separately, the difference in population make-up is again visible with the ratio being 15.2 elderly for every 100 people of working age in rural areas and 11.5 elderly for every 100 people of working age in cities (Adioetomo and Mujahid 2014). The proportion of the population that is over sixty differs from region to region. There are more older people proportionally in East and Central Java, especially in the Yogyakarta region, than elsewhere in the country and fewest in Papua and the islands of the Province of Riau (BPS 2009). As might be expected based on norms around the world, there are more older women than older men in every part of Indonesia, particularly as age increases. However, there are significant differences in the family status of older men and older women; 59.61 per cent of elderly women nationwide are widowed or divorced, but 82.78 per cent of elderly men are married (Kementerian Kesehatan 2017). This social pattern is important in understanding the experience of older people in Indonesia and likely reflects prevailing norms by which older women who are widowed or divorced tend not to remarry while older men in the same situation generally do, often to a woman who is somewhat younger.

Increasing age is generally associated with increasing levels of illness and poor health. While there are older people everywhere who have no health complaints, on average this demographic group accounts for a great deal of disease and typically makes heavier use of health care services than younger people. For many years, the health of the elderly was not a major priority of the Indonesian government because of the large proportion of the population composed of children and young adults. However, at the present time, the health of the elderly is a growing concern. The morbidity rate for people over sixty is about 30 per cent, meaning that, for every 100 elderly, thirty of them have some kind of ongoing health problem. In rural areas, the rate is 32.96 per cent; in urban areas, this rate is slightly lower at 27.20 per cent (BPS 2014). This differential is likely associated with income, a factor that is closely related to education and has the potential to affect health in a variety of ways (Berkman and Kawachi 2000). The level of poor health varies considerably across the country, ranging from a low of 23.67 per cent for this age group in Jakarta, the capital, to a high of 48.99 per cent in East Nusa Tenggara. Other areas with high levels of poor health among older people include Aceh (46.18 per cent) and Gorontalo (42.78 per cent), while comparatively better health is reported for the elderly in Yogyakarta (24.71 per cent) and Central Java (26.73 per cent) (BPS 2014). These differences are likely associated with level of development in the region in question as well as personal factors associated with individual older people (income, education, occupation, and so forth). However, it is also possible that cultural factors play a role; the people of Aceh are part of the larger Malay world, the people of Central Java and Yogyakarta are Javanese, while Gorontalo is a province located in the northern part of the island of Sulawesi whose inhabitants are also of Malay origin. While a majority of Indonesia's elderly report using modern health care facilities to address their health needs (60.47 per cent), a significant proportion use a combination of modern and traditional methods (27.63 per cent). In West Sumatra, the region occupied by the Minangkabau who are the subject of this book, 45.02 per cent of the elderly population, the highest in the country, use only traditional health care, which includes *dukun*, traditional practitioners who use a combination of home-made medicines and treatments and magic (BPS 2009). This probably reflects attitude more than opportunity as West Sumatra is one of the better developed provinces, and the majority of the population has access to modern health care facilities (Kementerian Kesehatan 2012).

Attitudes about health, health care, and ageing in general among the elderly are likely related to level of education and ability to access information in Indonesian. This is an important aspect of Indonesian society. For the vast majority of Indonesians, one of the nation's more than 700 local languages is their first language. This is especially true for individuals now aged over sixty years old, although most Indonesian young people also speak a local language first and begin to learn Indonesian formally when they enter school. Today, most have considerable exposure to the national language through television and advertising before they reach school age, but there remains a social gradient with respect to language. Because all public institutions, education, the media, government, and business use Indonesian, a person who cannot master the language generally cannot work outside the traditional environment where local languages are used. There are many people, especially among the large populations of rural to urban migrants in Jakarta and other large cities, who speak a highly colloquial, informal dialect of Indonesian in addition to their local language but cannot interact in the formal environment that uses standard Indonesian (Fanany 2012). Health information and health care services are part of the Indonesian language context and, while it is possible to find practitioners who speak particular local languages especially in the regions where the language is used, this social context is an Indonesian one. For this reason, use of modern health care facilities is associated with ability and ease of using Indonesian, which in turn is associated with higher levels of formal education and exposure to the contexts where the language is used.

In West Sumatra, only 7.88 per cent of the elderly have never attended school and only 45.06 per cent are illiterate (BPS 2014b). These figures are among the lowest in Indonesia. Nonetheless, West Sumatra is one of Indonesia's more homogeneous regions, occupied almost entirely by members of the Minangkabau ethnic group. For this reason, there is little reason for members of the community of any age to use Indonesian outside of the formal institutions, such as school or government. Many of the elderly in this region have little cause to use Indonesian, except perhaps to read the newspapers or watch television, and in practice, may not be comfortable using Indonesian in their day-to-day affairs. Observation suggests that many of today's elderly who live in West Sumatra understand Indonesian but do not speak it well or at all. They are often very unfamiliar with the highly colloquial Jakarta dialects favoured by many young people and used heavily in the entertainment media. For Minangkabau who live in other parts of Indonesia, Indonesian is a fully functional second language, and many speak it with native fluency. However, those that were born in West Sumatra retain an attachment to their first language which is an integral part of their identity. The prominence of the Minang language for all members of the ethnic group is a reflection of their environment and also their heritage and traditions as well as the matrilineal nature of Minangkabau society.

THE MINANGKABAU SOCIAL SYSTEM

Minangkabau society has a matrilineal social structure that is unique in Indonesia. Currently this group is the largest matrilineal society in the world (Cribb and Kahin 2004). It is thought that this type of social structure is very old and represents an ancient form of social organization (Holden, Sear and Mace 2003). For the Minangkabau, descent follows the maternal line, with children remaining members of their mother's family for life. Communal property, which may include a traditional house, rice fields, fish ponds, and other productive assets in the rural environment, belong to the extended family and are available for use by all of its members. The way in which these assets will be used is determined by a process of consensus within the family led by its senior women who are acknowledged to be the heads of the family. Personal income, such as from a paying job, is not part of these communal assets and can be used at the discretion of the earner. A leadership role comparable to that of older women exists traditionally for the male members of the family. The maternal uncle (the brother of one's mother) holds the status of *mamak* and has a special responsibility towards the children of his sisters. His own children are part of their mother's (his wife's) family, and the responsibilities of a father in traditional Minangkabau society tend to be less significant than those of the maternal uncle.

Extended families in a given location, as defined by descent from a common female ancestor, tend to be related through marriage or descent at some distant point in the past. In many cases, these past connections are obscure and have never been recorded, except in the understanding of members of the generation in question. Social relationships and obligations are very important, and people do tend to respect and understand the network of connections relevant to their own age and status. Traditionally, these networks were reinforced from generation to generation by specific types of desirable marriage. One of the most prominent of these was a match between the son or daughter of the *mamak* to the daughter or son of one of his sisters. The individuals involved belong to different families (making the marriage acceptable by traditional social rules) but has the advantage of keeping wealth within the extended family and concentrating the power that such wealth brings in the traditional context. There is some evidence to suggest that marriages of this kind are considerably less frequent than in the past because young people have wider circles of acquaintances and often meet people they wish to marry in the mixed community of universities or in other parts of Indonesia where they live and work. The problems associated with this type of cousin marriage were a common theme of early Indonesian literature by Minangkabau writers.

Marantau, a period of temporary migration, was an important feature of Minangkabau society in the past. Young men would typically leave their village of origin to live and work in another location for a period of time before, ideally, returning home to settle. In practice, however, many of these migrants stayed permanently in other parts of Indonesia and the larger Malay world, forming large Minangkabau communities in the neighbouring provinces of Riau, Jambi, and Bengkulu; in Jakarta and other large Indonesian cities; in Negeri Sembilan in Malaysia; and very recently in Sydney and Melbourne, Australia. The pull of the *rantau*, the destination of such migrants, has always been very strong, and the members of the Valley family described above are part of the large population of Minangkabau who choose to live outside of West Sumatra. Opportunities have historically been limited in West Sumatra, and life within the extended family can be restrictive.

There is evidence that the practice of *marantau* is very old. It is embodied in traditional expressions and proverbs and also defines the spatial divisions of the Minangkabau environment. Legend holds that all Minangkabau originated in the central highland regions of the area that is now West Sumatra. This occurred in the distant past, and, in theory, all Minangkabau can trace their origins to one of three original areas, referred to as *luhak*, that now make up the modern regions of Tanah Datar, Agam, and Lima Puluh Kota. There is some evidence that Tanah Datar is the oldest of the three because its traditional epithet is *luhak nan tuo*, the old or original region. By contrast, Agam is called *luhak nan tanang*, the tranquil region, and Lima Puluh Kota is *luhak nan bonsu*, the youngest region. Historically, every place else, including other areas that are now part of West Sumatra and are inhabited almost entirely by Minangkabau, was considered the *rantau*. This includes Padang, the provincial capital of West Sumatra, the coastal regions of Pasaman, Pariaman and Pesisir Selatan and other parts of the province. In most people's current conceptualization of place, however, the *rantau* is every place outside of West Sumatra and, at a more personal level, any place that is not the location a person was raised. In modern times, both men and women go to the *rantau*, typically to pursue educational opportunities or to work, and the idea that they should return to live in their place of origin seems to have faded in importance. In fact, the *rantau* communities of Minangkabau in Jakarta and elsewhere are permanently established, and most people in West Sumatra have relatives living outside the province in various parts of Indonesia.

While some observers believe it is in decline, the traditional matrilineal social structure is central to understanding the experience of the

Minangkabau elderly. In the past, most Minangkabau spent their whole lives in the village where they were born or in a nearby location. At least some of the people who went to the *rantau* did return and settled near their extended family. A majority of people lived in multifamily homes that were occupied by a female ancestor, her daughters, and their children. This remained common until fairly recently, and the older members of the family described above grew up in this kind of environment. In the past, Minangkabau society, especially in the villages, was segregated by gender. Women and their daughters, having the right to use and manage family property, lived permanently in the family home. Men, as permanent members of their mother's family, would spend the nights at their wife's house but might work on their mother's family land during the day and retained rights and responsibilities towards their own extended family, as *mamak* or in other ways. While girls learned from a young age how to manage rice fields and other productive assets, boys would be socialized into the world of men, which existed largely outside of the family home. An important institution in this context was the *surau*, or prayer house, where boys and teenagers would spend the nights with other boys and unmarried men. The *surau* were important centres for studying religion, martial arts, and other aspects of the traditional context that applied to men. Despite the apparent contradiction with the matrilineal social structure, the Minangkabau are Muslim, and adherence to Islam is considered a central aspect of membership in the ethnic group. This is comparable to all the ethnic groups that make up the Malay world (Lian 2001), and religious principles that come from Islam are important in forming the value system of the region.

Under this traditional system, the elderly had a permanent place within the extended family, at least in theory. Elderly women would live out their lives in the village of their birth and often in the same house their mother and grandmother had lived in. Having been trained from an early age in the agricultural work that provided a livelihood for everyone in the family and village and understanding the intricacies of managing family property, they would gradually progress to a position of authority in the extended family, although their exact role would be determined by the number of women of a comparable age and the assets of their family. As they aged, if they became ill or required support, it would be provided by their own daughters and granddaughters, as their position within the household was assured and was held for life. For men, the situation was somewhat different. In Minangkabau communities, almost everyone marries. For men, this meant a move from the household of their mother to their wife's home. The son-in-law was traditionally viewed as an honoured guest in his wife's house referred to as *urang sumando*. He was entitled to eat and sleep in his wife's family home but typically maintained extensive interaction with his own family and especially his sisters and their children. If he died before his wife while he was living in her house, his body would be returned to his family to be buried among their members. A man who outlived his wife, however, had no more claim on his wife's family and was expected to return to his own family. In practice, this usually consisted of his sisters who had a traditional obligation to take him in. His position with his mother's family was assured, and men in these circumstances were entitled to return to the household in which they had grown up. If the man had children, they would live with their mother's family where their father could visit them but not stay overnight. They would also be allowed to visit him and possibly spend the night if the families agreed. The same situation would follow divorce for both men and women. For women, there would be little impact on their circumstances as the divorced husband would have to return to his family. For men, divorce would mean a move back to his mother's home and life among his sisters and their families. Children would live with their mother and her family, and the arrangements for a divorced man to see his children might be more complicated than in the case of a widower.

Minangkabau are proud of the fact that their traditional system provides for all its members and especially prevents the possibility of women and children suffering deprivation as a consequence of death, divorce, or abandonment by their husband and father. In practice, however, there were many things that could go wrong with the traditional system. A family might have no daughters. Its assets might be inadequate to support its members, perhaps because there were a large number of female members. It might not be possible to reach consensus about how to use the assets it did have. Quarrels and feuds might develop between members. All of these eventualities were common in the traditional context and remain common today. In the modern context, however, many individuals have additional resources that were not common in the past. Even in rural areas, many people have salaried jobs in the modern Indonesian system that supplement income from family property. Schools, health centres, and village level administrative offices extend even to the most rural areas. A large number of people are employed in stores, restaurants, and banks in large and small towns. A significant number of people have their own businesses, some of which are very small and amount to little more than selling groceries from their house. Nonetheless, increasing levels of education and an extension of opportunities that are part of the modern Indonesian experience along with rising income have meant that fewer people live in multigeneration homes with members of the matrilineal family, and the nuclear family setting that is the norm in modern Indonesia is dominant, especially in Padang and the larger towns. Even in the villages, many people have built their own single-family dwellings on land belonging to their extended family such that they are living separately but adjacent to other members of the group. This allows some of the conflict inherent in the traditional system to be avoided and has resulted in a more important role for men in relation to their own children, as opposed to the children of their sisters.

This change has been very rapid. Indonesia gained independence in 1945 and immediately began to modernize under its first president, Soekarno, who held power from 1945 to 1965. Development was the primary aim of President Soeharto who governed Indonesia from 1965 to 1998. It was during this period, referred to as the New Order, that many parts of West Sumatra, and the rest of Indonesia, got electricity for the first time. A large number of schools, health care centres, and infrastructure were constructed as well that brought the institutions of the modern Indonesian nation into remote areas. Social change accelerated following the end of the New Order and gained enormous momentum in 2001 with the establishment of regional autonomy that gave unprecedented levels of authority to the local governments of regions and municipalities. The change over the past six decades has proven to be a challenge for the matrilineal system of the Minangkabau.

Nonetheless, values and traditions tend to change more slowly than behaviour and social practices (Inglehart and Baker 2000). The basic principles that governed the matrilineal system in the past remain an important force in forming the perceptions and attitudes of the Minangkabau. The Minangkabau themselves, and also other Indonesians who view their society from a distance, feel that *adaik* (*adat* in Indonesian), traditional law and customs, continues to play an important part in their society, their identity, and that they are still bound by many of their traditional values and considerations.

MINANGKABAU VALUES AND OLDER ADULTS

The values and perceptions of a given society are difficult to discern, but one method for identifying the kinds of ideas that are traditionally considered important by a majority of the members of a community is through the study of proverbs and other customary expressions that are metaphorical and fixed in form. It is important to note that these expressions typically reflect an ideal, the way things should be, rather than the way they are. In other words, proverbs and other similar utterances offer insight into a specific reality that exists to guide the actions and thinking of residents of the real world (see Fanany and Fanany 2003, for a discussion of proverbial reality in Minangkabau). The values of the proverbial world may be more aspirational than actual but they do reflect the concepts that are viewed as sufficiently important as to have been retained over a long period of time. As a result, proverbs often make use of archaic language and use surface imagery that derives from a long-gone traditional environment. Their underlying meaning, or the way in which native speakers of the language in which they occur understand them, though, reflects ideas that are still seen as having value for current society. Throughout the chapters of this book, proverbs will occasionally be used to illustrate traditional thinking in the Minangkabau community.

In order to better understand the traditional position of the elderly in Minangkabau society, or at least the position they might ideally enjoy, it is worth considering some of the large number of proverbs and proverbial expressions that deal with older members of society. These items exist in the Minang language, are well known to current members of the community, and are typically highly metaphorical. They represent a subsection of all such expressions that deal with virtually every aspect of Minangkabau life and human experience. There are two aspects of such expressions that can provide insight into the way a modern society views an issue of interest, in this case the position of the elderly. The first of these is the surface meaning of the proverb or proverbial expression. The surface meaning relates to the words that make up the utterance and the image they convey. The second aspect is the underlying meaning, or metaphorical intent, of the item. Proverbs and similar expressions are not meant to be understood literally. Their appropriate context of use and the situations which they are understood by users to apply to are part of the language and culture of the speakers of the language; it is this underlying meaning that makes proverbs and proverbial expressions seem out-of-context in relation to the discourse in which they occur if only their surface structure is considered.

A number of proverbs and proverbial phrases in Minang relate to the physical decline that often accompanies increasing age. These changes include decreased sensory ability, difficulties in balance and movement, loss of teeth, greying hair, and other physical and mental attributes associated with older age. Some examples include:

> *Urang tuo indak amuah duo kali kailangan tungkek.*
> An old person won't lose his stick twice.

While this proverb is used to mean "Once burned, twice shy", its surface image is of an elderly person who needs to use a cane for support.

> *Rawan murah, garaman abih.*
> Cartilage is cheap, but your molars are gone.

This proverb suggests that opportunity comes at times when it is not possible to take advantage of it and reflects a common circumstance that is often observed in life. The surface image, however, refers to an old person who has lost enough teeth to make it difficult to chew.

Other expressions refer to the nature of personality in old age, specifically to the fact that many older people believe that their ways and opinions are correct and appropriate, regardless of evidence to the contrary.

> *Dek ketek taanjo-anjo, lah gadang tabao-bao, lah tuo tarubah tido, sampai mati jadi parangai.*
> If they're spoiled when they're little, they'll carry it along when they're grown, it will be unchangeable when they're old, and it will remain their character until they die.

This item means "Spare the rod and spoil the child". It warns of the consequences of allowing children to do whatever they want. Its image, however, reflects a commonly observed characteristic of the elderly, namely that they are set in their ways and cannot (or will not) change, even if it would be beneficial to do so. Another item has much the same meaning.

Tabiaik pantang tarubah, biaso jadi parangai, lah tuo jadi pakaian.

Character doesn't change; a habit becomes nature and, when you're old, it becomes your clothing.

Another well-known utterance comments on the fact that the behaviour of the elderly can be erratic and even wilful and may well become more extreme as they age. In particular, it may be used to refer to the fact that older people can become childish in their demands and behaviour and be very difficult to deal with for that reason. The image is of the *keladi*, a plant of the *Araceae* family, that grows very prolifically in Southeast Asia and spreads over time to form large clumps or patches. It is distinguished by its heart-shaped leaves. This rhyming proverb is well known throughout the Malay world and occurs in Malay as well as in Minang.

Tuo-tuo kaladi, makin tuo makin manjadi.

(They) age like the *keladi*, the older they get, the more extreme they become.

A number of other items, however, note the importance of older people to the functioning of the community and as sources of knowledge and experience. The following expression, which is more properly termed an aphorism than a proverb because it is not metaphorical, reminds hearers of the accumulated wisdom of the elderly that has contributed to the formation of traditional law and customs (*adaik* in Minang).

Tiok nagari basuku-suku, nan suku babuah paruik, kato adaik mangko baitu, urang tuo lah lamo hiduik.

Every region has its clans, the clans consist of extended families, adat is the way it is because the elderly have lived a long time.

Another utterance that uses a similar structure reminds the hearer of the importance of taking responsibility for his or her actions and also of following advice.

Talangkah suruik, sasek kumbali, baitu faham handaknyo; kato rang tuo indak dituruik, binaso badan kasudahannyo.

If you take a wrong step, turn back; if you become lost, return the way you came; if you don't follow what our elders have told you, you will end in disaster.

Still other expressions describe the appropriate position of the elderly in traditional society. Utterances of this kind include:

Nan tuo dihormati, nan ketek disayangi, samo gadang dibao bakawan.

The old should be respected, the young should be treated with affection, those of the same age should be made into friends.

Elok nagari dek pangulu, elok kampuang dek nan tuo, elok musajik dek tuanku, elok tapian dek nan mudo.

The region is good because of its leaders; the village is good because of the old people; the mosque is good because of the religious scholars; the bathing place is good because of the young.

This last utterance sometimes occurs in a longer form which mentions additional institutions and the people associated with them. It suggests that the quality of the structures of traditional society depends on the quality of the people who use them. Old people, in this view, hold the village together and are its mainstay because they represent the oldest generation of the families that live there and are the ones most familiar with the traditions and rhythms of life in the community. This status comes with its own responsibilities and difficulties however. One of these is the need for older people to accept and put up with the activities of the young and their way of life. This is also expressed traditionally in an utterance that compares the emotional state of these two groups:

Adaik mudo manangguang rindu; adaik tuo manahan ragam.
The young must bear their longing; the elderly must endure.

OLDER MINANGKABAU AND SOCIAL CHANGE

In West Sumatra as well as in the rest of Indonesia, there is a great deal for the elderly to endure as society has changed enormously over the course of their life. The pace of change has been very rapid since Indonesia gained independence from the Netherlands in 1945 and picked up even greater speed since the end of the New Order government in 1998. This, followed closely by regional autonomy which took effect in 2001, has had a major impact on the way of life of all Indonesians. Economic growth has been strong since the end of the Asian financial crisis of 1997–98. By 2006,

Indonesia had a 2 per cent surplus in GDP (compared to a deficit of 3 per cent in 1996) (*The Economist* 2007). Growth of 5.1 per cent was achieved, with 5.3 per cent predicted for 2018 (World Bank 2017).

The strength of the economy has led to the development of a substantial middle class whose interests and activities parallel those of similar demographics around the world. A recent study by the Boston Consulting Group reports that there are some 74 million middle-class and affluent consumers in Indonesia whose ranks are expected to double in size by 2020 (Rastogi et al. 2014). Overwhelmingly, this growing middle class is interested in pursuing a modern lifestyle and participating in global trends. This is perhaps best reflected in the incredible take up of smart technologies and use of social media. Indonesia is the third largest user of Facebook and has more Twitter users than any other nation in the world, with 79 per cent of the population using social media in some form (Vaswani 2012). The negative impact of these trends on the maintenance of traditional culture has been noted as a serious concern by Indonesian scholars as well as members of the media and the public (see, for example, Muktiyo 2010; Jati 2012).

Of course, the rapid pace of change has serious implications for all of Indonesia's local cultures. Its impact on the Minangkabau is of particular interest, however, because of the nature of this cultural community. As discussed above, the Minangkabau are the only matrilineal culture that currently exists in Indonesia and is fairly large. Some 6 million people of Minangkabau origin live in the Indonesian province of West Sumatra with a similar number estimated to live permanently in other parts of Indonesia, especially in large cities like Jakarta and in the provinces of Sumatra that neighbour their region of origin (BPS Sumatera Barat 2016e). As a result of generations of *marantau*, members of the Minangkabau population have experienced many of the demographic and social trends that have shaped modern Indonesia, including domestic migration, urbanization, tension between traditional ethnic identity and national identity as Indonesians, adaptation to a multilingual and multicultural context, an ageing population, and issues of cultural consonance — the extent to which a person's experiences accord with his or her expectations. Their experience mirrors that of many other Indonesian ethnic groups, as well as people across Southeast Asia and other parts of the developing world. The Minangkabau population is of special interest, however, because their linguistic and cultural pride is high (Lewis et al. 2016) and, despite being highly integrated into Indonesian society, has been quite resistant to change. As a result, the impact of social, economic, political, and cultural shifts on the community has been especially visible. Additionally, awareness of the competing forces of tradition and modernization has long been present in Minangkabau society and was the subject of a number of classic novels from the early twentieth century by writers from this background as well as some modern literature from the region. The need to change and adapt to the social and cultural environment has been especially problematic because *adat* has been perceived as being able to withstand all tests of time. A proverb holds that: *Adaik indak lakang dek paneh, indak lapuak dek ujan* (*Adat* will not warp in the sun nor rot in the rain). Many observers feel that this is increasingly not the case, and the traditions of Minangkabau society now face challenges that can no longer be withstood. These changes have had a very significant impact on the experience of the current elderly who have seen the transition from a traditional to a modern society within the course of their own lives.

THE NATURE OF THIS BOOK

This book contains eleven chapters that describe the experience of ageing in modern Minangkabau society. Its aim is to provide a window into the experience of ageing among the members of one Indonesian ethnic community that is at the forefront of social change with the understanding that this will offer insight into similar forces that are being experienced all around the country by older individuals of all backgrounds and cultural origins. This, in turn, will allow for a better understanding of the needs of older Indonesians in the modern context and will support the development of more effective social policy, the provision of more innovative health and social services, and will suggest ways of addressing growing psychosocial problems experienced by older adults living in various environments.

The book's content is based on a long-term research project conducted over five years in the heartland of West Sumatra that represents the original Minangkabau homeland; in the city of Padang, the capital of West Sumatra, which was originally an area of migration but is now considered to be part of the Minangkabau world; and in the *rantau*, areas like Jakarta and other large Indonesian cities on the island of Java and in eastern Indonesia where significant Minangkabau communities exist but, while long established, are of more recent origin. Having interviewed a large number of older individuals and their family members in depth about their experiences and current situation, we focus on the ways in which individuals of Minangkabau background, who are now more than sixty years old, see themselves and their families in the context of modern Indonesia and the extent to which these perceptions replicate the situation they observed among their parents and grandparents. We are especially interested in these issues of cultural consonance in the context of a variety of social factors that characterize the modern Indonesian experience, such as language and religious issues, but also the nature of the living environment and interactions with family members and members of the wider public. An understanding of the experience of the elderly is particularly important now as the Indonesian population is ageing rapidly and more than 14 per cent of the population of West Sumatra itself is currently over sixty (BKKBN 2011a).

The picture of the experience of ageing in the Minangkabau community presented here is based on dozens of interviews with older members of this ethnic group who live in different Indonesian environments and whose life experiences span a large number of social contexts. In addition, the experiences of the members of a single, extended family are presented as case studies throughout the book to illustrate in greater detail the kinds of change individuals in this age group have faced and the ways it has affected their life course. These middle-aged and older people were interviewed repeatedly over the course of our study, and we also spent time with them among their family members and in the course of their daily activities. Their stories are complemented by several others of non-family members in order to illustrate the new social phenomena that affect older people, such as life in an institution for the elderly. The names and, in some cases, the exact place of residence of these older people, as well as the name of the village where the Valley family originates, have been changed to ensure their privacy, but their stories are accurate and they shared them willingly, and many times enthusiastically, as way of allowing others to understand their experiences and perceptions as members of the Minangkabau community and also as Indonesians.

THE VILLAGE TODAY

Mid-afternoon in the village of Koto seems unusually quiet. The sun is shining brightly, and everything is very green and fresh in the village where the Valley family comes from. However, no one is walking along the paths, and there are no children playing in front of the houses. This is a very different scene from just twenty years ago when there were many more people in Koto, and a large number of them were children and teenagers. Today, many of the people in the village are middle aged or elderly, and those that are not often have a reason or personal characteristic that has prevented them from leaving. Two of the younger members of the Valley family who are still in the village fall into this category. One has been disabled since childhood and, outside of a short time at a training programme for people with handicaps in another city, has always lived with her mother, who is the oldest member of the family still in their village of origin. The other is the thirty-year-old daughter of a member of the middle generation. She is viewed as "simple" and is felt to be unable to take care of herself. She lives with her mother, a retired school teacher, and interacts mostly with the few other family members still living there. One male member of the extended family is present. He is a grandson of Aminah and the brother of several of the people who were at the dinner in Jakarta described above. He spent some time working in other parts of Indonesia and then returned to the village where he lives with his wife at her family's house. The spread of the family across Indonesia is the subject of conversation this afternoon. This was triggered by a piece of news that came by SMS advising the family in Koto that one of the grandchildren was getting married. The younger members of the family who are present on this afternoon are impressed by how quiet things have become. However, Maryati, their great aunt who is the youngest daughter of Aminah from whom the family descends, sees things differently. "The family has expanded", she notes with pride. As a very old woman, she remembers how things used to be and can make comparisons that perhaps the others can't.

2

Ageing in the Past and Present

THE CONCEPT OF VILLAGE

The village, or *kampuang*, is the social unit that defines the living environment of people from West Sumatra. In addition to its obvious physical characteristics, the concept of the village is an important organizing feature in the way people think about themselves and others. One of the first questions people ask someone they just met is, *Kampuang di ma?* [Where is your village?]. Even though a large number of Minangkabau now come from large cities and the question really means "Where are you from?", Jakarta or Padang has the same cognitive status as an actual village in the Minangkabau heartland in the mountains of West Sumatra. The village is a place to live but also an encapsulation of all the elements required for human existence in the Minangkabau context.

Until comparatively recently, the majority of Minangkabau really did come from a village or maintained a close relationship with the village of their ancestors. Folklore holds that all Minangkabau originated in one of three regions in the highlands of what is now West Sumatra. These areas are referred to as *luhak* and represent the original homeland of this ethnic group and the centre of its traditional culture. The myths of the region indicate that the Minangkabau came down from Mount Merapi to the area of Pariangan. Later, they spread out into the original *luhak*, and even later to the coastal plains which were the first *rantau*, an area outside of their region of origin that served as a destination for migration. This happened, according to legend, at an unrecorded point in the distant past sometime after the original settlement of the area, which took place when the volcanoes that form the backdrop for the Minangkabau world were only "as big as a duck egg". Whether there is any truth to this idea, and if so, how much, cannot be discerned from the archaeological record of the region. However, it is the case that traditional literature, including proverbs and proverbial phrases, maintain the view that traditional customs and way of life developed in the highlands and spread down the mountains into the regions that have been inhabited by the Minangkabau in modern times. By contrast, newer influences of all kinds are seen as entering the Minangkabau world from the lowlands and travelling up the mountains into the traditional homeland regions. A well-known proverb states:

> *Adaik nan manurun; syarak nan mandaki.*
> *Adat* went down; religion came up.

This utterance refers to the idea that traditional law and customs originated in the mountain heartland of the region, but Islam came to the region from the coast (a *rantau* area) and moved into the older settlements in the mountains from there.

Among the traditions of the Minangkabau heartland is the nature and configuration of the village which is also specified in traditional law and custom. These customary rules, however, derive from practice and reflect the encoding of a pattern of life that likely existed since ancient times. The requirements of place reflect a transition through population growth from settlement, to village, up to a functional unit called *nagari* that is composed of several villages and contains representatives of all four major clans in the Minangkabau world. The nature of the human environment is a direct reflection of the needs of people in the traditional context which include: rice fields (*basawah*); dry fields (*baladang*); a meeting hall (*babalai*); a mosque (*bamusajik*); a road (*balabuah*); a cemetery (*bapandam*); and a bathing place (*batapian*). Life in the village has always revolved around the events of the residents which, like most places in the world, tends to focus on milestone events such as births, deaths, and marriages; changes in leadership and governance; and the economic and occupational interests of the population.

Village institutions order social life and, in theory, are responsive to growth and change. For much of Minangkabau history, people's lives centred on the houses they lived in; the rice fields, gardens, and ponds that supplied food and that were the source of livelihood; the bathing places along rivers or streams where they socialized and did chores; and the surrounding jungle that formed a boundary between areas of habitation and was also a source of danger. Islam, which is thought to have been adopted by the Minangkabau kingdom in the late fourteenth or early fifteenth century (Houben 2003), made a mosque and prayer houses a necessity in every village, and these institutions eventually became a focus of social life that has continued to the present time. Even more recently, elementary schools have become another institution in the villages. While junior and senior high schools are still mostly located in towns of some size, many villages have a school that was built or expanded during the New Order period of Indonesia's history that lasted from 1965 to 1998. Many villages now have small stores and perhaps a coffee shop, but the existence of these facilities is more dependent on the initiative of individual residents than the demands of the social environment.

The nature of village life in Minangkabau evolved within the constraints and opportunities of the physical environment. These have remained comparatively unchanged over time and represent a backdrop to village life that is stable in larger outline but that changes constantly with the seasons and cycles of the natural world. This physical environment is amply documented in Minangkabau traditional literature, which suggests that the villages of ancient times were part of their natural surroundings in much the same ways as their modern incarnations and also that the larger outline of life in the village has remained fairly stable.

The staple food of the Minangkabau is rice, and rice fields are vital for survival as well as for wealth. Depending on the terrain, these fields may be flat or terraced and require a great deal of upkeep to maintain against the forces of weather. Food plants of other kinds are ubiquitous, with bananas, coconuts, and other types of fruit trees growing throughout areas where people live. Some of these were planted by individuals; others grew naturally in their location and were simply maintained by nearby residents. Vegetables are planted wherever suitable land is available, in gardens but also in small plots near houses. Water is easily available in most areas and is vital for rice cultivation as flooded field techniques are largely used. In addition to a source of water for irrigation, fish ponds are common, and streams and larger bodies of water may run through a village area. Animals are numerous in the villages. Chickens and goats tend to be allowed to wander freely as are dogs and cats. Horses are not common, but water buffalo are and are relied upon for plowing and other agricultural work.

The areas where people live tend to be clustered along a road or in an area that can be readily accessed. People generally prefer to live in proximity to each other, rather than in an isolated house separate from the rest of the village. Because land is owned by extended families defined by the female line, new dwellings, as well as other types of structure such as rice barns or enclosures for animals, will be located on land that belongs to the residents' family. The building of communal institutions, such as mosques or schools, requires that a family donate land within the village where the structure can be built. In practice, this causes many problems because people tend to be very reluctant to give up any of their property. This continues to be a major problem in West Sumatra that is widely seen as impeding needed development (Fatimah and Andora 2014; Padang Media 2014). Many public facilities are built on land which is still owned by an extended family, with the developer having a right only to the improvements made. In the past, it was sometimes possible to develop unowned land on the fringes of the village and claim ownership. This possibility is severely limited in the modern context, however, because any usable land in the vicinity of the village is now owned by some extended family.

Of all the elements of the village environment, the houses in which people live tend to reflect most closely their traditions and customs. In the past, it was usual for several generations of a family to live in a single large home. These communal houses, or *rumah gadang* (literally "big house"), were built with roofs shaped like water buffalo horns in one of two broad styles that are associated with specific views about *adat* (traditional law and custom) held by different segments of the community. The roof shape is usually viewed as representing the importance of the water buffalo in Minangkabau society as well as to commemorate an ancient battle against a Javanese kingdom fought using water buffalo that was won by the Minangkabau. The word *kabau* that appears in the name of the group means "water buffalo" and is thought to commemorate this same event (Andaya 2000).

These houses, raised off the ground on stilts and with very high roofs, are particularly suited to the climate which is both wet and hot. Recently, there has been some interest in traditional building techniques in the context of earthquakes because of a local belief that *rumah gadang* are more resilient to natural disaster than modern houses (see, for example, Setijanti et al. 2012). However, many traditional houses are no longer in use or have disappeared from the villages, largely because they do not fit with the current lifestyle and aspirations of the residents who are shifting to a living arrangement based on the nuclear family. In the past, the communal traditional houses were occupied by the members of a family in the female line who were descended from a common female ancestor. Typically, several nuclear families would live together in this way as the women of each generation had a right to reside in the traditional home along with their husbands and children. In practice, this was not always the case, but it was also possible to add rooms to accommodate to the needs of a growing extended family.

TRADITIONAL SOCIAL STRUCTURE

In the past more than today, a significant part of the Minangkabau population spent most of their life in or near the village where they were born. While *marantau*, or temporary migration, was an integral part of the culture especially for men, many of whom settled permanently elsewhere, many others did return to the village to live or never left in the first place. It was less common for women to leave because this meant leaving behind assets one was entitled to use under the matrilineal system. Nonetheless, women did sometimes marry men from other places or whose work required them to live in another part of Indonesia and went with them to the *rantau*. Still, a large number of people were born in the house of their mother's family, lived there as a child and into adulthood. Women would continue to live in the family home or at least on family land for life. When they married, their husband would come to live with them and their mother's family, and any children would be members of this maternal clan. Men, while remaining members of their mother's family for life, would be socialized into the world of males from a young age. This involved spending a great deal of time at the *surau*, or prayer house, with other boys and unmarried men. When they married, they would live at their wife's house but typically spent much of the daytime on their own family's land, where they retained a stake and had a special responsibility for their sister's children as their *mamak* (maternal uncle).

It is difficult to assess the degree to which this social structure operated in its ideal form in the past. While modern Minangkabau tend to be very proud of their matrilineal culture and what they view as its social benefits, especially in terms of guaranteeing the welfare of women and children, there is some evidence that the system, which relies on rigid social rules, may never have functioned as smoothly as modern Minangkabau imagine. Examples of family feuds and long-standing bad feelings between close relatives are plentiful today and are also recalled from the past. Most families can cite examples of people who did things that are outside the Minangkabau system or violate its traditions and values. Nonetheless, many aspects of the traditional matrilineal system are still in place, suggesting they have always been important and really did shape the way people lived their lives. Among these are the fact that land and other assets are passed down in the female line and are used by the women of the extended family. People have a very clear idea that it is appropriate for men to live with their wife and her family, and not vice versa, and this is commonly seen, unless the couple happens to have bought or built their own home on land they purchased. This is more common among people living outside their village of origin, such as in the provincial capital of Padang or elsewhere. Even so, Minangkabau generally consider the wife to be the head of the household with a specific responsibility for the home and family. Men, as lifelong members of their mother's family, are traditionally expected to return to this family if their marriage ends due to death or divorce, especially if they do not own a home outside of the matrilineal system.

In the past, the connection to the family of one's mother was often stronger than in the present, and this was certainly the case for Minangkabau who had reached old age. It is worth noting that what constitutes elderly is rather fluid in Minangkabau society. In the past, many people had a loose conception of age and dates, and a person's exact age was not important as birthdays are not traditionally celebrated. Generally, if a person's children were married and had children of their own, he or she was considered old, a designation that related more to social status than to age. Participation in employment was less of a marker because many elderly people in the rural environment often did (and still do) various kinds of work, even when they had left or retired from jobs in the formal sector.

For women in the Minangkabau village of the past, old age caused very little change in their day-to-day life, except in that they would normally take on greater responsibility for the extended family and its property gradually as the generations changed. In many cases, they would continue to live in the same house where they had been born and where their status would evolve from a child to a young adult to a middle-aged person to an elder. At all stages of life, they would be surrounded by female relatives who might include a grandmother and great aunts in childhood; a mother and aunts; and sisters and female cousins in later life. A number of male relatives might also be present, at least part of the time, and would include the brothers of their mother and grandmother, the husbands of various female relatives, and their own brothers and male cousins. Nonetheless, as noted, the presence of these male relatives was more transient because those who were members of the family would spend time at their own wife's house and the husbands of female members, while eating and spending the nights, might be out much of the time working and dealing with their own maternal family. There are separate terms of address for members of the maternal family that are not the same as those used for comparable relatives on the father's side, and most people think about their family in terms of which side of the family they come from. They often know more about the family on their mother's side and sometimes lose track of paternal relatives they do not have personal contact with.

From a young age, Minangkabau girls would be taught how to manage the family's land and other assets by helping the adult women and listening to family discussion. As older female relatives died, they would move up in seniority and take on more responsibility for the larger family group. In many cases, this increasing authority had to be shared among all the women of the same generation, which, for any individual, included siblings and cousins who were the children of one's mother's sisters. However, if it happened that there were few women in any generation, the women or woman at that level would represent a concentration of power that would last until the next generation came into control. If there were no daughters in a generation, as does occasionally happen, a family could die out. For this reason, modern Minangkabau are often very concerned if a woman has sons and no daughter or is childless, even if they do not live in the village and no longer depend on traditional assets.

In an ideal situation, an older woman would live among her daughters and their children in the village where she had been born and often in the same house where her mother and grandmother had lived. As a member of the oldest generation of the family, she would be entitled to a certain amount of respect and consideration and could expect help and support if she needed it. It was unusual in the past for old people to live alone (although this did sometimes occur) because of the large number of children in each generation. Even a woman who had no children of her own would likely have nieces and nephews who could be relied upon for assistance in old age. The younger generation of the maternal line typically provided care for older family members who had become ill or infirm and took on an increasing responsibility for household chores and management. In the Minangkabau village, as in the rest of the world, there tended to be more old women than old men, and it was common for women to outlive their husbands.

The availability of younger family members to care for an older woman was seen as more important than the presence of a husband. Men, in the traditional system, are referred to as guests in their wife's house and are termed *urang sumando*. It has been suggested that the term *sumando* comes from an archaic word meaning "pledge", indicating that the man was given to the woman's family as a husband but would retain his main allegiance to his mother's family. Modern usage of cognate terms in Malay (*semenda, bersemenda*) simply mean "related by marriage" (Dewan Bahasa dan Pustaka 2005). Blood relationships, as defined by the matrilineal system, have always tended to be more significant, both socially as well as in people's feelings, than relationships by marriage, including between spouses. This is manifested explicitly, such as in language use where a Minangkabau husband is typically referred to using the term that means "older brother" and is, in fact, used for actual siblings, but also implicitly in the way people perceive the roles of family members as well as their own, relative to their social relationship and position. A traditional metaphor in Minang that refers to a man's position in his wife's family is "like ash on a tree stump" [*bak abu di ateh tunggua*], meaning that, just as a slight breeze can blow away the ash, it does not take much for him to leave.

In the traditional Minangkabau village, then, elderly women always had a place in their family home and expected to live out their life in the same environment in which they had always lived. While it was unusual for an older woman to find herself completely alone, she would nonetheless have the benefit of whatever her mother's family owned and could generally avoid the worst kind of poverty by exerting her rightful claim to what the extended family as a whole could produce. In addition, older women enjoyed a social status that was respected within the village environment and were seen as having authority over younger family members and also a right to be seen and heard. This guaranteed position within the family and village can be seen as one of the protective aspects of the matrilineal system in Minangkabau which helped to guarantee the well-being of an elderly woman without a spouse and even without children. This is visible in the experiences of Aminah, the founding member of the Valley family. Her story, and the stories of her descendants and others in the Minangkabau community, serve to illustrate the experiences of older people and interplay of forces that shape their lives.

Aminah

Aminah, the oldest member of the Valley family, died in 1977. She was 102 at the time, to the best of the family's knowledge. The exact dates of birth of the generation who had been born before Indonesia gained independence in 1945 were often unknown, although the older members of the family had a reasonably good idea of how old their parents and grandparents were when they died. At the time of this writing, two of Aminah's daughters were still living, as were a large number of grandchildren who had known her. At the time of her death, Aminah had been a widow for twenty-five years and lived in the house she had grown up in with four of her children and twenty-three grandchildren. She had been the only surviving daughter in her family, although she had several brothers. As a result of this, all of the family's wealth, which included a large amount of productive land as well as the home of the extended family and other assets, came to her when her own mother died. She had four daughters who lived with her with their husbands and children. They supported her in her old age and assisted her when she needed them to. The family property provided more than enough income for Aminah, her daughters, and their children to live comfortably, even though her sons-in-law had jobs and income of their own. When her husband, Musa, died, Aminah, who had been one of his three wives, did not experience much change in her daily routine, and her economic situation did not change at all. Her husband had never spent much time with her, and she was used to managing her own affairs and doing what she pleased. Her husband had spent the days at his mother's house managing his family's land and business. On most nights, he went to the house of one of his other wives. Aminah had been raised to manage the family's property from a young age and did not expect more than this from her husband. She enjoyed economic stability and material and

emotional support from members of her matrilineal family, which she felt
were due her. She attempted as much as possible to replicate her own
upbringing with her daughters and tried to ensure that they understood
the complicated processes involved in managing the agricultural cycle
and knew how to deal with the family's property and productive assets.
In this, her aim was to maintain the wealth and status of the family in
Koto, their village, and see that their economic gains continued into the
future. Like other women of her generation, Aminah believed this was
the appropriate role for her to play in her old age and expected that her
daughters shared her views and would accept her guidance, which for
the most part they did. In the context of Minangkabau society, Aminah's
experience was ideal and fulfilled the cultural and social norms of the
village. This gave her a secure place, the love of her family, and great
respect from people around her.

THE WORLD OF MINANGKABAU MEN

The experience of Minangkabau men in the past was different from that
of women. Men occupy a precarious position in traditional Minangkabau
society because of the way access to family resources is structured. While
remaining a member of their mother's family for life, men do not always
have a defined place in their matrilineal family, and what this place is
may depend on their personal achievements. Men do have a role in the
management of family assets and are expected to contribute to their
mother's family by working on the land, but much of the decision-making
authority lies with women who clearly control the family with the advice
and support of their male relatives. For this reason, in the traditional
context, boys and young men spent a great deal of time with their peers
and were expected to sleep at the village prayer house with other boys
and unmarried men. This was often an opportunity to learn about religion,
village lore, martial arts, and other aspects of folk culture. However, it
also meant that, from an early age, men were somewhat removed from
the mainstream of activities in the family home.

Upon marriage, a man went to live with his wife and her family. In
many cases, this meant joining a household that was composed of several
generations of women along with their husbands and children. Married men
often spent a considerable amount of time with their own family during the

day, returning to their wife's house in the evening. Wives often laid claim to the personal income of their husband (including any income generated by land belonging to his maternal family that his female relatives had allowed him to use), who was also expected to help work their land, but who continued to contribute to his own family's well-being by working for them and participating in the upbringing of his sisters' children as well. Because men were viewed as outsiders in their wife's family, it was easy for women to dissolve a marriage (although only men can initiate divorce under Islam) or treat a husband unkindly. In a situation like this, the man could in theory return to his own family, but in practice this was often awkward or impossible. Women tended to see men in terms of the value they could offer to the family measured by genetic and financial contribution. In the traditional context, this supported two significant social phenomena.

The first of these was *marantau*, the practice of temporary migration. One of the ways a man could raise his social status and accumulate personal wealth was through *marantau*. Those who were successful in the *rantau* might return to the village and be seen as more desirable husbands. This might allow them to marry up and enjoy a more comfortable life or at least to gain the respect of a wife and her family. In some parts of West Sumatra, such as the Pariaman region, a dowry is traditionally paid for men; the amount is based on their perceived prospects and potential contribution to their wife's family. Even when a man was able to achieve success in the *rantau* and make a favourable marriage, however, his position might be temporary because, in the village, he would still be subject to the wishes of his wife and her family and might, at some time in the future, be viewed as no longer an asset to their family. If this did occur, he might be welcomed back into his own family, but this would depend on his sisters and other female relatives and whether they felt he was in a position to contribute to their economic needs and how they perceived his behaviour towards them.

Because success in the *rantau* did not give men a stable position in the village, many Minangkabau men stayed in other locations where they settled permanently. Some of them married women from the place where they were living. Others married Minangkabau women but were less subject to the demands of their wife's family because of their distance from the village. In situations like this where family property was not available, nuclear families were the norm and were supported by the personal earnings of both the husband and wife. These men also generally spent much more time with their own children than a man living in his own village might. At present, there are large communities of Minangkabau in many parts of Indonesia, including the capital Jakarta, as well as in Negeri Sembilan, Malaysia, and elsewhere. There is some evidence that these communities are very long-standing, although many have grown significantly since Indonesia's independence (Kato 1997).

The second social phenomenon that relates to the traditional status of men was the pattern of marriage and divorce that was common in Minangkabau villages. Perhaps because marriage was often based on economic potential, divorce and polygamy were common. Many women in past generations were married and divorced several times, which led to a situation where, in a small village like Koto, there is some past family connection between almost everyone. For women, divorce had little impact on their situation, either economically or socially. Men, who fared much less well when a marriage dissolved, often had multiple wives. This was allowed by Islam but served a more important social purpose in the Minangkabau context because having several wives meant a man had several families he was attached to. If one marriage did not work out, rather than return to his own family, he might continue to have a place with his other wives. While many women likely would have preferred their husband to be married only to them, the situation was understood and accepted by many because it did not seriously interfere with women's interests in relation to their own family, of which any children would automatically be a part. From the point of view of men, having more than one wife, assuming one had the means to enter into multiple marriages, was a way of planning for the future and trying to ensure a place for oneself in the village community. It also increased the chances that some of a man's children might be willing to care for him in old age if his own extended family was not.

Kamil

Kamil, who was born in the nineteenth century, was Aminah's older brother. He married the daughter of his maternal uncle with whom he had several children. This marriage was arranged by the uncle who preferred him to either of his two brothers as a son-in-law. There had been another sister in the family, who died as a teenager. Aminah, herself, had always been sickly, and the family, especially Maryam, Kamil and Aminah's mother, was very concerned that she might die as well. If there were no granddaughters in the female line, the family could become extinct and its land would be taken over by other people in the village. The family's hopes rested on Aminah.

As it turned out, Aminah's health improved greatly as she grew up, and she became cheerful and confident, even though her mother and three brothers spoiled her. She inherited Maryam's strong personality and was able to grasp early in life how much responsibility she would have when she grew up as the only daughter. As he had for Kamil, their maternal uncle, who held the traditional title of Datuak Sati Basa Batuah and was the *mamak*, or male leader of the family, arranged Aminah's marriage to a prominent man in the village who already had a wife. Aminah was delighted, if reluctant at first, because she knew how important it was for her to produce daughters and keep the family going. She eventually had eight children, five daughters and three sons. Although one son and one daughter died in childhood, everyone was happy, and the likelihood that the extended family would become extinct was now remote.

This situation was especially good for Kamil. When their maternal uncle, who was also his father-in-law died, he would inherit the title Datuak Sati Basa Batuah and assume the role of *mamak*. If Aminah had not had daughters to continue the family line, this position would have been meaningless because the family would have ended at that generation. Aminah's four daughters, Kamil's nieces, would now ensure the continuity, and even expansion, of the family. Kamil would have a special responsibility for his sister's children and grandchildren. His uncle had chosen Kamil to replace him and take on the role of male leader of the family, and Kamil marrying his uncle's daughter cemented the relationship. Kamil and Aminah, as two of the most important members of the family in the context of the traditional social structure, became very close and supported each other. Kamil spent as much time at his wife's house as he did at his parents' house where Aminah and her children lived.

Kamil enjoyed his role as *mamak* as well as the title he held. After the death of his uncle and mother, he and Aminah became even closer. They made decisions about family matters together. Kamil was as close to his nieces and nephews as he was to his own children. As custom required, he spent many hours a week talking to his nieces and nephews about life, the village, religion and *adat*. In this way, he was more significant in shaping their thinking than that of his own children who were educated in a similar manner by their uncle, their mother's brother. This brother was also Kamil's cousin but belonged to a different family, that of Kamil's mother-in-law.

Kamil believed strongly in the importance of the role of *mamak* as laid out by *adat* and carried it out to the best of his ability. Not every man in his position would have done this. Some men chose to spend more time with their own children. Others lived far from the village in the place their wife came from and saw their nieces and nephews only occasionally. But because of his personal situation and because he was willing to do what custom demanded, Kamil benefitted enormously in his old age.

Kamil died in the early 1970s at the age of about 104. He was bedridden for the last five years of his life after suffering a stroke. Both his wife and Aminah survived him and both wanted to take care of him. It pleased Kamil that he could have chosen to live with his wife or his sister during the most difficult part of his life when he had no choice but to rely on others for everything he needed. He knew his sister and wife loved him, as did his children and nieces and nephews. When Kamil fell ill, many members of this younger generation had children of their own, and they all liked to sit by his bed and listen to the stories he told. Despite the stroke and resulting disability, Kamil never felt sad, abandoned or isolated. He lived with his sister because she had a larger house, and her daughters and their children were available to support him. His wife had agreed to this arrangement happily because she shared the concern that there would always be someone around to take care of him.

THE IMPACT OF SOCIAL CHANGE

In recent decades, Indonesia has undergone very rapid social change associated with modernization, economic development, and global trends. This began after independence in 1945 and accelerated during the New Order when development was a main focus of the thirty-two-year government of President Soeharto. In West Sumatra, as was the case in many parts of Indonesia, this was the period when electricity became available, numerous schools and health care facilities were built, roads and other infrastructure were improved, and an Indonesian national culture began to be apparent (Dove and Kammen 2001).

This national culture, which was consciously supported by the New Order government, was aimed at promoting stability and national identity (Sen and Hill 2006). It included such unifying factors as intensive promotion and development of the Indonesian language as a vehicle for communication in the public environment and also for interaction between ethnic groups but also high levels of control over the media and other forms of expression (Keane 2003). Administrative structures were strictly hierarchical under the New Order, and Jakarta was the centre of governmental and professional activity of all kinds. The capital became a magnet for the most capable and ambitious but also for large number of unskilled job seekers who hoped the urban environment would offer more opportunities for work.

For increasing numbers of Minangkabau who were born in West Sumatra, Jakarta became even more attractive during this period in Indonesia's history. Large numbers of people moved to the capital; some of these had no intention of returning to their village of origin, while others saw themselves as participating in a more traditional form of *marantau* from which they hoped to return someday having become wealthy. More than in the past, the possibilities offered by the capital attracted two types of migrants that included those following a more traditional pattern but also those who were highly educated and aspired to positions within the formal sector.

Traditionally, Minangkabau who migrated to other parts of Indonesia mostly became traders, selling clothing and other items in markets and small stores; setting up restaurants of all sizes and levels of sophistication; or becoming self-employed service providers or craftsmen. While there were always some highly educated individuals, such as teachers or religious scholars, who went to the *rantau*, the majority of migrants entered Indonesia's large informal sector composed of mostly undocumented individuals who did whatever they could to make a living. It was migrants of this kind that started the very large Minangkabau community in the Tanah Abang area of Jakarta and who still make up the majority of traders in the wholesale and retail garment industry concentrated in that neighbourhood, which has gained a reputation for being notoriously difficult for the city government to regulate (Suprapto 2009; Kompas 2013).

Another traditional aim of *marantau* was to take advantage of educational opportunities that were not available in West Sumatra. Those migrants who left the region and graduated from schools and institutions elsewhere in Indonesia often found greater opportunities for employment where they were, and many did not return to live permanently in their region of origin. This trend accelerated greatly during the New Order because the potential for advancement within the highly centralized system was much more significant in Jakarta than in regional areas. Many university-educated professionals left West Sumatra during this time to work in the capital more or less permanently. Increasingly, women took part in this migration because of the potential for economic gain and personal advancement. While exact figures are difficult to find, the provincial government of West Sumatra acknowledges the enormous contribution these Minangkabau make to the local economy through funds that they send to family members in the village that are used for the development of the regions (Kartika 2013). This issue is discussed in more detail in Chapter 8.

Education had always been important in the Minangkabau community and was seen as a significant form of social capital because of its impact on earning potential and also because the ability to complete higher levels of education was seen as indicative of intelligence, which, especially for men, was a desirable characteristic in a spouse. Even before independence, West Sumatra had had a number of famous schools for both boys and girls as well as prominent educational leaders (see, for example, Ahmad 2009). A large number of writers from the area shaped early Indonesian literature and language use in modern Indonesia (Anwar 1976; Phillips 1977), and many Minangkabau became major public figures. Mohammad Hatta, Indonesia's first vice-president, for example, was Minangkabau, as were a number of subsequent government ministers and other leaders.

During the New Order, the number of educated Minangkabau who moved to Jakarta and other large Indonesian cities, including Padang, the capital of West Sumatra, increased greatly. Cities came to be seen as offering the greatest potential for advancement with opportunities being even more plentiful in the national capital because of the centralized system. It was during this period that urbanization began to be a social issue in Indonesia as a whole, as the experience of the Minangkabau was replicated across the country and among virtually every ethnic group (Evers 2007). For members of the Minangkabau community, successful migration during this period was enhanced by their comparatively high level of mastery of Indonesian and the established attitudes favouring education for both boys and girls. In 2013, for example, the participation rate in education among thirteen- to fifteen-year-olds in West Sumatra was 92 per cent; for sixteen- to eighteen-year-olds, the figure was 74 per cent. In West Java, the province surrounding the Special Capital Territory of Jakarta, and historically a more developed region of Indonesia, the comparable figures were 89 per cent and 59 per cent respectively (BPS 2014).

The increased desirability of migration along with the rising importance of participation in national culture through language use, formal education, and employment in the formal sector spurred an extremely significant change in West Sumatra. For the first time in Minangkabau history, the importance of land and traditional assets held by the matrilineal family began to decrease for many individuals who viewed their prospects as being better within the modern domains of the nation. In practice, many people began to consider that they could compete in the modern economy and the rewards of doing so might far exceed what they could reasonably expect in the traditional context where social position was much less mutable and was difficult for the individual to change. Even in rural areas, more young people aspired to study at a university, despite the fact that this meant moving to a larger town in the province as a minimum. Once they graduated, it was still more appealing to work as a teacher, health professional, or in a government office, while living in the village than to engage in a traditional occupation. The ability to earn income outside the traditional context became a liberating force for both men and women as it allowed the individual to be more economically independent without the constraints of family consensus.

The first generation to benefit significantly from the social change that affected all of Indonesia in the decades following independence was that whose members were born in the 1950s, once the modern nation began to take form. While many Minangkabau had held professional positions within the Dutch-controlled administration prior to independence, this career path had not been widely available, and the traditional social context remained important. This first generation born since independence is now reaching the age where its members are considered *lansia* (elderly), and their own experiences, as well as those of their elderly parents and grandparents, are very different from those of people of a comparable age in the past.

For the current generation of older Minangkabau, it has not been unusual to spend one's whole adult life in the *rantau* — Padang, Jakarta, or another part of Indonesia. It was only after the inception of regional autonomy in 2001 that there started to be more opportunities in the regions. Regional autonomy resulted in a significant decentralization of governance and services from the hierarchical structure of the New Order to a system where the units of authority are the *kabupaten* (county-like divisions of provinces often referred to as "regencies") and *kotamadya* (municipal areas). Because the regions were given the right to run their own educational, health care, and governmental institutions and also authority over a range of services, it has become possible to have a professional career, including in the lucrative field of politics, in every part of Indonesia. In some parts of the country, regional autonomy has been associated with a return to their region of origin by experienced and successful people who had been working in the capital and elsewhere. The skills and experience of these individuals are needed in the regions, but this phenomenon has been associated with the social issue referred to as *daerahisme* (regionalism) which relates to the marked preference for employing people who come from the region in question over those who come from someplace else (Djohan 2007). In many parts of Indonesia, an associated trend has been observed, namely an increase in the status and importance of membership in an ethnic group, use of the local language, and the integration of certain aspects of local culture into the public realm. In parts of Java, for example, this has manifested as a series of local laws requiring that Javanese be used in the public sector at certain times (even though this contravenes national law requiring Indonesian to be the language of official interaction) (Solo Pos 2011; Republika 2014b; Kompas 2014a). In West Sumatra, a comparable cultural movement has emerged called *Kembali ke Nagari* (Return to the *Nagari*), which involves restructuring local administration to correspond to the traditional administrative divisions of the Minangkabau world that were broken up under the New Order (Biezeveld 2007).

In practice, however, the enhanced opportunities at the local level have had comparatively little impact on the current generation of older Minangkabau, having been instituted relatively recently when they had already spent a significant part of their career in other places and were facing older age, retirement, and the possible social and personal changes associated with this period of life in places other than their village of origin. As a result, most of them have not been in a position to benefit greatly from these social changes. Nonetheless, many older individuals in the Minangkabau community must now cope with the social and cultural impacts of a changed (and changing) society that is very different from what they experienced for most of their life. For those involved, this is presenting special challenges for which there is no precedent in Minangkabau culture and which can be seen to be creating a tension within the traditional system.

Pulai

Pulai was Aminah's oldest daughter and one of her six children who survived to adulthood and had their own children. Pulai had a great advantage over her three sisters in terms of position and power in the extended family. Not only was she the oldest of Aminah's children, but her three sisters were the youngest in the family. Pulai was very close to her mother, not just because of age, but because of circumstances. Aminah had married very young, and, at one point, she and Pulai were pregnant at the same time. Aminah's youngest child, Maryati (Chapter 1) was a few months younger than her nephew, Amran, who was Pulai's oldest child.

Another important reason Pulai had the most power in the family after her mother was that her married life was also most similar. Like Aminah, Pulai's husband was already married, and she was his second wife. Like her mother's husband, Pulai's husband was much older than she was when they married. None of Aminah's other children had a polygamous marriage. Because of the large age difference, both Pulai and Aminah spent decades as widows. Unlike Aminah, however, Pulai's husband was a low-level, but important, official in the Dutch colonial administration in Central Sumatra (as the region was then called).

It was easy for everyone to understand why Aminah was so close to Pulai, trusted her judgement, and listened to her whenever there was an important decision to be made, such as how to share the income from the harvest or how to allocate land to members of the family to use when they married. Pulai's position became even stronger when Aminah's brother died. He had been the *mamak* of the family, and his role was taken over by Kadir, Pulai's brother who was immediately below her. They were close in age and able to understand each other better. In addition, as it happened, Pulai and Kadir were seriously injured when the family house was struck by a mortar during the 1959 civil war in which West Sumatra rebelled against the central government. They were both taken to the nearby town of Bukittinggi for treatment and spent several months in recovery. Kadir's wife, who was at the Valley family's house at the time, was killed. This incident brought Pulai and Kadir closer, and both benefitted from this when Kadir become *mamak* of the extended family.

Soon after the war ended in 1961, Pulai, with the support of her husband's family and his children with his other wife (her husband had died by this time), built a house on land belonging to the extended family. She was the first in the family to do so. The house was brick and cement with a tin roof and was one of the most modern houses in Koto at the time. This raised her standing greatly, in the family as well as in the village. Because she was widowed and her two oldest children, both boys, no longer lived in the village, she would allow and even encourage the young children of her sisters to stay over at her house.

Like her mother, Pulai learned very early how to manage all the responsibilities of the head of the family. She knew all about the property the family had and how to take care of it. More importantly, she learned from her mother how to manage the family members, who became increasingly numerous as her sisters married and had their own children, some of whom were girls. Pulai herself had only one daughter while her sister, Nurijah (Chapter 2), had eight children, four of whom were girls. Erni (Chapter 3) had seven children, two of whom were girls, and Maryati (Chapter 1), the youngest sister, had four children, all girls. At some point, there were bad feelings between the sisters when the younger ones felt that they had not been given a reasonable amount of land to support their families. They felt that Pulai and Kadir used their power to overrule them and could usually influence their mother in this way. Each of the younger sisters would try to stay on the good side of these three most powerful family members, but Aminah usually agreed with Pulai and Kadir.

Like her mother, Pulai was not very affected by the death of her husband. He had rarely been around anyway because he had to spend time at his other wife's home as well. She lived in a different village, and Pulai and her children sometimes did not see him for days at a time. In addition, Pulai was not dependent on her husband for financial support and always had plenty to eat, a comfortable home that belonged to the extended family, and enough extra income to send her children to school. Her children's education was one of the reasons she tried as hard as she could to convince Aminah and Kadir that she needed more land. Her sisters were much younger so her claim was that her children were significantly older than her sisters' children and should take priority. Her youngest child, Inang (Chapter 5), is the same age as the oldest child of Nurijah (Chapter 2), the oldest of Pulai's younger sisters.

In many ways, Pulai benefitted from the traditional social structure almost as much as her mother. Aminah, however, had been the only daughter. With three younger sisters, Pulai had to compete seriously for power and resources. She was luckier than some women in the village who had sisters who were closer in age to them.

When Aminah died, Pulai lost her main ally in the extended family but she still had Kadir whose support for her grew even stronger. Her younger sisters, however, became more persistent in challenging her on issues that were important to them. The friction within the family grew considerably and, while Kadir was able to mediate to some extent, the relationship between the sisters worsened, even though the conflict never became public. If anything, the Valley family was seen by the whole village as an example of a harmonious family. Many children from other families would come to the Valley to learn to read the Quran and study with the Valley children. Some would sleep at the Valley house, while others spent the night at Pulai's. This went on throughout the 1960s and 70s.

Overall, Pulai, with a great deal of support from Kadir, managed the extended family quite well after the death of her mother, and the people of Koto thought very highly of her. She took care to suppress internal conflict that emerged within the family and, in large part, she and Kadir dealt with it successfully. Nonetheless, this was a much harder task than it had been for her mother, and Pulai was the last family member whose life mostly conformed to the traditional patterns of Koto.

OLDER MINANGKABAU IN THE *RANTAU*

One aspect of this change is for the individuals who have spent their whole adult lives away from their place of origin living in a non-Minangkabau community and taking part in the broader, more Indonesian context. These individuals gave up their direct access to family assets early in life, even though in theory they might be able to claim a share or voice in how those assets are used, and have lived largely outside the traditional system. For them, personal earnings are their main form of support, and they generally do not participate directly in the events of the village and the day-to-day decision-making of the extended family. Both male and female Minangkabau living in the *rantau* often marry people from other ethnic groups, which, in some cases, loosens their ties to the village and sometimes to their extended family as well. In many cases, people in this situation visit their family in the village only in the holiday period at the end of the Muslim fasting month of Ramadan and not usually every year. Nonetheless, the influx of Minangkabau who live permanently in the *rantau* to West Sumatra at this time is a significant social phenomenon that generates a great deal of news coverage and excitement locally. For the visitors, this is a time to see friends and family and show off their success. As is the case elsewhere in Indonesia, many more people return to the cities after the holiday than left at the beginning. A glimpse of those who have apparently made it in places like Jakarta seems to be an irresistible draw for people in the village who might have been thinking of leaving, even though the majority of Minangkabau who live in the *rantau* do not achieve great success or wealth. The perceived potential of opportunities outside of West Sumatra, or at least away from the village, seems to have grown over time to the point where it is contributing to a noticeable decline in the number of young adults and middle-aged people in the Minangkabau heartland.

Despite having spent many years outside of the village or West Sumatra, many older migrants are beginning to experience new problems associated with increasing age. One of these relates to their lack of social status once they stop working. For many of the Minangkabau who spend their whole working life in another place, their self-esteem and personal conception of identity is associated largely with their job. This is especially the case for professionals. It is often difficult for them to adjust to the loss of status associated with stopping work, especially as it is not replaced by a position within the extended family that might bring respect and purpose. For those who have worked in the informal sector, selling goods in a market for example, it is often not possible to stop working entirely. This situation exists across Indonesia, where the majority of elderly people must continue to work to support themselves. Without the safety net traditional social structure provides, old age may be extremely stressful for those who cannot expect help from a network of family members they should have been able to rely upon in the context of the traditional environment.

However, a second and, in some cases, more concerning problem is emerging for the ageing population of Minangkabau migrants. This relates to the need to care for their own ageing parents, many of whom remained in the village. In the past when more people spent their lives in the village, often in the same household as older relatives, the transition between generations occurred gradually, and there were recognized social structures available to care for elderly family members who might need a great deal of assistance, as in the case of Kamil. Even if these mechanisms did not function in an ideal manner, they were widely understood and agreed upon such that they provided a guide for how a family could manage even a very serious illness in one of its older members. At the current time, however, many very old people have been left behind in the villages without members of the next generation to help support them. This has had a number of impacts which there are no precedents to address.

Some of these very old people have children who live in other parts of Indonesia or West Sumatra and may be able to live with them in those locations. While this arrangement frequently seems ideal to both the child and the elderly parent, in fact, it is often fraught with problems. The parent often imagines they will be part of a household of the type they may recall from their youth where they are in constant contact with their children and grandchildren as an integral part of their daily life. In practice, however, younger people, especially in Jakarta and other big cities, may work long hours and typically spend a great deal of time commuting. Grandchildren who were born in the *rantau* often speak only Indonesian and cannot communicate easily with elderly grandparents who speak only Minang. They may also be busy and rarely at home. This means that the old person who has been brought from the village must spend a great deal of time alone or in a family setting they cannot really participate in because of language difficulties and unmet expectations. If their health is poor and their children have the means, a maid may be hired to help them during the day. However, because the Minangkabau do not have a servant culture, this type of situation is typically very awkward and uncomfortable for the older person involved. The elderly in this situation may have no friends of a similar background in the city and nothing meaningful to do. If they are in poor health and have to rely on children and grandchildren, they may be aware of the financial and emotional burden they represent, and this is an additional source of distress. For this reason, most would choose to remain in the village if they could.

Nurijah

Nurijah is Aminah's third child and second daughter. She was considered among the luckiest by practically everyone in the extended family. She married Jalal, who came from a village about 30 km from Koto. Jalal was born and grew up in Malaysia, which had long been an attractive destination for *marantau*. This gave him very high social status in Koto because, when he and Nurijah got married in the late 1940s, Malaysia's currency was strong, and it happened that Jalal's family had done well there. In addition, he had gone to English schools such that he spoke the language quite well, and this was considered highly desirable in Indonesia.

He was asked to teach English at the local high schools and later at the one college in the town of Batusangkar.

Nurijah was convinced that her future was secure. She and Jalal had eight children. More importantly for Nurijah, four of the children were girls. She would have a strong claim to the family property since she had contributed four girls to the family line that began with her grandmother Maryam, Aminah's mother. Soon after their marriage, she and Jalal built a large house for their nuclear family on family land about 500 yards from the original family home.

As things changed in Indonesia, so did Koto. While Aminah was illiterate and Nurijah had barely any formal education, all but one of her children finished high school, and three of them earned university degrees. All four girls eventually became school teachers, a remarkable achievement by the standards of Koto. At the time they entered the job market, teachers did not require university training.

Nurijah is now in her mid-eighties. She has been sick for the last ten years, having suffered a stroke that left her paralysed. She has serious difficulty speaking and cannot take care of herself in any way. She is bedridden and must depend on a wheelchair to move around. More importantly, she now has to live in Jakarta with one of her daughters, something she says she never expected.

When asked about her experiences, Nurijah expresses only sadness and talks about how she never imagined, when she married Jalal almost seventy years ago, that she would end up like this in her old age. She lives far away from her home in the village without her husband (who died years ago) in a city she does not like, with neighbours she knows nothing about and has barely met. She thought that she would be surrounded by her grandchildren in her old age. While this has occurred, the reality is far from what she expected. All her grandchildren were born in Jakarta and do not speak Minang, the language she feels most comfortable using. While she can understand standard Indonesian, she can barely make sense of what her grandchildren say, as they speak mostly in the local dialect of Jakarta. However, all her daughters live in Jakarta and the surrounding regions, and she cannot live alone.

When asked where she would rather live, without hesitation, Nurijah says Koto. But the big house she and Jalal built is empty most of the time now. The only one of her children who still lives in Koto is a son who is married to a woman from the village. He lives with his wife and children not far from Nurijah's house. Every now and then, he checks to make sure nothing has happened to the house. He does some yard work and cleans the inside of the house as necessary. According to *adat*, it would not be appropriate for Nurijah to live with her son who lives in the house of his wife. Nurijah cannot live in her house in the village by herself because of her ill health. While Jakarta would not be her first, or even second or third choice, she feels she has no alternative. The most important thing for her now is to be with one of her daughters. She feels lucky that her children are willing to take care of her in her condition but she always thinks about Koto and how she misses the village and her home.

THOSE LEFT BEHIND IN THE VILLAGE

Not surprisingly, many of the very old prefer to stay in the village. They tend to be very reluctant to leave their house and land and are concerned that the assets of their family will be taken over by other people, even if their children live elsewhere and have no particular interest in property in the village. This may be a very pressing and stressing issue for older women whose traditional responsibilities include management and development of family assets. In some cases, the older people who remain in the village have no children or have lost contact with children in the *rantau* who left the village long ago. A lack of female descendants has always been a problem in Minangkabau because of the resulting extinction of the family line. In the modern context, though, it has other implications as well that relate to the safety and well-being of the elderly. In the past, when more people stayed in the village, or returned there after a period spent in the *rantau*, there were generally members of the next generation available to assist older people, even if they were not their children. Other members of the extended matrilineal family might also play this role, and it was not unusual for an old person to be supported by nieces and nephews as well as their own siblings and cousins. As the social networks of the village have become more depleted, a far greater number of elderly people in West Sumatra are being classified as *lansia terlantar*, an Indonesian term used in the health care and social services sector to mean "neglected elderly".

The national Ministry of Social Affairs estimates there are about 2.8 million *lansia terlantar* in Indonesia (Jamsos 2012). An older person falls into this category if he or she does not have access to an income that allows for a reasonable standard of living and also does not have a social support network that can provide assistance with day-to-day living as well as in relation to health needs. While programmes are in place to provide a kind of pension to people in this position, the fact that the Ministry of Social Affairs can only address the needs of a minority of individuals in this way has been widely reported and discussed (see, for example, Purbaya 2013; Suara Pembaruan 2013).

In West Sumatra, as well as in other parts of Indonesia, the existence of a growing number of older people without family to support and care for them has given rise to a new phenomenon that is familiar in the West — the establishment of nursing homes designed specifically to meet the daily and health needs of elderly people who do not have other alternatives. At present, there are four institutions of this kind in West Sumatra. Two of these, PSTW Sabai nan Aluih and PSTW Kasih Sayang Ibu, are run by the Department of Social Affairs. PSTW Sabai nan Aluih is located in the town of Sicincin, not far from the provincial capital of Padang. PSTW Kasih Sayang Ibu is in Cubadak in the Tanah Datar region near the village of Koto where the Valley family comes from. Two private facilities are also in operation: PSTW Syekh Burhanuddin located in Pariaman, which, like Sicincin, is part of the traditional *rantau* and is located on the coast near Padang, and PSTW Kasih Ibu in the town of Payakumbuh, which, like PSTW Kasih Sayang Ibu, is also in the heartland of the Minangkabau world.

The need for institutions of this kind in Minangkabau has been problematic because the idea of leaving older people in the care of people who are not relatives in the context of the matrilineal family is both foreign and disturbing to many people. Nonetheless, the provincial Department of Social Affairs reports that the residents of these institutions include, not just those who have no family, but also elderly people whose families have brought them there for care. The public homes receive funding from the Department of Social Affairs to support their activities, but the private institutions must rely heavily on donations and other sources of funds (Antara 2008). This creates a continuing problem in providing adequate food and care for the residents, especially since the number of older people needing assistance has grown enormously in recent years.

At present, the two public facilities are operating over capacity. From only a handful of residents when they first opened in the early 1980s, each institution is now full and cannot accommodate all those brought to them for care. In a speech made on National Old Age Day (*Hari Lanjut Usia Nasional*) in June of 2014, then Governor of West Sumatra Irwan Prayitno called for people to care for their older relatives at home in a way that accorded with traditional culture and values. He also noted that building more nursing homes was not considered an appropriate solution in the local context, especially as many of the families of current residents were known to be able to afford care for their relatives at home (Hendra 2014).

A number of other initiatives have also been established in West Sumatra to serve the growing number of elderly people as well as to meet the needs of families who are trying to care for them. These have included health care centres that specifically treat older people (*puskesmas lansia*); health posts, associated with health care centres, that monitor the condition of the elderly in their own communities (*posyandu lansia*); and also programmes to facilitate older people remaining in the family home. A number of social and health care organizations, some of which are run by religious groups, are starting to offer "day care" for older people who live with younger relatives who work during the day (Antara 2012). Similar to such institutions elsewhere in the world, these are places older people can spend the day where they will be assisted with their basic needs and encouraged to take part in activities intended to interest and occupy them. Similar programmes exist across Indonesia and are recognized as a necessary extension of the health and social services system to respond to the growing population of elderly people (JPNN 2014).

For the Minangkabau community, changes to the social, political, economic, and cultural environment have taken place very quickly. People who are now entering older age largely grew up in an environment that closely approximated the traditional ideal in terms of the matrilineal social structure and observed first-hand the experiences of their grandparents and other older relatives who had lived their whole lives within this system. They were raised to view dependence on family land and real assets as appropriate and desirable as a manifestation of the continuation of the matrilineal social system. For a not inconsiderable number of Minangkabau, however, social change associated with the development of Indonesia as a modern nation gave them choices that were not available to earlier generations.

As noted above, the possibility to benefit from higher education and advanced training, to move to other parts of Indonesia as a professional, and to earn an income that far outstripped what was available in the village in terms of what it could provide expanded greatly during the New Order years. The current period which has been characterized by regional autonomy has offered similar but even greater opportunities to many younger people. In the past, even people who had been extremely successful in the *rantau* tended to return to their village in larger numbers. They had an established place in the village hierarchy and a home (that of their mother's extended family) where people would have to accept them. Nonetheless, those who returned to the village were often treated in accordance with their perceived ability to contribute to the family. Those who had made a lot of money were often received more readily than those who had not by members of their family in the village. Migrants who decided to stay in the *rantau* and who became wealthy were often resented when they tried to participate in family decision-making or to influence the ways of the village because they were seen as having given up the right to make those kinds of contributions when they left, even though their money was usually welcome. This problem persists today and is a frequent subject of discussion among Minangkabau intellectuals who have been successful outside of West Sumatra.

Minangkabau who are retiring from professional positions in the *rantau* increasingly feel that they can choose not to return to the village. Many can support themselves in older age and wish to avoid what they see as endemic infighting in the village and the restrictions of the complex network of family connections with their accompanying social obligations. This is the norm among many of the most successful Minangkabau professionals. Despite having been raised within the traditional context of the village, they are abandoning their ties to the extended family and its communal property and, as a result, are breaking the cycle of migration and return. The result of this is that many family homes are empty, positions of leadership that are properly filled by older members are vacant, and, according to some observers at least, certain aspects of *adat* can no longer be fulfilled because the traditional social structure is incomplete (Sumarty and Azizah 2007; Oktaninda 2009).

Muhsin

Muhsin, sixty-six, is the oldest child of Erni, Aminah's third daughter and Nurijah's younger sister. He lives in Padang, the capital of West Sumatra, about 113 kilometres from Koto. While Padang is not the cultural capital of the Minangkabau world, it is the political and economic centre of the region. Muhsin has a successful career as an academic. He is a professor at a public university in Padang and served as Rector of that institution for the two terms (eight years) allowed by the law. He is married to a woman from a well-to-do family who comes from a village not far from Koto. They have five children, three girls and two boys, all of whom have at least an undergraduate degree. Muhsin enjoys both prestige and financial security in his old age. Because of his high rank, he has not yet retired. Generally, public employees retire by the age of fifty-six in Indonesia, but, because of his rank, Muhsin can continue working until he is seventy if he chooses to.

Muhsin feels very secure in his old age. He has four brothers and two sisters, all of whom have university degrees and professional jobs. Muhsin would easily be able to take up the family title of Datuak Sati Basa Batuah, but when it was offered to him by members of his extended family soon after the fall of the New Order government when the push for a return to tradition was strong, he turned it down. He preferred to remain in Padang with his family, deliberately isolating himself from life in Koto. When his parents were alive he would return to the village regularly but only to see them, not to take part in the affairs of the extended family. Citing his responsibilities at the university, he rejected any traditional role in the village. He was fully aware that the consequence of this choice would be that he would not be able to return to the family home in the village in his old age should he need to. As a result, he bought and/or built five houses in Padang. Some of these are now used by those of his children who are married and have children. He and his wife live in one with two of his married daughters, along with their husbands and children. A son, who recently finished medical school, is now married and lives in another town.

Muhsin, like many Minangkabau in his position, chose to build his life around his nuclear family, a pattern that is more associated with modern Indonesia than with traditional Minangkabau society. In Muhsin's case, this has been highly beneficial. Neither of his two sisters, both of whom are professionals who live in the village and work in nearby towns, have children so he does not have the burden of having to support nieces and nephews, one of the main responsibilities of a maternal uncle. Muhsin is content and happy with his life in Padang, completely free from traditional obligations. Recently, he announced that he and his wife want to be buried on land they purchased in Padang and have chosen their exact burial sites. This is a very significant symbolic decision that exemplifies the distance he wishes to maintain from the village and its customs and traditions.

THE PATTERNS OF AGEING IN
MINANGKABAU SOCIETY

It is difficult to overestimate the impact of social change on the traditional patterns of ageing in the Minangkabau community. Centuries old traditions have changed very rapidly, and the individuals who are currently considered *lansia* are living in a time that seems to be a cultural tipping point when the course of events appears to favour change and is creating the need for institutions, like nursing homes and day care for the elderly, that were unheard of just a few decades ago. For the first time in Minangkabau history, the traditional social structure defined by the matrilineal extended family is less important than the social status that individuals can create through their own efforts. It is possible to earn more money and acquire greater assets than would be available even under the best circumstances in the village for those who have the education and training to have benefitted from a professional career. However, those who did not have this kind of experience and may even have spent their whole lives in the village are also being affected by the inability of traditional social structures to compete with modern alternatives. The growing phenomenon of neglected elderly is a direct consequence of this because, in the past, older people would have always had relatives in a position of social obligation to them who would have to help them in old age. In other words, on the one hand, the traditional system is losing its appeal for those who have been able to acquire significant wealth in the modern system as well as for those who aspire to wealth, even if they live in the village. On the other, it is no longer strong enough to withstand the pace of social change, and traditional safety nets are failing.

These tensions in the Minangkabau community are being intensified by the nature of the life course in Indonesia. As life expectancy increased, very much like the situation in many Western countries, Indonesia's population of old people has grown as has a smaller but not insignificant number of the very old. For the first time, many Minangkabau (and Indonesians in general), who are themselves retired or approaching retirement and can already be classified as *lansia,* are also responsible for extremely elderly parents who often have significant health problems and mobility issues. This situation is largely outside the capacity of the traditional system to accommodate. While there were always individuals who lived to a very old age, they often remained in reasonable health because the kind of modern health care that allows a person to survive a catastrophic illness, such as a stroke or cancer, has only become available recently. For the Minangkabau community specifically, this situation is compounded by the tradition of *marantau* which, combined with the increasing lure of larger cities, is emptying the villages of younger people who often prefer to live elsewhere. As the Indonesian population continues to age, it is likely that the experience of the Minangkabau at this time will soon become the norm for other groups across the nation.

3

Adat Traditions and the Elderly

ADAT IN MINANGKABAU

The term *adat* in Indonesian means "traditional law and customs". The cognate term in Minang is *adaik*, which has the same meaning. *Adat* is used throughout this book because it is most frequently used in writings about Indonesia in English and has no exact equivalent. *Adat* is an aspect of culture that is well known throughout Indonesia, where each ethnic/ linguistic group has its own customs and traditions that relate to its specific social and historical context. *Adat* existed long before the modern state of Indonesia, and most regions have traditional interpretations of locally relevant, culturally enforced law that relate to issues like land ownership, property rights, and inheritance; marriage, divorce, and other aspects of family law; life course events of local significance (birth, death, circumcision, and so forth); and many other elements of culture that reflect the traditional interpretation of shared experiences in a given location or among members of a specific group. Modern law, which was first instituted by the Dutch colonial government and which has been revised and updated in the context of the independent nation of Indonesia, addresses some of the issues to which *adat* also applies, although these two types of law have generally been seen as separate. *Adat* relates more to individuals' relationship to their own ethnic culture, while modern law defines a similar relationship to the state (see Lindsey (2008) for a discussion of the nature of the law in Indonesia).

In recent years, the concept of "local wisdom" (*kearifan lokal*) has become part of the national intellectual paradigm and is often applied in situations where it is felt that local ways may have value in addressing some issue or solving some problem that is of current concern. This is in contrast to a historical tendency in Indonesia to adopt approaches and solutions that come from the Western intellectual environment without much consideration of whether they apply in the local context. Much of the content of local wisdom derives from *adat*, which is seen as providing a socially acceptable approach or suggesting potential solutions that draw on the shared experience of the community where they are to be implemented.

Since the establishment of regional autonomy, local culture has become more significant at the regional level. The devolution of real power to local authorities in control of sub-provincial administrative jurisdictions has, in practical terms, caused the populations of many governmental areas to be more homogeneous than the population at the provincial or other level because they are so much smaller, and many ethnic groups are geographically localized. What this has meant is that members of the public in various regions are more likely to share certain aspects of culture that may potentially inform policy at the local level. This is frequently mentioned as a possible avenue to support development in various parts of the country (see, for example, Widyanto 2012; Ghofar 2013; Sudadi 2014).

In West Sumatra, the idea of *adat* has always been strong, even before the establishment of regional autonomy and the current interest in traditional practices. However, this may be a function of the way the Minangkabau tend to view their *adat*, rather than the way *adat* functions in current society or the role people are willing to give it in modern life. Even among non-Minangkabau, there is a persistent idea in Indonesia that Minangkabau *adat* is both strong and of extreme importance to members of the community. The nature of *adat* (*adaik* in Minang) is described in traditional literature as follows:

> *Adaik nan indak lakang dek paneh, nan indak lapuak dek ujan, paliang-paliang balumuik dek cindawan.*

> *Adat* doesn't crack in the sun; it doesn't warp in the rain; at most it becomes covered by moss and mushrooms.

The proverb above, which likens *adat* to a piece of wood, is used to suggest its timeless nature and stresses the fact that it does not wear out. It indicates that social change as well as outside pressures and influences (represented metaphorically by the sun and rain) do not damage it or impair its usefulness. Another proverb states:

> *Adaik dipakai baru, kain dipakai usang.*
> When *adat* is used, it stays new; when cloth is used, it wears out.

This expression is used to emphasize the perceived flexibility of *adat*, which is seen as being appropriate and adaptable to every generation. The following proverb explains the source of this flexibility:

> *Adaik nan basisampiang, sarak nan batilanjang.*
> *Adat* wears a *sampiang*; the law goes naked.

A *sampiang* is a type of sarong worn over pants by men that reaches from the waist to the knees and is part of ceremonial dress. Its colours and patterns vary from region to region and also have specific meanings in the context of tradition. The proverb means that *adat* has many aspects and variants that derive from custom. The law, in this case religious law, by contrast, has a specific meaning that is fixed and applies to everyone in the same way. Traditional thinking also holds that *adat* is eternal in nature:

> *Adaik sapanjang jalan, cupak sapanjang batuang.*
> *Adat* is as long as a road; a *cupak* is as long as a segment of bamboo.

This proverb suggests that *adat* has no limitations and applies in every situation and at all times. A *cupak*, which is a locally standard measure for rice, is made from a segment of a type of bamboo. It is a symbol of laws that are made within the context of *adat* and can be changed as long as they remain compatible with its precepts. This is comparable to the size of the *cupak* used in a given area which can be changed by making a new one.

These proverbs, and many other similar items, encapsulate the way *adat* is viewed in the Minangkabau way of thinking and would be agreed with by most members of the community, at least in theory. *Adat* is seen as being capable of application in all eras, to every generation, and in all contexts people in the society might reasonably encounter in relating to other people and the institutions of their community. While traditional thinking allows for *adat* to be adapted for a given situation, this may be difficult in practice because of the requirement for consensus among those affected and the fact that there are often a number of different views and interests in any group that may affect the process of change. For this reason, *adat* often changes gradually and imperceptibly as people begin to do things in a slightly different way because of their situation without consciously considering that *adat* is changing. This is reflected in normal Minang language use where the term *adaik* refers to "traditional law and custom" but can also be used more generically to mean "the way things are done".

The origins of Minangkabau *adat* and some of its content are discussed in the traditional literature of the culture, which includes the examples shown above. This parallels the way certain aspects of the Judeo-Christian ethic are contained in the Old Testament and other writings. Other elements of *adat* have never been formally recorded but are known to members of the society as the way things have always been done and, often, the only way things can be done. For this reason, some parts of Minangkabau *adat* are consistent across the population and are understood in much the same way by people everywhere. Others of its aspects vary somewhat from place to place and reflect a certain level of diversity in the community. The elements of *adat* that relate to the structure of the society and the nature of the family, its main constituent part, are agreed upon, at least generally, in all segments of the Minangkabau community.

ADAT AND MATRILINY

As discussed in Chapter 2, Minangkabau society is matrilineal and is based on family membership that descends from a female ancestor. Individuals remain a member of their mother's family for life. In the past, it was the norm for people to live in close contact with their matrilineal family, often on family-owned land. In recent times, however, a trend towards a nuclear family structure has been observable that reflects an accommodation with the needs of modern life and the national culture of Indonesia. The extended matrilineal family unit was the functional entity in traditional society, with land and other real property held communally by the group. Individuals could also own property bought with their own earnings, but this was difficult in the villages because all of the useable land had come under the control of one or another extended family in the distant past. It is extremely difficult to buy land anywhere in West Sumatra today because of this pattern of traditional ownership. In order to sell or dispose permanently of a piece of traditionally held property, the whole matrilineal family must agree. In practice, this agreement is very difficult to achieve, and many people are extremely concerned about losing family assets or will not compromise on how the profits from such a sale will be divided or used. Consensus of this kind is supposed to be unanimous, with family members who hold opposing points of view responsible for winning others over to their way of thinking.

For this reason, a system of land mortgaging developed and is institutionalized by *adat* in the Minangkabau community. This process, called *manggadaikan* in Minang, gives the right to use the land to an outsider for a period of time in exchange for a sum of money that is agreed upon by the parties involved. While consensus within the extended family that owns the land is required, this is an accepted way to raise money enshrined in *adat*, which allows such an act for several specific reasons. They are: a position of traditional leadership is vacant and funds are needed to install a member of the family and confer the family's traditional title; the family home (specifically the *rumah gadang* with its buffalo horn roof) has fallen into disrepair and must be restored; a daughter of the family is to be married and money is needed to pay for an appropriate wedding; or someone in the family has died and funds are needed for an appropriate funeral. In modern times, some families add the need to pay for the formal education of its younger members or to fund the Muslim haj pilgrimage to this list, but these are recent additions to *adat*.

Land that is in use for various productive purposes is referred to as *pusako tinggi* (high inheritance) and belongs to the extended family. It is passed down through the generations in the female line as discussed above. For this reason, this type of asset is sometimes referred to as *pusako basalin* (inheritance by birth). By contrast, *pusako rendah* (low inheritance) are assets that were gained by other means and can be sold or mortgaged by the family members who are entitled to them. *Arato pancarian* (earned assets) are wealth that is earned by a husband and wife during their marriage. If the marriage is dissolved, these assets can be divided by agreement of the spouses. *Arato surang* (individual assets) are those that are earned by an individual and belong to him or her alone. This could include assets brought into a marriage by one partner which would return to him or her if the marriage ends. *Adat* provides guidelines for dealing with all these forms of wealth and also with *tanah ulayat*, land that belongs to the extended family but has not yet been used productively. The rules for inheritance are of extreme concern in the Minangkabau world because of the need to protect the holdings of the extended family, and *adat* institutionalizes the way in which this should occur.

In the past, the assets of the extended family included some kind of communal home that housed the living female members of the family, their spouses and children. These women would continue to live in the family home for life and would bring their husband into the household for the duration of the marriage. Who is entitled to live in this home is also outlined by *adat* which provides a place for all members of the matrilineal family should they need or want it. This includes all the female members of the family as well as their direct descendants but does not include members of the family by marriage once the marriage is no longer in existence. A man whose wife dies, for example, must leave her family's home and return to the home of his mother and other matrilineal relatives. Female members of the family may always claim a place as well as a share of the assets of the extended family.

Minangkabau families are further organized into larger groups referred to as *paruik* that represent a number of extended families that are related in the matrilineal line. *Paruik* is the ordinary Minang word for "stomach". In the case of the family, the term is understood more as "womb" and suggests a common origin. These families can trace their heritage back to an identifiable female ancestor but have branched and expanded and may include a large number of members. Very large *paruik* may split, with the resulting groups establishing their own leaders and, in a sense, becoming new extended families. They may take control of the communal assets most closely associated with their members and to continue to function in the way they had before but with a smaller number of people.

At the societal level, these large networks of families related through the maternal line are ordered by clan membership. There are felt to be four main clans in the Minangkabau world, although local branches often have their own names. These numerous local classifications, however, are each associated with one of the four major clans, which are Koto, Piliang, Bodi, and Caniago. At some time in the distant past, the Koto and Piliang clans and the Bodi and Caniago clans aligned according to their interpretation of *adat*. Nonetheless, these four clans, through their many branches and local components, remain extremely important conceptually, and *adat* requires that members of all four clans be present in a given settlement for it to be considered a village. Because, historically, the village was one of the significant administrative divisions in people's living environment, it was necessary for all the clans to be represented to ensure that the village was a meaningful representation of the community as a whole.

The clans are also important in the context of family relationships because *adat* does not allow marriage between members of the same clan. The long-term result of this in a village like Koto is that unions that occur among members of each successive generation reinforce the links between the clans that are present in the community. It is for this reason that it is considered acceptable for a person to marry his or her first cousin if the potential partner is the child of a maternal uncle. This cousin will belong to his or her mother's family and, of course, have membership in her clan. A similar cousin on a person's father's side is also a possible match but is not marked in the matrilineal system because of the much looser and more distant relationship with one's father's family. Marriage between first cousins in the maternal line, as described above, tends to be prized in Minangkabau society and was quite common in the past when many families tried to ensure at least one such match occurred in each generation.

Anthropologists have long been interested in the advantages of this type of marriage in Minangkabau society, and a number of possible explanations for its social value have been suggested. For example, several Dutch scholars who became interested in this issue beginning during the colonial period suggested that this pattern of cousin marriages served to fulfil the requirements of reciprocity between families who acted as "wife givers" and "wife takers" at various times (see, for example, Josselin de Jong 1980). More recent scholars have viewed this social practice as representing an "exchange of men" (see, for example, Peletz 1987). By contrast, it has also been suggested that the practice is not so much an example of Levi-Strauss' (1969) theory of exchange but can be seen as a system to increase social value within the family group, rather than create cohesion within a family lineage (Krier 2000). Indonesian scholars who have discussed this issue have generally accepted the views of Western anthropologists that the system ensures a type of exogamy and represents spouse exchange between families and clans but have also noted that this kind of marriage does not appear to be as attractive to members of the Minangkabau community as in the past (see, for example, Junus 1964; Ali 1997; Arifin 2004).

For many members of the public, however, the desirable nature of marriage between first cousins within the matrilineal system often has a more practical purpose, that of trying to ensure smooth social interactions between people who will be compelled to deal with each other within the traditional social structure. Another strong motivation seems to be a desire to know as much as possible about a marriage partner for one's child. In other words, members of the community generally do not see a larger, society-wide result of this practice but instead view it as a strictly local and personal issue that can make life easier for the people involved, including themselves. People do recognize the difficulty of dealing with in-laws and in finding out exactly what their antecedents are. This is important in maintaining the social standing of the family. These aims were recognized by some of the earlier scholars who studied the Minangkabau community (see, for example, Loeb 1934). There is also an idea that a cousin comes from a known background and would be less likely to disrupt the way that particular family deals with its members and assets and also raises its children. There is some indication that marriages of this kind were never considered greatly desirable among young people, even though many recognized the importance of agreeing to this type of match for the sake of the family's interests and to please their parents. Among members of the younger generation today, marriage to a first cousin is increasingly unusual. Even when parents and other older members of the matrilineal family would like to have such a marriage in the younger generation, young people, who increasingly work outside the village or who have graduated from a university and work in a professional context, have much wider circles of friends and acquaintances and are more likely to find their own marriage partner from among the people they know and work with.

Kadir

Like his own maternal uncle, Kadir, one of Aminah's sons, married his maternal uncle's daughter. Also, like the uncle himself, this marriage was arranged by Kadir's uncle and the whole family. Kadir was very happy with the arranged marriage. In fact, he was proud that his uncle preferred him as a son-in-law over his only brother, Lukman. He had not been surprised, however, that his uncle, and indeed the rest of the family, wanted him to be the one to continue the long-standing tradition that one son in each generation would marry a daughter of their maternal uncle. Kadir was better educated and considered more suitable by the family to inherit the role of *mamak* in the Valley family when his uncle died. As a result of this marriage and the family's traditions, the two extended families were very close. They socialized more with each other than was the norm for families where there was no marriage involving cousins. Kadir's children and the children of his sisters were all childhood friends.

Kadir married in the second half of the 1940s and, by 1959, already had six children, all of them girls. In that year, his wife was killed when a mortar hit their house during the civil war between the Revolutionary Government of the Republic of Indonesia (known in Indonesia as PRRI) and the central government. He was seriously injured at the time but survived. When the war ended a year later after the PRRI rebel army was defeated, Kadir married his late wife's sister. *Adat* approves and even recommends this kind of marriage under these circumstances, when a wife has died and has already had children. There is a term for marrying the sister of one's deceased wife, *pindah lapiak*, which means "move to another (sleeping) mat". In the case of Kadir, both his family and his wife's family urged him to do this. He had five more children with his second wife, four girls and a boy. He died in 1998.

Kadir, his mother Aminah, and the whole Valley family were very happy that he had so many daughters because his sisters had had a large number of sons between them. The family was certain that the tradition of one of their boys marrying one of their uncle's daughters would continue. The issue came up whenever one of the boys in the family reached what was considered an appropriate age to marry. When a family came to propose that their daughter be married to one of the Valley family boys, consideration was always given to whether the boy should marry one of his uncle's daughters instead. In the end, however, no cousin marriages occurred among this generation of the Valley family, perhaps because of the level of education and experiences of this generation.

FAMILY LEADERSHIP UNDER *ADAT*

Adat dictates how many aspects of daily life should be conducted, and this extends to leadership within the matrilineal extended family. There are well-established leadership roles for both men and women in the Minangkabau family, and the individuals who play these roles are typically older people who have shown they have the experience as well as the personal qualities necessary to manage family assets but also the people who are their responsibility. Older men are often referred to collectively as the *niniak-mamak*. They have a special responsibility for the young people of the family who are sometimes referred to collectively as *kamanakan* (nieces and nephews), a term which acknowledges the special responsibility of the maternal uncle for his sisters' children.

In the traditional context, as described in Chapter 2, older women gradually took over most of the responsibility for the management of their family's assets, a process they had been socialized to do from their teenage years. Decision-making as it related to the household, its expenses, living arrangements, and milestone events involving its members was generally subject to their views which carried the most weight and which were seen by both men and women as the right of women to determine. In practice, this system often led to problems between the women of an extended family of the same generation as well as between women of different ages. Since each female member of the household had a personal interest in obtaining access to resources for her children and was often very competitive with her own sisters and cousins as well, the multifamily, multigenerational matrilineal household was frequently tense, and bad feelings between members were common.

Often, it was very difficult for the senior women of a family to unite in agreement about what the family as a unit should do, especially in situations where financial or other benefits might result. *Adat* places a high premium on consensus, but the women of a family often had difficulty reaching an agreement that all of them could accept. The result of this has been that large tracts of family-owned land have often remained inactive for generations because the extended family that owns them cannot agree about how they should be used and by whom. The risk of this lack of action is that other people will simply take over land that seems to have been abandoned, causing loss by attrition to the established owners. Over time, the land may pass to the takers in a *de facto* sense because most family-held land in West Sumatra is not titled, with ownership being recognized only in the traditional, *adat* context.

Among the senior women of a family, it is often the oldest of each generation who can exert the most dominant role. Nonetheless, this is not fixed by *adat*, and a range of personal factors can come into play that affect which person will be recognized as the head of the family. In some situations, a woman may have been the only female child of her generation. In this case, leadership will naturally come to her when her mother and aunts die. In other cases, where there are several older women, who may be sisters or cousins (children of all the sisters of the previous generation), some may not live in the village, perhaps having moved away to work or because their husband works in another location. Other potentially eligible women may be incapable because they do not have the force of personality to manage their sisters and cousins as well as the younger generations. Others may be uninterested or lack the organizational skills to deal with complex problems of land and wealth management.

Erni

Erni, Aminah's fifth child and third daughter, was considered the least lucky in marriage when she wed a man from a very ordinary family in Koto. Unlike her oldest sister's husband, who was an important local administrator in the Dutch colonial administration, and different from Nurijah, her next sister, who married a man who was raised in Malaysia, Erni's husband was from the village and did not graduate from high school. He also did not have a regular job. When they got married in 1949, he taught religion without a permanent appointment in primary schools that needed his services. The work was unpredictable, and the pay was minimal. In addition, he often gave sermons at the mosque at the midday Friday prayers. This was unpaid. As a result, the extended family did not think highly of him, and Erni suffered the consequences.

Whenever the Valley family discussed who should have the right to cultivate specific pieces of land, which they rotated every three or four years, Erni always ended up with the least desirable field because it was the least fertile, difficult to irrigate, too far from the house with more inconvenient access, or had some other problem. Whenever she complained and demanded that she be given a better field, she was always outvoted or outmanoeuvred by her two older sisters. Erni, when asked, often talked about how difficult her life was and how her sisters disliked her. More often than not, they managed to influence their *mamak* as well as their mother. Sometimes Aminah felt sorry for Erni and went against the wishes of her older daughters, but this was rare.

The tension between Erni and her sisters and their negative view of her husband sometimes manifested in inappropriate behaviour or lack of consideration towards Erni and her husband. For example, Nurijah's husband, Jalal, used to teach English to the village children at the family home in the Valley. This always took place at night. The house had four bedrooms with a large common room that separated them. Jalal always conducted these classes right outside Erni's room. Erni often complained about this especially because the class was noisy and inconsiderate, often disturbing her and her husband late into the night.

As a result of the problems with use of family land and the way her sisters treated her, Erni and her husband left Koto soon after their first son was born. They did not return to the village and to the Valley house to live permanently until twelve years later. Several of her children were born outside Koto. During their time away, Erni's husband managed to get employment as a primary school teacher. He taught at several schools around the province before moving to the primary school in Koto and, several years later, to a secondary school in the town of Batusangkar. By this time, he had managed to earn a high school diploma and bachelor's degree.

Erni encouraged her husband to move back to the village and urged him to ask the government to place him at the school in the village because, by that time, her two older sisters had built their own houses on family land near the old house. Even though they still viewed her in the same way as before and often united against her, this bothered Erni much less than when they had lived in the same house. In addition, Erni was much more experienced and better able to deal with the difficult situation. Perhaps more importantly, her husband now had a regular job with a dependable, if low, salary. She could ignore her sisters' behaviour most of the time now since they lived in separate houses. Erni lived in the original family home with her younger sister and the sister's husband, with whom she got along much better, as well as their mother, Aminah. Her husband was also much more relaxed at home so the whole situation was far more tolerable to them than when they first got married.

THE MATERNAL UNCLE

The male leader of the matrilineal extended family is the *mamak*, or maternal uncle, of the oldest generation living at any given time. While many women have more than one son, as may their sisters, generally only one of the potential male members of the family will become the *mamak* and take on the responsibility for his sisters' children. Nonetheless, all the male members of the family, including those who do not have a formal leadership role, may contribute to consensus discussions about family matters. The *mamak* of the extended family has the right to use the family's traditional title and may be very influential in family decision-making. Historically, the ceremony to install a new leader and confer this title to its next holder following the death of the old *mamak* was very elaborate and expensive in accordance with tradition and the family's status. Financing this is one of the traditionally acceptable reasons to mortgage land, which is a reflection of the long-standing importance of traditional leadership to the smooth functioning of the community. The generic identifier for men holding this position is *Datuak*, a term which refers to the position and will be part of the full title the man is entitled to use.

Among the various *Datuak* of a *paruik* or clan, one serves as the *Pangulu*, who represents the various extended family groups in the wider community. A senior man in Minangkabau society might be a *Datuak*, which would be his title in the context of his extended family. He might also hold a position of broader leadership as a *Pangulu* within his clan. Finally, he would be a member of the *niniak mamak*, which is one of the cultural institutions of the Minangkabau community. The majority of older men in Minangkabau, however, do not have access to these roles and participate in their matrilineal extended family only as a husband and father and with a limited role in the upbringing of their sisters' children. As is the case for women, the men who are placed in leadership positions by their family are those the members believe can best champion the interests of the group, who are most capable of influencing the opinions of family members, and, increasingly, have been more successful in the wider society. In traditional society, one function of *marantau*, at least in theory, was to give men a chance to gain experience and assets that would be useful in providing leadership to their extended family when they returned to the village.

Marantau, it can be argued, traditionally served another purpose, although this was largely unstated and is rarely consciously recognized by members of the Minangkabau community. Conflicts often arose between the *mamak* and his teenage or young adult nephews. The powerful position the *mamak* holds according to *adat* often resulted in a desire on the part of the incumbent to dictate the way the family's property and resources would be used and also to limit or control the behaviour of its young people. While the intentions of the *mamak* may have been good and intended to protect family interests, they might also have been seen as oppressive by young men, whose role in the matrilineal family is more distant and limited than that of young women. *Marantau* served as means for young men to leave the village and escape the influence of their *mamak*. It was an opportunity for them to prove themselves among strangers and show that they could succeed on their own merits away from the extended family. This acted like a release valve for some of the social tension and overt and suppressed conflict that might seriously damage family relationships if allowed to develop in the context of village society. A proverb recognizes the way in which young men were viewed traditionally in terms of their value to the family and community:

> *Karatau madang di ulu, babuah babungo balun; marantau bujang daulu, di rumah baguno balun.*
>
> Mulberry trees grow upstream, they have no fruit or flowers yet; go to the *rantau*, young man, at home you have no purpose yet.

This rather blunt statement, which compares the young man it addresses to a fruit tree, suggests that the value of young men is limited in the matrilineal context. Their potential function in traditional society is to work and to act as husbands and fathers. This role, which is defined in terms of the women of the extended family, does not leave much space for personal initiative or ambition. These qualities were seen as properly being developed away from the village where time would show whether a person had the character traditional society demanded. In practice, many young men did not return to the village, regardless of their success or experience in the *rantau*. Those who did well had no incentive to return, while those who failed to make a good living often felt embarrassed to return. This can be attributed in large part to the very competitive nature of life in the village with respect to social status, influence, and personal freedom, especially for men.

As might be expected, open conflict between the *mamak* and his nephews is not uncommon and can be significant. These problems have the potential to disrupt the functioning of the whole extended family and seriously impact the coherence of the group. Infrequently, this type of problem can escalate to violence. In the traditional context, the people involved had to be separated, with one leaving the village at least temporarily. Not surprisingly, it has always been the nephew who had to accept the majority of blame for the situation and who was sent away.

Hamzah

Hamzah is Nurijah's second child and first son. From a very young age, he was rebellious and was seen as difficult by his *mamak* Kadir, *Datuak Sati Basa Batuah*. The *mamak* succeeded in persuading the whole family, including Hamzah's parents, that he was a problem child and needed special attention. By the time Hamzah reached his early teens, the *mamak's* sisters had nine boys between them, two of whom were older than Hamzah, one who was his age, and the rest were younger than him. The boys all believed that their *mamak* was too strict and did not like the way he disciplined them. The *mamak* did not hesitate to strike them and would punish anything he considered bad behaviour with very severe corporal punishment. The nephews felt that much of what they did was not serious and should not have been punished at all.

Hamzah was the most rebellious of the nephews and defied his uncle openly. As they grew older and bolder, the others rebelled more openly as well. Eventually, they would purposely do the things their *mamak* had forbidden them to. This included stealing his chickens, fish and rice from the mill he managed, which they cooked together outside the house without the knowledge of their mothers. They also smoked cigarettes, which was strictly prohibited by their uncle, and gambled, which was both prohibited and against the law.

From the very beginning, their *mamak* knew what was going on. Being young adults and inexperienced, they often left evidence of their actions even when they thought they were being careful. However, their uncle soon realized that even the severest of punishments was not stopping the bad behaviour which he understood was directed towards him. He also knew that Hamzah was the ring leader and punishing him only made Hamzah angrier and more determined to defy his uncle.

Their *mamak* then used a different tactic. He thought that if he could control Hamzah, the other nephews could be brought under control as well. So, he gave Hamzah special status. He started treating him well and giving him responsibility within his businesses in the Valley. He would ask him to care for the chickens and ponds and paid him for the work. The rule had been that no one was allowed to smoke until they could earn their own money. Now that Hamzah had income from his work for his uncle, he was allowed to smoke. This strategy seemed to be working. The thefts decreased, even if they did not entirely stop. The *mamak* would often talk to Hamzah about the importance of honesty and proper conduct.

The uncle thought that Hamzah had changed. What he didn't know was that, while Hamzah managed to stop his brothers and cousins from stealing from their *mamak*, Hamzah continued to do so. His dislike of his uncle that had developed during the years of what he considered unfair and oppressive treatment had not diminished. In fact, it had turned into hatred, but he managed to conceal it when he was given access to the things he wanted. Where he and his cousins had stolen from their uncle in the past, Hamzah now did so with his friends from the village. Even his cousins didn't know about this.

Nonetheless, the *mamak* did not fully trust Hamzah even though he seemed to have changed. He would use various people he knew in the village, including the women who brought their rice to his mill, to keep an eye on what Hamzah did. Eventually the *mamak* learned that Hamzah was still stealing from him and was taking even more than before. The fact that Hamzah had involved people from outside the family infuriated his uncle. This behaviour, in the *mamak's* eyes, shamed the family on top of being amoral and criminal. He beat Hamzah so viciously that even Hamzah's mother and her sisters tried to intervene. This did not have the effect the *mamak* wanted, and Hamzah, in fact, planned to take revenge.

One day, Hamzah waited for his uncle to come to the Valley in the early afternoon as usual. He had a machete and had decided to kill his uncle. Hamzah was fifteen years old at the time. Luckily, the family realized what he was planning before his uncle arrived. It took the whole family to disarm him. His mother and his grandmother, Aminah, managed to convince Hamzah that killing his uncle would not solve his problems or be good for anyone, including for Hamzah himself.

Extended family meetings followed. A decision was made that the *mamak* and Hamzah should be separated. This could only be accomplished by sending Hamzah away. Nurijah was devastated. While she understood there was no other way, she could not imagine her young son being expelled from the village. He had not even finished junior high school, but she had to accept the decision of the family since she did not have an alternative.

The family was lucky in a way because it happened that the oldest son of Aminah's oldest daughter, Amran, was a policeman in the city of Makassar in South Sulawesi. He was a district commander at the time, and the family agreed that the best place for Hamzah would be with him. Being a police officer with that kind of position in the 1960s was prestigious for someone with a village background, and Amran was considered by his relatives to be successful and good example for the rest of the children in the family. Hamzah, too, accepted that this would be a good place for him to go. South Sulawesi was far from West Sumatra. At the time, it took two days to sail from Padang to Jakarta and another three days to reach Makassar once a ship was available. In all, it took Hamzah almost two weeks to reach Makassar and the conditions on board ship were poor. Hamzah realized at the time that he would never return to Koto. The emotional distance was too great, and this was the purpose of sending him away as far as the family was concerned.

Hamzah is almost seventy years old now. He married a local woman and still lives in Makassar.

OLDER MEN AND OLDER WOMEN

Just as the extended matrilineal family often experiences tension between its male members and also among its women, particularly the older ones who hold a great deal of decision-making power, the relationship between senior women and the comparable male members is also often problematic. The reason for this is that many Minangkabau have an understanding of the matrilineal social structure that focuses on the advancement of the family as a unit and enhancing its standing in the village. This kind of local social status depends on wealth, success of members both socially and financially, and the ability to maintain and develop the assets of the group. These largely economic concerns have meant that men are often viewed by their sisters and other female relatives in terms of what they can contribute to the family and how much they are able and willing to support the female members financially as well as in family decision-making.

This reality has often meant that men's position in their matrilineal family is tenuous, and they may not be able to claim their entitlements as prescribed by *adat*. For example, a man whose marriage ends because of death or divorce is supposed to be able to return to his matrilineal family home to live. In theory, he should be received there by his sisters and other female relatives and exert his traditional right to reside in the family home, participate in its activities, and be supported by its wealth.

Similarly, if a man has been living in the *rantau* and decides to return to the village, he should be able to rejoin his matrilineal family and live with his mother, sisters, and other female relatives in the household he grew up in. In practice, however, the ability to do so rests more with the decision and interests of his female relatives than with the precepts of *adat*.

Mansur

Mansur, the father-in-law of one of Aminah's grandsons died in 2011 at the age of eighty-four. He had been a widower for some time, his wife having died several years before. Two of his sisters had long since left Koto with their husbands and lived in other cities. A third sister had lived in the village like Mansur but was also dead. The children of this sister lived in Koto as well but did not want Mansur to live with them after his wife died. This was a terrible blow to Mansur because he and his sister had been very close. He had always assumed he would live with this sister and her family if his marriage ended because the sister had been living in their mother's house where Mansur and his siblings had been born. When his sister died, however, a bitter dispute about the inheritance of family property had arisen. This damaged Mansur's relationship with his nieces and nephews beyond repair, and they were not willing to associate with him. Mansur had no choice but to beg his own children to let him live with them. Two of his five children lived in the village, but this type of arrangement did not fit with the requirements of *adat* and was considered shameful by people in Koto. Nonetheless, Mansur's children reluctantly agreed, rather than see their father homeless. Mansur was desperately unhappy because the whole village was talking about what a bad person he must be. In their eyes, nothing else could explain why his own family had abandoned him such that he now had to live at his wife's house, even though she was dead. Mansur was deeply ashamed and no longer left the house. Unable to bear the overt and implied criticism of the community, he even stopped going to the mosque for the Friday prayer because he knew that people were talking about him and his aberrant situation.

ADAT AND THE CARE OF OLDER PEOPLE

Adat places elderly people in a position of respect within the community. This is reflected in various traditional expressions and sayings that remind younger people especially of the value of experience and knowledge that can only be gained over time. The idea that older people are valuable is deeply engrained in *adat*, as in the following saying:

> *Tirulah iduik buluah batuang, maso rabuang carian urang, lah tuo banyak gunonyo.*
>
> Be like the bamboo plant: when it is a young shoot, people seek it out; when it's old, it has many uses.

This proverb likens the human life course to that of the bamboo plant. Bamboo shoots are a popular vegetable that can be cooked in many ways. For this reason, people look for them and cut them to eat. Similarly, young people are important to the community. However, mature bamboo is an extremely important building material that is very versatile and has a long history of use in Minangkabau society. This is like the elderly, who have a lifetime of knowledge and experience that is of value in many situations.

As is often the case, it is likely that the large number of proverbs and expressions that remind the Minangkabau community to treat the elderly well and benefit from their knowledge are aspirational, rather than a reflection of how things actually were at some time in the past. Nonetheless, Minangkabau *adat* does institutionalize the position of the elderly in the community. Their specific functions in the context of *adat* are supposed to ensure that older people remain a part of their family and village society for life. This may once have been the case, but it is likely that many of the modern stresses that are easily observed in extended families have always existed. However, people may have had to accept the arrangements that *adat* required because there was no alternative, and individuals of every age had fewer choices and possibilities than they do today. In other words, it is probable that there have always been matrilineal families who did not wish to receive elderly men back into the family home, children and grandchildren who would have preferred not to be responsible for ageing and perhaps infirm mothers and grandmothers, but there was no other mechanism to address the needs of these older people. It is only in the very recent past that alternatives, whether in the form of institutions that offer care for older people or access to personal income that allows younger people to abandon the village entirely, have been available to growing numbers of Minangkabau. The result is that, for increasing numbers of people, the potential advantages of the traditional system are outweighed by the personal gain possible in other ways of life.

As discussed in Chapter 2, the number of residents in nursing homes in West Sumatra is growing. In light of the difficulties of the traditional system, this should not be surprising, despite the demands of *adat* and its placement of elderly people in a position of respect. This is one manifestation of the choices available to younger people who, for the first time, can choose not to care for elderly relatives and have an option to replace this with care that is outside the traditional system. This is an important difference that is emblematic of the way social change in Indonesia has affected the Minangkabau community. In the past, many people may have had felt compelled to behave in certain ways that were prescribed by *adat* because there was no way to live outside its requirements and still remain in the village. It was always possible to leave the area and settle somewhere else, but this was not an option for many people who lacked the means and personal initiative or who were already enmeshed in the village system and could not bring themselves to leave everything and go, even if they would have liked to.

The social penalties for violating the customs of the village and going against *adat* are very severe. Minangkabau society tends to be communal, and people are used to living in close contact with others. They are, as a rule, concerned with what others think of them and how they are viewed by the community. Because village society is generally very enclosed, it can be impossible to avoid everyone knowing anything that goes on and forming an opinion about the people involved. Because there is some kind of relationship between almost everyone due to the intergenerational networks that connect the extended families, most people may feel they have a personal or family interest in what happens to others and generally do not hesitate to comment on and discuss the matter openly.

In the past, everyone who lived in his or her own village had, to some extent, to conform to expected behaviour at a personal level and also in the context of *adat*. Today, however, the institutions of the modern Indonesian state reach into local areas and exist alongside traditional social structures. More importantly, access to financial resources beyond the assets of the extended family are available to many more people, even in remote and rural areas. In many cases, people who live in villages like Koto can earn considerably more money from modern employment than they can get from the family property. The appearance of nursing homes set up by the Ministry of Social Affairs, as well as private providers, and linked to the modern health and social services system are a response to this. For the first time, there is a reasonable alternative that guarantees some sort of care for elderly family members outside of the village and the traditional system controlled by *adat* that offers a viable alternative to the customary ways of accommodating the needs of the elderly. In addition, many people can afford to pay for this kind of care for older relatives.

Like all Indonesians, individuals in the Minangkabau community see themselves as members of their own ethnic group, which is closely associated with *adat*, the Minangkabau language, and their village of origin. However, they are also Indonesians and members of a national society that has its own social and institutional structure. For many, especially those who are better educated and who work in the formal sector, national institutions and social structures may seem as relevant to their daily life as *adat* and the ways of the village, if not more so. For this reason, the choice to make use of a facility available in the Indonesian context, rather than the comparable institution in the traditional context, can be viewed as a reaction to enhanced possibilities. The social penalty for choosing an alternative available in the modern context is likely to be smaller than that associated with violating *adat* in the context of the village because the choice lies outside the traditional system.

This is not to say that there are no social penalties for choosing an alternative to the traditional approach embodied in *adat*. There often are, but these reactions on the part of the community are not institutionalized the way direct violations of *adat* are. In the case of nursing homes, for example, the facilities themselves are new, and there is no precedent in village life that suggests how placing an elderly resident in this type of care fits into *adat* and the traditional ways of thinking in the community. While the social penalties for a family, who is required by *adat* to take care of an elderly relative who is part of their matrilineal extended family, may be very severe, especially if that older person then has to resort to living in a way that violates *adat* or that is seen as inappropriate (a person living by him or herself, for example, when matrilineal relations are available), the removal of the same older person to a modern institution may be commented on but is likely to have fewer repercussions to the family because the whole issue has been taken outside the traditional context. This is especially the case if the reason for choosing a nursing home or other facility is because appropriate relatives no longer live in the village and cannot, or prefer not to, move the elderly person into their home wherever it is.

The nursing homes that currently operate in West Sumatra were originally intended to provide accommodation and care for older people who had no children or whose children had gone to the *rantau* and could not afford to support them. The fact that many of the current residents do, in fact, have family members they could appropriately live within the context of the matrilineal social system and *adat* and who have the means to care for these older people is increasingly an issue of concern (see, for example, Hendra, 2014; Antara, 2014). This is likely a reflection of some of the tensions inherent in the matrilineal system and the lack of fit between its requirements and the demands of modern life.

The local media in West Sumatra has also addressed this phenomenon in editorial comments, some of which are quite strong in their criticism of the institutionalization of older people in the Minangkabau community. The daily newspaper *Haluan*, for example, which is published in Padang, noted on National Old Age Day of 2013:

> *Jika penerapan ABS-SBK*[1] *benar-benar ada dalam keseharian orang Minang, tidak mungkin akan ada orang tua di ranah ini yang jadi penghuni panti jompo kecuali orang tua yang benar-benar sudah tidak memiliki kaum lagi. Selama masih ada persukuannya ia tetap akan memiliki ninik mamak pimpinan kaum yang akan menjadi pelindungnya.*
>
> *Kini dengan HLUN,*[2] *yang perlu disentuh di Sumatera Barat adalah bagaimana caranya agar semangat dan budaya merawat orang tua itu menjadi bagian dari keseharian dari sebuah keluarga. Jangan sampai panti jompo jadi penuh di Ranah Minang, itu pasti sangat memalukan kita.* (Haluan, 30 May 2013)

---

1. ABS-SBK is shorthand for the way *adat* is supposed to be understood in the Minangkabau world. The abbreviation stands for the proverb: *Adaik basandi sarak; sarak basandi Kitabullah*, which means "*Adat* is based on the law; the law is based on the Holy Book [the Quran]". ABS-SBK, as a catchphrase, has been popularized since the establishment of regional autonomy, with its accompanying rise in the status of traditional culture and thinking, although the proverb itself is much older. The term is frequently used in discussion about the nature and implementation of *adat* in the current political and social environment of West Sumatra.

2. HLUN stands for *Hari Lanjut Usia Nasional*, or National Old Age Day.

[If *adat* were truly followed in the daily life of Minangkabau people, it would not be possible for there to be old people in this area who live in nursing homes, except for those who really have no extended family left. As long as members of their own clan are available, the leaders of that clan should be their protectors.

Now, on National Old Age Day, the issue of how to make care for the elderly part of the culture and spirit of the family must be addressed. There should be no nursing homes in West Sumatra. This is certainly extremely shameful for all of us.]

As this newspaper editorial suggests, the idea that Minangkabau *adat* is strong and should guide the behaviour of members of the community is well established and would likely be supported by a majority of individuals. However, while this view is clearly related to traditional thinking about *adat*, as exemplified in the proverbs and sayings noted above, it does not reflect real experience at the present time and is likely an idealized version of what happened in the past as well. In fact, for many individuals as well as families in the Minangkabau community, the precepts of *adat* have become much less important as determinants of personal and group behaviour, and the penalties for violating them have shrunken in a commensurate manner, as a consequence of rapid social change and the emergence of alternatives.

This poses a special problem for older members of the community who often grew up in families that were much more bound by *adat* than families generally are at present. They observed the position of the older people they knew, those belonging to the generations of their own parents and grandparents, and came to understand that the appropriate place for the elderly was with their own children or with their matrilineal family, as relevant to the specific situation. They are experiencing a collective crisis in cultural consonance, where the unmet expectations they have for their old age are contributing to the emergence of significant health and well-being problems that have not been seen before in the Minangkabau community. This issue is discussed in detail in Chapter 10.

4

Religion and the Elderly

RELIGION IN THE MINANGKABAU COMMUNITY

All Minangkabau are Muslim, and identification with this religion is part of the ethnic identity of the group. For this reason, it is not possible for members of the ethnic group to profess another religion; if they do convert, for example, they effectively remove themselves from the rest of the community. There have been one or two cases of a family member of a prominent Minangkabau figure converting to Christianity which, when known to the public, immediately became a major topic of discussion among the public, and this is increasingly a topic of discussion in Minang language social media. One such case involved the half-brother of Hamka, a prominent writer and religious leader. A recent biography documents this and other aspects of the life of this half-brother, which some readers consider despicable and have linked with the recurrent issue of a missionary presence in West Sumatra. It is unclear to what extent Christian missionaries have actually approached members of the Minangkabau community in the past, but there have been several conspiracy-type accusations that circulated among the public in recent years (see, for example, Minang Lamo 2013). Anecdotal evidence suggests that conversions from Islam rarely occur. However, religion is a central element of identity perception among the Minangkabau and one whose practices frame its experience.

In this, the experience of the community parallels that of several other groups in the Malay world, most notably the Malay themselves, for whom adherence to Islam is a fundamental characteristic that determines ethnic identification (Lian 2001).

For the Minangkabau, as is the case for many of Indonesia's ethnic groups, Islam represents a comparatively new influence in their history. Islam is viewed as having reached Indonesia in the eleventh century (Ricklefs 2008), likely introduced by traders and travellers from India and the Middle East. The religion gradually spread, replacing the older Hindu and Buddhist practices that were already in existence (Clarke et al. 2004). These older practices, which had long since entered the region from India, had mixed with indigenous religious beliefs that are thought to have had a strong supernatural dimension (Brakel 2004). The original religious practices of Indonesia never completely disappeared however, and it is not uncommon to see traces of them in modern society. These extremely ancient practices, which are often rooted in observations of the natural world, frequently emerge in response to unusual events. For example, a solar eclipse in early 2016 triggered the appearance of ancient religious rituals in parts of Indonesia that were once believed to ward off the negative impacts of such an occurrence. In ancient times on the island of Halmahera, one of Indonesia's easternmost islands, for example, an eclipse was believed to be caused by a vicious giant who was trying to devour the sun. Local practice required that members of the public use noisemakers to frighten the giant away because darkness during the day was seen as a portent of danger and misfortune (see Tempo 2016).

For this reason, the various religions in Indonesia are often said to be syncretic, suggesting that elements of earlier belief systems have mixed with or are practised alongside religions adopted later (Brakel 2004). These later religions include Islam, but also Catholicism and Protestantism as well as other Asian religions. A large part of the population of Bali remains Hindu, for example, and there are Buddhists as well as Confucianists throughout Indonesia. All of these beliefs exist in forms that are distinctively Indonesian and have incorporated many aspects of the indigenous religions that preceded them but did not disappear completely from the communities involved. For this reason, many individuals who feel that they are deeply religious and a member of one of Indonesia's modern religions nonetheless maintain a belief in supernatural beings, superstitions, and behaviours intended to ensure good fortune and health that derive from much older belief systems.

For the Minangkabau specifically, Islam is an important aspect of their identity that directs the rhythms of daily life and structures the environment to support religious practices. One of the requirements for a settlement to have the status of village is the presence of a mosque or prayer house. Many people use the five daily prayers as time markers in ordinary speech, suggesting, for example, that a meeting take place "before *Asar* (the mid-afternoon prayer)" or "after *Maghrib* (the evening prayer said at sunset)," rather than at a clock time. Similarly, all public events and work occasions are structured to enable participants to pray at the required times. Other religious duties, such as fasting during the month of Ramadan, are enforced through social control in the Minangkabau community, and local authorities in West Sumatra generally do not tolerate restaurants operating openly during daylight hours when the majority of people are supposed to be fasting (Nusa News 2016). Various regional governments in the province require that nightclubs and other entertainment venues close during the fasting month or that Internet cafes shut during the hours between fast breaking (about 6:30 p.m.) and the start of the *tarawih* prayer held only during Ramadan (about 8:00 p.m.) (Taufik 2015). As a result of practices of this kind, the Minangkabau are generally perceived to be both religious and conservative by other Indonesians. One reason for this perception is that there have been Minangkabau migrants in other parts of Indonesia for generations, some of whom became formal or informal religious teachers, often in addition to other work (see Ali 1975, among others). Nonetheless, many Minangkabau also believe in various supernatural beings and powers that preceded the coming of Islam and sometimes figure prominently in the experience of individuals, as in the case of Pokiah presented below.

The integral nature of Islam in individual and group identity today is expressed in a very well-known proverb that is often referred to by government officials, religious leaders, and other community figures in discussing or justifying certain courses of action that will affect the broader community. This expression, *Adaik basandi sarak, sarak basandi Kitabullah*, means "*Adat* is based on the law; the law is based on the Holy Book [the Quran]". Often abbreviated ABS-SBK in the media and other contexts, this proverb suggests that the institutions of the community and their function are grounded in Islamic principles and practices such that *adat*, the traditional laws and customs of the community, cannot be separated from the precepts of religion and these two conceptual domains are interrelated in a way that requires *adat* to comply with religious principles.

Nonetheless, another older version of the same proverb remains known in the Minangkabau community and reflects a past interpretation of this relationship that was common until several decades ago (see von Benda-Beckmann and von Benda-Beckmann 2013). This expression holds that "*Adat* is based on (religious) law, (religious) law is based on *adat*" (*Adaik basandi sarak, sarak basandi adaik*). This older expression likely reflects a more traditional interpretation of the relationship between *adat* and Islam which gave them equal importance and recognized their interdependence. This may have been a reflection of the fact that Islam came late to the Minangkabau community at a time when *adat* was already established, as indicated by the saying, "*Adat* went down, religion came up" (*Adaik nan manurun, sarak nan mandaki*). According to the traditional legend cycles of the Minangkabau people, the origin of the group was in the central highland region of the area that is now West Sumatra. Over time, they moved down the mountain slopes to the coast and spread out to occupy the whole area of the modern province. Islam, the source of religious law, came from outside and entered the region from the coast, gradually spreading up the mountains into their original homeland. This indicates that, while extremely important in structuring individual and group experience, Islam is a much more recent force that represents an overlay of values and principles supplementing *adat*. The saying also stresses the fact that *adat* is indigenous, while Islam came from outside and was adopted by the Minangkabau. Interestingly, there are indications that the community did not take readily to Islam and that some early Muslim travellers in the region felt the community to be "too pagan" to accept the religion (Ali 1975, p. 66).

A dilemma inherent in this situation that has long been recognized by scholars (Biezeveld 2007; Stark 2013) is that the traditional social structure of the Minangkabau, as defined by *adat*, is matrilineal. Islam, by contrast, is patrilineal and prescribes very different roles for men and women than traditional Minangkabau society does. Nonetheless, the Minangkabau adhere to both *adat* and Islam, although their domains of application are slightly different. *Adat* is currently most important in managing the assets of the extended family and dictating relationships and responsibilities within the group. Religious law, by contrast, is most significant in the context of validating milestone events, such as marriage and death, although these aspects of the life course also have significant *adat* dimensions. Islam is also the source of various family law issues in the modern context and provides the legal basis for divorce, inheritance, alimony and child support outside of the traditional context. In addition, Islam is also an important element of identity that many individuals try to show in their outward appearance, in dress, for example, as well as in speech where they may use Arabic words and phrases when speaking Minang or Indonesian. For many individuals, however, the practices introduced by Islam have become incorporated into their understanding of *adat*, making the division between the two difficult to elucidate. A similar ambiguity is observable between the principles and values introduced by Islam and those that existed previously that derive from an earlier system of belief, and it is not uncommon for people to consider a range of supernatural meanings for their experience in addition to those suggested by formal religion.

Pokiah

Pokiah lived his whole life in the village of Koto in the Minangkabau heartland. Two of his relatives in the extended family (children of his mother's maternal cousins) were prominent religious scholars in the village; they delivered sermons in the mosque at the Friday midday prayer and taught religion to the village children in the afternoons. Pokiah, himself, was not very religious. While he did participate in some of the public religious rituals of the village, such as going to the mosque on Fridays and taking part in the special evening prayers during the month of Ramadan, his private behaviour was not religious. He rarely performed the five required daily prayers and was a prominent member of the village's branch of the communist party before it was banned following the 1965 coup. In addition, he was a respected *dukun*, a traditional healer who used magic as well as other means to address the problems of those who came to him for help. In his old age, when he could no longer work in the rice fields, which was his main occupation, he focused his attention on his *dukun* practice. He built a hut in the middle of his coffee grove where he spent most of his time and where he died one day.

Unlike many of the village elderly, Pokiah did not become more religious in his old age. People wondered how he spent his time in the hut because he rarely interacted with the rest of the village. People speculated that he had turned to black magic and had befriended supernatural beings such as jinn and the spirits of the dead from beyond the grave. It was rumoured that people would come to him to make people they didn't like fall sick or that young people would ask for his help to make someone they liked fall in love with them. Pokiah knew about these rumours because members of his family, usually the children of his sisters, would bring him food or help him pick his coffee and would tell him about what the village was saying. Pokiah enjoyed having people talk about him. He decided to let the village know that, now that he was old and would probably die soon, that he was planning to pass on his knowledge as a *dukun*. A few young men from the village studied with him as well as some others from neighbouring villages.

Against his father's will, the son of one of Pokiah's brothers, was interested in learning Pokiah's black magic. Ilham, the son, was attending a religious high school at the time. He did not want to become a *dukun* himself but wanted to understand the practice and what Pokiah thought about it. Ilham, now an older man himself, says that Pokiah really believed in the power he possessed, and that others could possess, and knew it was possible to make people sick or fall in love using powers that contradicted the teachings of Islam. Pokiah explained to Ilham that he had befriended some jinn (whose existence is mentioned in the Quran), and these jinn friends could help him achieve such feats. When Ilham told him that, in Islam, only God can determine a person's fate, and this was the reason everyone was supposed to pray and do what God wanted them to, Pokiah said that God didn't act directly. God created the means, and a *dukun* learned those means, including by studying with the jinn. To Ilham, this all sounded like *syirik* (heresy). But Pokiah increasingly believed and acted on his view that asking for help from something other than God was perfectly acceptable.

When Pokiah died in his hut one night, and people from the village didn't find his body until late the next morning, it was understood as a bad sign, a warning from God. Even on earth, people told each other, God had punished him for being a heretic.

RELIGION AND AGEING

A great deal of work has been done on religion and ageing around the world. Over the last fifty years or so, a body of literature has been developed that generally indicates the importance of religious faith and religious participation in the health and well-being of older adults for whom greater religious involvement is often associated with better physical and mental health (Levin, Chatters and Taylor 2006). This trend is observable across methodological approaches and seems to apply to individuals from a range of cultural and social backgrounds. However, the underlying cause of the relationship between religious participation and better health and well-being is less clear, despite the volume of work in the area. A number of theoretical perspectives have been applied to this issue since the 1980s, but, of this early work, the concept of multidimensional disengagement has been suggested to best describe what has been observed in various groups and populations (Levin and Chatters 2008). Multidimensional disengagement, developed by Mindel and Vaughan (1978), suggests that, as an individual ages, he or she tends to withdraw from formal, institutionalized religious activity and increase informal, private religious activity. In other words, an older person might be expected to attend organized religious services less frequently but pray or study scripture more in compensation.

More recent work has focused on the development of models that describe the relationships between various measures of religion, health, and well-being. Many of these build on the work of Wheaton (1985) on the role of coping in alleviating stress. Subsequent investigation has included investigation of the hierarchical relationship of relevant factors (Krause 2003); structural relationships between religions and health (Krause 2004) and epidemiological study of group experience (Krause et al. 2002). Another model developed by Ellison (1994) also considers the mediating effect of various factors that relate to religion and health. Ellison's wok indicates that religion can reduce the impact of chronic and acute stressors that may negatively affect mental and emotional state; provide a framework that supports coping and resilience; offer social resources deriving from the communal aspects of practice; and support the development of psychological resources that may enhance coping and the growth of positive feelings. In general, it has been noted that older people tend to become more religious, perhaps because this period in life tends to be more stressful in many ways (Koenig, King and Carson 2012).

Much of the literature on the relationship between religion and physical and psychological health reports on research conducted in Western settings.

However, there is a body of work on the ageing experiences of Muslim communities who are part of the larger, multicultural context of nations like the United States (see, for example, Salari 2002; Al-Heeti 2007; Ajrouch 2008). Much of this relates specifically to the needs of older immigrants, who are ageing in a culture other than their native one and where the usual experience of ageing does not conform to what they might have experienced in their culture of origin. This important work addresses issues of cultural consonance and culture specific expectations but provides little insight into the ways in which Islamic principles and practices might affect the experience of ageing in communities where a majority of individuals are Muslim and where there is no complicating influence from immigration and acculturation pressures. One of the main difficulties associated with the study of ageing in non-Western societies has been the selection of appropriate indicators that are meaningful in understanding the role of religion in ageing in the community of interest. Moberg (2009) mentions Indonesia specifically in this context.

The selection of relevant indicators can only be accomplished if detailed information about the views and practices of the individuals involved have been explicated in a way that defines their experience in depth. Some work of this kind exists for different locations and ethnic groups in Indonesia but has tended to focus on the general or health experience of the elderly without specific consideration of religion (see, for example, Keasberry 2001; Van Eeuwijk 2003; Jena 2014). While it is beyond the scope of this text to identify such indicators for Indonesian society in general or for the Minangkabau community specifically, it is expected that the current discussion of the role of religion in the lives of older people of Minangkabau background will serve as an important contribution to this area of research.

Religion is widely viewed as an appropriate area of interest and concern for older adults in Indonesia. Older people, who may no longer be working and who often have adult children and grandchildren, often choose to display more overt religious behaviour as this is associated with an appropriate social role for the elderly. Individuals often adjust their self-perception based on their age and family status and consciously adopt a more religiously observant persona in order to conform to this social norm. For example, older Minangkabau tend to dress more conservatively and adopt specific types of clothing if they have been on the haj. Men who have completed this pilgrimage often wear a type of white hat that signifies their status. Both men and women prefix their name with the letter H, which stands for *Haji* (for men) or *Hajjah* (for women) and has a certain prestige in the community like other titles associated with education or rank. Similarly, younger people tend to expect more religious behaviour from older relatives and see a greater interest in religion as usual and appropriate for parents and grandparents. The manifestation of this idea is readily observable in advertisements for products and services with a religious dimension. For example, food and beverages advertised on television for inclusion in fast-breaking meals during the month of Ramadan often feature scenes of extended family life where the associated religious observation or holiday activities are led by an older family member, such as a grandparent. Similarly, older, retired movie stars or other celebrities are often featured in advertisements of this kind or that promote the Islamic services sector. On the one hand, this approach caters to the needs and interests of older people but, on the other, reinforces the idea that religious activities and institutions are most suitable for them.

An interesting example of this relates to the yearly haj pilgrimage to Mecca. The haj represents one of the five pillars of Islam that is supposed to be undertaken by observant Muslims once in their life if they are financially able to. This journey involves travelling to Saudi Arabia during the haj season in the Islamic month of Zulhijah[1] and following a prescribed route to take part in a series of religious activities associated with the history and practice of Islam. In Indonesia, with its large Muslim population, the haj is big business. To control the influx of people from around the world, Saudi Arabia uses a system of quotas that allow a specified number of pilgrims from each nation to take part in the haj each year. In Indonesia, the number of people who wish to do so far exceeds the places available, and waiting lists in some regions are more than twenty years long. The

---

1. Indonesia uses the Western (Gregorian) calendar in all official contexts. The Islamic calendar is used to mark religious holidays and events, but most Indonesian Muslims are not aware of the Islamic date on a daily basis. Commercial calendars with parallel dating systems are widely available, however, and the date in the Islamic calendar is published in some newspapers and online news sources alongside the Western date.

application process is managed by the Ministry of Religious Affairs, which also informs those who have registered of their departure date and group. Currently, the waiting list for residents of West Sumatra extends till 2034 (Kementerian Agama 2016*b*).

Participation in the haj is especially attractive to older people in Indonesia, in part because it is seen as a meaningful way to use their life savings and complete a religious duty at a time when they may have more time and fewer family responsibilities at home. However, there is also a deep-seated belief that a person who dies during the haj or in the regions holy to Islam will more easily enter Heaven. For this reason, many elderly people choose to make the trip despite chronic, serious health problems with full knowledge that they might die in Saudi Arabia. In fact, it has been suggested that many older Indonesians go to great lengths to hide these conditions during the health examinations required to participate in the haj. This is a major issue for the government of Saudi Arabia that is also of concern to Indonesian authorities (Hidayatullah 2014; Republika 2014*a*). Nonetheless, the religious desirability of dying during or immediately after the haj are widely discussed in Indonesian social media and online forums about Islam (see, for example, Perpustakaan Muslim Indonesia 2015), and, for this reason, the Ministry of Religious Affairs has recently implemented a procedure to move older applicants up in line, although this is currently limited to prospective pilgrims aged seventy-five and over (Kementerian Agama 2016*a*).

In West Sumatra specifically, the Minangkabau community has strong expectations that older people will be interested in and wish to participate in religious activities. This interest is viewed as likely to be expressed in increased attention to the personal ritual aspects of Islam (praying at the appropriate times daily, fasting during the fasting month, and so forth) and also to self-improvement through study of religion (personal study, Quranic recitation, etc.). Formal religious activities are seen as a support to this type of personal activity, including prayer, which many people view as preparation for an afterlife whose nature will depend on religious faith and devotion in the later stage of life. Not surprisingly, there are, for this reason, certain forms of religious observance that are carried out almost entirely by the elderly. For instance, it is generally believed that even a person who has lived his or her life in a way that is proscribed by religion will go to Heaven if the last words he or she utters are, *Lailaha illallah*, the declaration of faith that represents the first pillar of Islam. This is seen as so significant that Abu Talib, the uncle of the prophet Muhammad and his greatest protector, is said to have to wear shoes of fire for all eternity because he never adopted the religion of Islam.

One example of this increased attention to religious obligations in older age is referred to in Minang as *sambayang ampek puluah* and denotes to a practice thought to have come to the region with the Salafi movement which promotes a purist approach to the interpretation of religious precepts. *Sambayang ampek puluah*, which is taken part in almost exclusively by elderly people, involves a period of forty days, of which thirty fall within the fasting month of Ramadan, where all five of the daily prayers are done communally in a mosque or prayer house with a congregation. In order to do this, many old people sleep and eat at the mosque for the duration of the period each year, bringing their own food and bedding from home. In several parts of West Sumatra such as the Dharmasraya region that borders the province of Jambi, this practice takes place in virtually all mosques and sometimes also involves praying at the grave of religious figures thought to have mystical attributes (Afrianti 2013). By contrast, in the provincial capital of Padang, there is only one mosque where this practice, which is referred to as *suluak* by some Minangkabau, still takes place (Iwan 2014). The aim of this observance is to carry out all the required prayers for forty days in a communal manner as a kind of religious deed that will ensure entrance to Heaven because such a practice is thought to be many more times more valuable if done during the fasting month. Despite the fact that religious authorities in West Sumatra have repeatedly explained that this custom has no basis in orthodox Islamic teaching, it remains a widespread annual practice among elderly Minangkabau.

While *sambayang ampek puluah* is associated specifically with the fasting month of Ramadan, many older Minangkabau make an effort to conduct the five daily prayers communally as much as possible. This often means praying in the local mosque as often as possible so as to be among a congregation. In fact, many older people have formal and informal arrangements with contemporaries to carry out specific prayers together. These visits to the mosque are an important means of socializing for these elderly as well as a way to enrich their religious practice. Praying communally is viewed as more beneficial and more rewarding but is often not a possibility for younger people who work during the day and typically have more responsibilities in the home. For this reason, many older people in the Minangkabau community view the ability to engage in more communal religious activity as a benefit of age that they were not able to enjoy when they were younger.

Similarly, many elderly people in West Sumatra choose to fast on Mondays and Thursdays, which is not required, but is seen as a beneficial religious practice that is recommended for those who are capable of doing so. As is the case with required fasting during the month of Ramadan, Monday and Thursday fasting requires abstinence from food, drink, smoking, and so forth during daylight hours. Many elderly Minangkabau view this as another way of ensuring their entrance to Heaven by gaining greater approval from God. Fasting in the Minangkabau community is widely accepted as encouraging self-control and management of negative emotions. For the elderly, this is consistent with displaying a calmer, more religious demeanour. There is a clear distinction in Islamic teaching between practices that are required and those that are recommended, even though they are optional or voluntary, although these voluntary activities are viewed as beneficial if carried out. For many older people who have the time and means, intensified religious practice is a socially accepted type of behaviour that also allows them to maintain and expand a network of friends and associates. It is for this reason, that many older Minangkabau take part in group activities, such as Quranic interpretation classes, intended for the elderly and arranged either by groups of older people in the community or by institutions providing social and health care.

Katuang

Katuang was not an extraordinary member of the village of Koto in any sense, including in terms of religion. When he was young he went to Pekanbaru, a city in the *rantau* not too far from his village and where some other young people from the village had gone to seek their fortune. While some stayed in the *rantau* and never returned to the village again to live, Katuang returned within a few months. He couldn't get along in the *rantau* and didn't like living outside the village. Like many people with only a primary school education, he married early, had children, and worked on his wife's land. He was not especially religious in his youth but would carry out the required rituals, like praying, fasting, and paying *zakat* (religious tax).

As he grew older, Katuang became more religious. He would perform additional prayers that were recommended in addition to the required five daily prayers. He would fast outside the month of Ramadan. Over time, he grew more and more open about these activities by praying at the mosque as opposed to at home, telling people about his fasting, and so forth.

When Katuang was too old to work as much or as hard in the fields, he became even more religious and began to do things he had never done before. He used more Arabic expressions in speech, greeting people with, *Assalamu Alaikum*. Before taking any action, he would say *Bismillahirrahmaniirrahim*, and, when he was done, *Alhamdulillahi rabbil alamin*, out loud, especially if other people were around. He carried out the five daily prayers in the mosque as often as he could rather than pray at home and took part in the weekly Quranic translation class at the mosque taught by one of the villagers. As his other activities receded due to his age and declining health, he increasingly filled in the time with religious observance that was agreed to be a worthwhile occupation for the elderly in the village. This included more intense religious activity as well as participation in religious practices most often seen among older people that he had never had time for when he was younger.

RELIGIOUS INSTITUTIONS AND OLDER MINANGKABAU

A high level of consensus in the community that religious activities are appropriate for and desired by older people has meant that local governments within the province have set up a range of programmes intended to support this. These include training and orientation programmes for those planning to participate in the haj, instruction in Quranic recitation, and training in religious practice, which supplement a number of more general programmes related to health and well-being and run through village and district level offices, including public health care centres. An important component of these public programmes is the distribution of *zakat* to elderly people classified as indigent. While this does not relate to the religious behaviour of the older people involved, it does reaffirm the role of religious organizations and institutions in addressing the needs of the elderly.

Zakat is a religiously prescribed tax based on income, the giving of which is the fourth pillar of Islam. In Indonesia, while individuals can pay *zakat* directly to entitled recipients, a public agency, Badan Amil Zakat Nasional (Baznas), was set up in 2011 by the Minister of Religious Affairs to coordinate the payment and management of *zakat*. As a result, it is now possible for individuals to pay *zakat* electronically and online as well as by direct salary deduction and for funds to be targeted to community development projects consistent with the rules governing this type of charity in Islamic law. One of the specific concerns of Baznas' West Sumatra branch is providing for elderly people who are living in poverty through grants of food and money (Kantor Wilayah Kementerian Agama Provinsi Sumatera Barat 2016). This return of religious charity to the oldest members of the community is strongly supported by the provincial governor and other public figures in the region who see it as demonstrating community-wide concern for the elderly, which is considered to be a reflection of Minangkabau traditional culture and also a means for alleviating poverty in a vulnerable part of the population.

The large number of older people with insufficient income and resources is a growing issue in Indonesia and one which a number of religious organizations, as well as the government, are attempting to address. It has been noted that a large number of elderly people in Indonesia cannot afford not to work, despite chronic illness or disability and as much as 40 per cent of the population aged over sixty remains in the workforce (Berita Satu 2014a). For much of Indonesia's large lower socioeconomic class, the need to support elderly relatives represents a serious drain on their income. For this reason, many older people try to remain productive for as long as possible. In West Sumatra, the matrilineal family structure should, in theory, provide a place, and access to resources, for everyone, but in practice, there are people who cannot be accommodated within the system, either because of quarrels and disagreements among members, because the family has died out, or because the family has insufficient productive land.

With the increase in numbers of older people, there has come a need for institutions of a kind that did not exist up until very recently in West Sumatra and other parts of Indonesia. These include public and private old age homes, government agencies that provide for a range of needs in this part of the population, and health care services aimed at older people. While much of this support is public in nature and run by various local administrations or at the national level, Indonesia's largest religious organizations have also expanded their activities to include social care for the elderly. The Muhammadiyah organization is an example of this type of private sector support.

Muhammadiyah is a modernist Islamic organization founded in 1912 in Yogyakarta, Central Java. At present, it has national reach and some 29 million members. The organization's activities include political and social concerns and also have a strong focus on education. Muhammadiyah has more than 5,000 schools across the country as well as a number of hospitals and other health and social welfare institutions. It has a number of associated organizations, for women, students, and special interests, and often supports non-religious programmes at the national level that are intended to benefit the population as a whole. One recent example of this has been a public health campaign about avian influenza, which is a national environmental health concern in Indonesia (Perserikatan Muhammadiyah 2016). Among its present concerns are offering charity care to older people living in poverty, often in the form of programmes associated with religious holidays or events and setting up and running old age homes that are culturally appropriate and protect older people from abuse. The aim of these homes is to accommodate elderly people who have no family or resources in a setting in which they will feel comfortable and that provides religious support. In recent years, a number of foreign health care providers have begun operation in Indonesia, some of which are now expanding into care for the aged. These providers are seen as mercenary, and resistance to the idea that older people should be seen as a commodity is beginning to emerge. The Muhammadiyah organization is positioned as an alternative to this kind of commercialized care and is also culturally appropriate (Sutrisno 2016).

Both public and private organizations that work with older people in West Sumatra, as well as in Indonesia as a whole, tend to focus strongly on supporting the religious beliefs and behaviours of their clients. In addition to being seen as a socially appropriate activity for the elderly, greater religious understanding is expected to encourage resilience and foster coping for older people who often experience declining health, loss, and separation as part of the normal life course progression in addition to possible economic deprivation. Because many Minangkabau view themselves as deeply religious (regardless of personal behaviour), older people tend to be more open to advice and behaviour change that is presented in the context of religion. For example, it is generally accepted that lack of mobility may worsen chronic conditions experienced by older adults (see, for example, Langlois et al. 2012; Hogan, Mata and Carstensen 2013). The concept of exercise as an adjunct to health is new in Indonesia and does not fit with traditional patterns of behaviour, especially for the elderly. However, programmes in which older people participate in group calisthenics as a way of maintaining flexibility and promoting mobility have been quite successful. These programmes, which are often run by local health care centres and are among the activities of old age homes, are often associated with religious teachings about health that suggest the individual should take reasonable means to improve and protect his or her well-being. This approach has long been used in health promotion in West Sumatra, such as by associating environmental hygiene with religious texts promoting cleanliness, and has proven successful in changing behaviour.

At the individual level, older people seem to be more willing to change their behaviour, even when this requires participation in activities for which there is no traditional precedent, when the need for change can be seen to be associated with religious doctrine. However, it is also the case that group exercise of this kind is, in fact, consistent with more traditional behaviour in one important way. It provides a group context within which older people can socialize and represents a basis for shared experience, which is extremely important to most Minangkabau. An additional benefit of these programmes is that they may enable older people to carry out their daily prayers for longer without pain or impairment. The five required Islamic prayers are accompanied by a prescribed series of physical motions that involve bending forward, kneeling, and placing the forehead on the floor. Many older people have increasing difficulty achieving the full range of required motions, and it is permissible to pray in other positions (such as sitting on a chair or lying down) if the person is physically incapable. However, being able to carry out the daily prayers with their accompanying movements is a point of pride among the elderly and is also a measure of their physical health. For example, if a person has been ill and has been unable to pray standing up, being able to sit and then pray normally is often used as an indicator of their recovery.

In addition to modern activities of this kind, the institutions in West Sumatra that support the elderly facilitate various types of religious activities that include events celebrating religious holidays, Quranic recitation classes and events, and lessons on religious doctrine. For example, many government institutions, such as the Department of Social Affairs and the Department of Religious Affairs at provincial and lower levels, support religious activities in the community that are open to any older person living in the area. Similar programmes are offered by private providers as well, generally targeting the population in a specific area. However, in addition to formal activities of this kind, many older people take part in religious activities they themselves set up as small groups. This might include a group of older people who all use a local mosque hiring a religious teacher to present a lecture or class on some aspect of religious practice or the establishment of a group to practise Quranic recitation or study its interpretation.

These communal religious activities run by loose groups of older people in a neighbourhood or village are a way of maintaining the kinds of social networks that were characteristic of people's experience in the past before a majority of the Minangkabau public had modern occupations. The elderly, who represented the senior members of their extended families, often had more time, as agricultural work and chores around the house were taken over by younger members of the family, and tended to socialize with others of their own generation. Some of this interaction related directly to the kinds of religious activities that are still common to this group. Because religious participation is viewed as seemly and appropriate for older people, these activities contributed to the perception that the village was enhanced by the presence of the elderly who would serve as models for younger people. In addition, for the older individuals themselves, greater attention to religion may have provided a means for managing their emotions and coping with change in their own physical health, in the dynamics of the family, and in the behaviour of younger relatives. As research in other parts of the world has shown, older members of the Minangkabau community also find comfort in religion and feel that it provides a way for them to adapt and accommodate to their situation.

Muhammad

Muhammad, the husband of Erni (Aminah's fourth child and third daughter), was very active when he was young. He taught religion at the primary school level and moved many times from school to school in different parts of West Sumatra before returning to the village of Koto a few years before his retirement. In addition to teaching school, he always ran after-school religious classes for the local children, usually at night. When he returned to his village in the last few years of his career as a teacher, Muhammad began to think about his retirement and what he would do. In Indonesia, school teachers are required to retire at the age of fifty-five, when many people have many more productive years left. Muhammad knew that the evening classes alone would not replace his main job as a school teacher in terms of his interest and feelings, and he began to consider what he could do with all the free time he would have.

In anticipation of his retirement, Muhammad helped establish a kindergarten in his village and an orphanage in the nearby district capital. He had always been active in the Muhammadiyah organization so the two institutions were set up in association with this group. While Muhammadiyah did not provide funding for these initiatives, the association gave them credibility, standing and immediate acceptance in the community which allowed Muhammad to raise the required funds. In addition, many of his friends in the organization helped run the school and orphanage.

Muhammad had always been known to be an observant Muslim, not just because he taught religion in school and to local children at night, but because he had always been involved in community religious activities. After his retirement and for many years after that until his death just before his eightieth birthday, Muhammad spent all his time making the kindergarten and orphanage a success. He became more active in community work, raising money to help children from poor families so that they could go to school. He found a more religious lifestyle fulfilling and satisfying, which made his retirement bearable and even enjoyable. All of these helped him cope with the many difficulties he faced in his old age, the most trying of which was the death of his wife. In Minangkabau society, there are few circumstances more difficult for a man than the death of his wife. *Adat* makes it awkward for a widower to continue living in his wife's house with their children, and the man is expected to return to his mother's family. However, contrary to the dictates of *adat* and also to what usually occurred in the village, Muhammad's children wanted him to stay after their mother died. He decided to accept their offer and, while the first year was especially hard, he lived with his two daughters until his death nine years after his wife's. He often said that it was his religion and the kindergarten and orphanage, as well as the social network he developed through them, that allowed him to be happy in his old age.

RELIGION IN THE WIDER MINANGKABAU COMMUNITY

Many observers in Indonesia today believe that religion is increasingly important as a way of addressing a large number of social problems affecting modern society. At the same time, there has been a visible increase in religious symbolism in the public environment, which has intensified since the establishment of regional autonomy in 2001. In West Sumatra, many elected officials are more conservative than in the past and project a religious persona that is part of their public presentation. This is a reflection of public sensibilities and the fact that the Minangkabau continue to view their religion as inherent to their ethnic identity and as a lens through which they evaluate and interpret their experience. It is also seen as a source of solutions to observed problems, and many people, including those in leadership positions, suggest that issues like crime, drug abuse and mental illness can be eliminated from Minangkabau society if the public returns to a more rigorous religious stance.

In relation to the elderly, this view has led West Sumatra's governor and other officials to repeatedly call upon the public to act in accordance with ABS-SBK ("*Adat* is based on (religious) law, (religious) law is based on the Holy Book") and use religious sensibilities to guide their relationships with older relatives. Religion is also widely seen as an appropriate basis for psychological counselling, which is increasingly viewed as a necessary response to rising levels of depression among the older members of the community, those in institutions as well as those living in the community. There is a concurrent interest in developing counselling methods based on Islam for other population groups as well.

While difficult to judge, many people in the Minangkabau community, including many members of the social work and health care professions, believe that depression, especially among the elderly, is a new phenomenon. It is the case that no term exists for this condition in either Indonesian or Minang and the English loan term *depresi* is generally used. If this perception is accurate, and it is the case that feelings of depression, sadness, isolation, hopelessness and loneliness, that are now commonly reported by the elderly in West Sumatra, were not widespread among older Minangkabau in the past, it seems likely that the increase in such feelings is related to social change and cultural consonance, not solely to a need for more religious behaviour and understanding. Nonetheless, it is significant that the belief that religion might provide a solution to the problem is so widespread. This is a factor that is amenable to change in the Minangkabau community, whereas changes in the nature of the family and its relationships, new desires and aspirations on the part of younger people, more difficult economic conditions that require more income than traditional assets can provide, and new opportunities that are making the traditional matrilineal social structure less significant for many people are not. In other words, an increased intensity of religious behaviour can potentially be achieved by the elderly people in question through their own efforts or in the context of organized activities offered at the community level, and these might provide additional resilience at comparatively little cost. However, despite the acknowledged importance of religion to the Minangkabau public and in the lives of its elderly, it remains to be seen whether it is an adequate response to decreasing cultural consonance and the fading of traditional patterns of care for the elderly.

5

Language and the Elderly

THE LINGUISTIC CONTEXT IN INDONESIA

The linguistic context in Indonesia is extremely complex. Since achieving independence in 1945, Indonesia has used *bahasa Indonesia* (literally, "the language of Indonesia") as its national language, a situation that was anticipated by the nationalist movement as early as the 1920s. In fact, the origin of the national language is usually dated to the Youth Pledge (*Soempah Pemoeda*) made by nationalist leaders in 1928 that called for a future nation of Indonesia whose language would be Indonesian (Foulcher 2000). However, despite the fact that this formalization of the language came less than 100 years ago, there had been a de facto Indonesian language in use for centuries before this time.

Modern Indonesian is a standardized form of Malay, a member of the Austronesian family of languages, that had been in use as a lingua franca in the region that now makes up the modern nations of Indonesia, Malaysia, Singapore, and Brunei Darussalam. In its earliest period of usage, Malay was likely a trading language used to facilitate interaction among people who spoke different languages that were also indigenous to the islands that would become Indonesia. Over time, it spread and developed and eventually came to be associated with Islam and the religious and cultural practices that were related to the religion (Adelaar and Himmelmann 2005).

Indonesia eventually became the Netherlands East Indies, first under the control of the *Vereenigde Oost-Indische Compagnie* (VOC) and later the Dutch government when the VOC collapsed in 1800, after nearly 200 years of operation. Portuguese traders and missionaries were also active in the eastern part of the region before the VOC consolidated its holdings. The British, who had colonized the Malay peninsula, held the region of Bengkulu on the island of Sumatra from 1685 to 1824. There was great interest in the area by European explorers because of the availability of a wide range of spices that had been known in Europe for centuries but that had been controlled by middlemen in the Arab world and India (Ellen 1977; Ricklefs 2008). Despite intense interaction with European powers over a period of centuries, the languages of the colonizers remained a source of loan words but never became widespread media of communication in Indonesia. Instead, the Dutch colonial government, as well as other European groups in Indonesia, tended to use Malay, rather than try to teach large numbers of local people their language (Sneddon 2003*b*).

By the twentieth century, many people in the territory that would become Indonesia, were able to speak Malay, and the language, as used in the region, had already begun to include characteristic usages that were different from other areas where Malay was also in use (Teeuw 1959). At about this time, serious literature written in Malay began to appear, which further helped standardize and popularize the language. Interestingly, this early literature featured the work of a number of Minangkabau writers, who are often credited with contributing to the formation of modern Indonesian through their books published in the 1920s and 30s (Teeuw 1972).

While there were (and still are) groups in Indonesia, and especially Malaysia, whose first language is Malay, a majority of the Indonesian population speak another local language as their first language. It is estimated that there are some 700 languages in use in the nation (Lewis, Simons and Fennig 2016). Of these, some are linguistically related to Malay, while others, particularly a number that are in use in eastern Indonesia, belong to another language family (Musgrave 2014). For many Indonesians, one of these local languages is their first language and the language they use in the full range of informal interaction with family and friends in their day-to-day affairs. However, the national language, Indonesian, is used in all formal contexts, most importantly in education and the media. In practice, children begin to be acquainted with the standard usages of Indonesian when they begin school, but they often have considerable exposure before this time through television and other incidental contact. Indonesia has been extremely successful in establishing the national language, and literacy rates in Indonesian have reached 98 per cent for people aged fifteen to forty-four. Literacy among older people aged over forty-five is about 89 per cent. In West Sumatra, fewer than 1 per cent of people aged between fifteen and forty-four cannot read and write, and only 3.5 per cent of those aged over forty-five fall into this category (BPS 2016). This likely reflects a long-standing concern with education among the Minangkabau and also their ability in and attitudes towards Malay that have deep historical roots.

However, like many of Indonesia's local languages, Minangkabau, the first language of almost all of the residents of West Sumatra, is rather small in terms of number of speakers. The largest local languages, Javanese and Sundanese, are estimated to have about 84 million speakers and 34 million speakers respectively (Lewis, Simons and Fennig 2016). Not surprisingly, these languages have had a significant influence on the nature and structure of modern Indonesian usage (Soderberg and Olson 2008). While Minangkabau writers were influential in setting the form of standard Indonesian in the early twentieth century, the influences from Javanese especially are more widespread today because of the impact of technology in popularizing and spreading dialect usage. A prominent example of this is the very informal, colloquial dialect of Indonesian associated with urban speakers in the nation's capital, Jakarta. This dialect is used heavily on television in entertainment programmes of all kinds that are intended for younger audiences. Its characteristics are very different from standard Indonesian, and younger speakers across the country are eager to speak in this way (Smith-Hefner 2007). Many older Indonesians are concerned about this situation, and comment in the media on the declining standard of Indonesian usage is frequent. Much of the blame for this is ascribed to the media itself (see, for example, Kompas 2009) as well as to the impact of English which is the most widely taught foreign language in Indonesia, although mastery remains low (see, for example, Harimansyah 2015). Many observers believe the attractiveness of English is leading to a dangerous deterioration in Indonesian usage (Mulyana 2016).

In recent years, and especially since the establishment of regional autonomy in 2001, the language context in Indonesia has been changing. On the one hand, the nature of regional autonomy and the accompanying devolution of authority to relatively low levels of administration have meant that many regions are more ethnically homogeneous, which has created a demand for local regulations that call for the use of local language in the public environment. Such local regulations on language (*perda Bahasa*) have been passed in a number of regions, especially in Java, where the vast majority of the public speaks Javanese as a first language (see Pemerintah Kabupaten Banyumas 2013; Pikiran Rakyat 2015; Kabar Nias 2015). Indonesia's 1945 Constitution protects local languages and recognizes their significance to Indonesian citizens and society but mandates the use of Indonesian in all formal contexts. For this reason, there has been some discussion that local laws requiring the use of a local language in government, education, the media, and so forth at certain times (often one day a week) is not constitutional. However, proponents of these local laws on language believe that they are needed to prevent the deterioration of ability in the public's first language.

The province of West Sumatra does not currently have local regulations relating to language use (although Regional Regulation of the Province of West Sumatra No. 6 of 2014 on the Strengthening of *Adat* Institutions and the Preservation of Minangkabau Cultural Values (Peraturan Daerah Provinsi Sumatera Barat Nomor 6 Tahun 2014 tentang Penguatan Lembaga Adat dan Pelestarian Nilai Budaya Minangkabau)) is seen as encompassing language issues in addition to *adat* concerns. The reason for this is that the population is almost entirely made up of people of Minangkabau ethnic background, and the Minangkabau language is heavily used in all informal contexts by a majority of the population. While there are serious concerns within the community that younger speakers are no longer able to use all varieties of Minang fluently and are not familiar with the highly metaphorical language of traditional cultural expression, the language is not threatened, and most of the public of all ages can use it fluently.

For many of the people in West Sumatra who are now over the age of sixty, Minang is their main language of expression and the one in which they are most fluent. Individuals of this age began any formal education they might have in the 1950s or earlier, soon after or just prior to Indonesia's independence in 1945. This schooling would have taken place in Indonesian, which had not yet undergone the process of standardization carried out in the context of language planning undertaken by the government in the 1960s and 70s. Those who eventually entered professional careers, perhaps following a university education, generally became fluent in the formal, standard language of academic pursuits, but many have used Minang in more informal interaction for their whole life. Others, who had less formal education, can often read and understand formal language use (such as is used in television news broadcasts) but are less able to comprehend the highly informal language varieties that characterize youth culture. These informal varieties of Indonesian are heavily influenced by Javanese usage and a type of slang associated with the highly urbanized context of the capital (see Smith-Hefner 2007 for a discussion of this). This type of language is common on the Internet and can be heard on television in entertainment and comedy programmes. It has proven very appealing to younger Indonesians, who often imitate these dialects, even when they are not commonly used in their region of origin. There can be no doubt that the dynamic nature of Indonesian, the appearance and popularity of non-standard varieties, and the widespread use of English for reasons of prestige represents a challenge to many older individuals and may seriously impede their ability to interact fully, except in their local language.

Inang

Inang has spent almost her entire life in the village of Koto where she was born. As the only daughter among four children whose mother was the oldest daughter in a family with two sons and four daughters, Inang enjoyed affection and attention from everyone. She would be expected to play the role of the senior woman that her grandmother and then her mother also held in the extended family. For this reason, she was given the best opportunities that the family could afford and that the community considered a girl like her should have. One of these was formal education.

In the late 1940s, a few years after Indonesia's independence, when Inang was born, schools were available near to or even in remote areas like Koto, but most people could not afford for their children to attend. As a result, even a very small amount of formal schooling was considered extremely prestigious in the village. When Inang reached school age, she was able to attend a primary school in the town of Batusangkar. There was no school in the village itself at the time. After that, she attended the vocational junior high school in the same town and studied home economics. Her family wanted her to continue her education at the corresponding senior high school and, for that, she had to move to the provincial capital of Padang, three hours by bus from the village. At the time, most children of her generation did not attend school at all; very few graduated from primary school. So, Inang's achievements dramatically increased her own standing in the community and, importantly, that of the whole extended family. There were many aspects of prestige associated with formal schooling. One of them was fluency in the national language, *Bahasa Indonesia*.

Even though Indonesian had been used before independence in Indonesia, especially in literature and by the nationalist movement, it was not until after independence that the language spread much more quickly and reached the villages through formal education. While Inang's first language was Minang like her peers, unlike them, she had completed twelve years of education and had achieved native fluency in Indonesian.

Because there were so few schools and a very small proportion of the population that attended school at the time, Inang was able to secure a teaching position after graduating from high school. She taught at the junior high school she had attended in Batusangkar and spent her whole career there until retiring a few years ago. So, after having spent three years away from the village but still within West Sumatra and the Minangkabau cultural and linguistic environment, Inang returned to the village, raised a family and carried out the traditional duties expected of her in the extended family as well as in the community in addition to her professional activities as a school teacher.

Because she had a job and had to teach in Indonesian every day, Inang's command of Indonesian did not diminish after leaving school. In fact, it improved because of her work. Throughout the course of her career, and especially in the decades before her retirement, Inang had seen additional schools built in Batusangkar as well as a primary school in the village. Electricity, and, with it, television, came to the village during this time. New government offices opened, community organizations were established, and the village became more connected to the developing national culture. People with better command of the national language were more able to participate in new institutions and enjoy opportunities that were increasingly available. Inang belonged to a number of social organizations and was active in her profession as well.

Throughout her life, Inang has used Indonesian and Minang with equal frequency and intensity. Over the years, she has become a true bilingual speaker and can use both languages with equal facility in all social contexts. She can also switch effortlessly between them and, in this way, represents the ideal of language mastery envisioned by the nationalist movement when Indonesian was chosen to be the national language of the nation.

LANGUAGE AND OLDER PEOPLE

There has been a growing interest in the language use of the elderly for several decades. The cognitive abilities associated with language comprehension and production are extremely complex (Burke, MacKay and James 2000; Kemper and Mitzner 2001), and there is an idea among both old and young that this facility diminishes with age (Ryan et al. 1992). It has been found that deterioration in the ability to use and comprehend language can interfere with the ability of older adults to interact and socialize as they would like (Kemper and Lacal 2004; Hummert et al. 2004). Much of the body of literature on this topic relates to word, sentence, and discourse issues in the speaker's native language and has been reviewed in detail by Thornton and Light (2006).

Language ability in the elderly has often been viewed in terms of language attrition, especially in the context of bilingualism. This approach assumes that certain aspects of language use are more likely to be affected by changes in cognitive processes associated with ageing and that such changes are likely to occur in the same way for various populations, regardless of language spoken and other background factors (Seliger and Vago 1991; Goral 2004). In fact, considerable variation exists between individuals, even when overall patterns of language change are similar. Of particular interest in relation to the linguistic situation in Indonesia is the research that relates to specific linguistic skills. For example, several studies have shown that vocabulary use and syntax are not affected by the normal ageing process and may even improve as the individual ages (Wingfield and Stine-Morrow 2000; Goral et al. 2008). Lexical retrieval, however, has been found to decline with age (Baressi et al. 2000; Mackay et al. 2002), as has comprehension of complex ideas (Wingfield and Stine-Morrow 2000; Waters and Caplan 2001).

A comparable body of research relates specifically to bilingual speakers. This work has identified two parallel processes, decreased use of one of the languages (intralanguage attrition) and influence of one language on the other (interlanguage attrition). Much of this work does not address the issue of original level of mastery, however, nor clearly distinguishes between issues relating to performance as opposed to competence. For example, the situation of an individual who mostly uses his or her second language and experiences attrition in the first language is likely to be very different from another speaker whose second language use declines with age and, as a result, is subject to attrition. This situation is further complicated by the fact that some bilinguals do not attain native speaker competence in their first language (if, for example, they enter the second language environment as children and their language development is not yet complete), while others do not achieve native speaker competence in their second language (see Goral 2004, for discussion of this issue). Research suggests that an important aspect of language attrition for bilingual speakers is lexical retrieval, which involves increasing difficulty recalling a term in one of the languages spoken. Studies of speakers of a number of languages indicate that code-switching and code-mixing become increasingly common with age and that these phenomena may involve the first or second language (Hansen 2001; Hulsen, De Bot and Weltens 2002; Schmid 2013).

LANGUAGE USE AMONG OLDER MINANGKABAU SPEAKERS

Among older Minangkabau speakers, it is possible to observe the various patterns of language use and attrition reported in the literature. However, their nature and occurrence are related to a number of factors specific to the social patterns of the group. Many older speakers who have lived their whole lives in their village of origin or similar area (as in the case of older men who have lived since marriage in proximity to their wife's family in her village) were never fluent speakers of Indonesian and rely on Minang as their main language of communication. Unless these individuals had reason to use Indonesian, such as in the context of employment, their mastery of Indonesian may be limited to comprehension (often of more standard usage only), and they may have little productive ability in the language. Speakers of this kind are normally extremely fluent in Minang, however, and are capable of using it in all contexts. They may also show mastery of the highly stylized varieties of language used in traditional literature and *adat*. A second group of Minangkabau elderly exhibit true bilingualism in Minang and Indonesian. These individuals are often professionals whose formal education and employment required the use of Indonesian at a high level but who continued to use Minang in a full range of social contexts outside these two domains. Speakers of this type often live in Padang or other West Sumatran cities, where a majority of the community is Minang-speaking and there is environmental reinforcement of both Minang and Indonesian. Some of these speakers exhibit considerable borrowing between Indonesian and Minang, especially when discussing matters associated with the domains for one language in the other. However, many of them have equal facility in the two languages and can switch between codes effortlessly as the situation requires. This pattern of language use is often observed among older Minangkabau who have lived much of their adult life in the *rantau*, where they have generally been exposed to a much more diverse language context and speakers from other parts of Indonesia with different language backgrounds. Many of the individuals in this situation are able to use one or more varieties of Indonesian. Mastery is often dependent on level of education and occupational status, with those who are university educated professionals, for example, generally having greater competence in several varieties of Indonesian, while those who worked in trade or in the informal sector are often only able to use the highly informal urban dialects that characterize the lower economic classes of Indonesian speakers. Some of these speakers also have considerable exposure to another local language and may have some facility in that language as well. In terms of their retention of Minang, older individuals who have spent their adult lives in the *rantau* also show considerable variation, which is related to a number of social factors but also to inherent language ability.

Not surprisingly, the degree to which an older individual living in the *rantau* can maintain his or her ability to speak and understand Minang is directly connected to his or her personal situation and social network. For older Minangkabau who are married to another Minang speaker, Minang has generally remained a language of daily communication within the home or at least between the spouses involved. Children born in the *rantau* often do not speak Minang, although many can understand; instead they are often native speakers of Indonesian and exhibit full mastery of relevant varieties as well as the dialect used in the place they live. Older speakers in this situation, regardless of their mastery of Indonesian, often retain high-level ability in Minang, which is supported by participation in ethnically based social groups and, in many cases, strong connections with their region of origin in West Sumatra. Many older Minangkabau who have spent their adult lives outside of West Sumatra are married to non-Minangkabau or to people of Minangkabau descent but who were born outside of West Sumatra. In situations of this kind, Minang is not typically the language of the household. Instead, daily conversation may take place in Indonesian or, occasionally, in another local language. Individuals in this situation vary greatly in their involvement with Minangkabau social groups and organizations and the degree to which they interact with extended family and friends in West Sumatra. There is some evidence that language use in marriages where one spouse is a Minang speaker and the other is not is related to whether the Minang speaker is male or female. The matrilineal social structure of the ethnic group means that Minangkabau women living outside of West Sumatra sometimes remain closer to family in their region of origin and may also be in closer contact with other Minangkabau in the place where they live. The fact that any children of marriages like this will be considered Minangkabau under *adat* also supports the maintenance of ethnic identity, but this does not always guarantee access to social contexts that support language maintenance. For Minangkabau men married to non-Minangkabau women, the connection to the extended family and region of origin is often more tenuous which sometimes results in less contact with other Minang speakers. The location where both male and female Minang speakers live is also significant in marriages where the other partner speaks a different local language and considerable variation can be observed. For example, if the family lives in a region where the non-Minangkabau spouse's local language is used, that language may take on greater importance and will likely be spoken by any children of the marriage in addition to Indonesian. It may also be the language used in the home. If the family resides in an area that uses a third language that is not spoken by either spouse, the home language is often Indonesian, and children sometimes have some knowledge of the mother's language, whatever it is. These phenomena have been observed for a number of Indonesian ethnic groups, not just the Minangkabau (see, for example, Sakur, Baruadil and Lamus 2015; Juliani, Cangara and Unde 2016; Tamrin 2016).

Needless to say, the ability of elderly Minangkabau to use Minang and Indonesian is not completely dependent on their social context but has a strong dimension of inherent ability as well. While less amenable to quantification and evaluation than degree of mastery, it is well documented that some individuals are more "language bound" than others in terms of relying on the structures and conventions of the first language, which may impede the ability to develop fluency in a second language (see Day 1979, for discussion of this). Similarly, attitude and self-perception may also have a significant impact on an individual's mastery of a second language (Butler and Hakuta 2004).

It is also worth noting that Minang, which is an ancient language believed to be related to a form of early Malay that ultimately gave rise to the modern variants of the language that include Indonesian (see, for example, Blust 1982), has a number of dialects and varieties that are in use in West Sumatra. To many modern Minang speakers, the dialect used in Padang has the status of a standard variety, even though the language has never been subject to any formal language planning or standardization. Pronunciation and word use vary between the coastal usages and those common in the upland regions, and Minang speakers tend to be sensitive to dialect differences that can often be used to identify a person's place of origin. Any consideration of language maintenance, therefore, must take into account these language varieties as well as to the dynamic between Indonesian and Minang. For example, an older Minangkabau who has lived for decades in Padang is almost certainly completely fluent in Minang as it is used in the provincial capital but may feel awkward using a regional dialect, even if this dialect is his or her native one. By contrast, an older Minangkabau who has lived in the *rantau* for much of his or her adult life may be able to speak the specific dialect he or she grew up with but can no longer use other varieties of Minang. There has been considerable research on Minang dialects carried out by Indonesian linguists that provide insight into this matter (see, for example, Zulfihendri 2015; Nesti 2016, among others).

The language context of elderly Minangkabau is closely related to their perception of well-being, which may be severely challenged by language attrition of either Indonesian or Minang. However, it is also important to consider the enhancing effects of exposure to multiple languages over the life course for those individuals who have been able to master them. Because older age typically allows more time for non-work pursuits, individuals who have better mastery of Indonesian, in particular, but also potentially Arabic or another foreign language or even an additional local language may be able to use such competencies to greatly enhance their experience through reading, television, and increasingly the online environment, all of which require language competence. This is especially relevant for those older Minangkabau who have had professional careers in which they used Indonesian at a high level. This often coincides with higher levels of formal education, which may also have created the habit of reading in the people involved. The ability to read fluently in Indonesian, for example, is often taken advantage of in retirement to deepen religious knowledge or to satisfy personal interest in various areas or disciplines. Similarly, for those whose Indonesian is fluent, an increasing variety of television programming, combined with the easy availability of satellite dishes, means that leisure time can be used to watch a range of programmes that include movies, serials, sports, game shows, and variety shows. Foreign programming is widely available as well and is watched by many Indonesians even when they do not speak the language used.

Language, then, can affect older Minangkabau in two opposite ways. For those who experience some form of language attrition or gap in their mastery, loss or lack of ability to interact fully in either Indonesian or Minang can serve to isolate and act to the detriment of social inclusion and participation. The converse of this is also the case, however, with greater language facility, especially in Indonesian, acting to enhance well-being by allowing access to a much wider range of types of entertainment and personal development. Within the community of Minangkabau elders, both extremes exist, as do numerous individual situations that lie on a spectrum between the two poles. Individuals who, through a combination of inherent ability and personal circumstances, achieve, or end up with, lower levels of mastery, however, may experience serious impacts on their ability to socialize and interact effectively with their peers. This type of linguistic isolation may be very serious in terms of the individuals' affective state and may also be a major contributing factor to depression and loneliness.

Salim

One of the most difficult circumstances a man can find himself in in Minang society occurs when he has been married, has children, and is subsequently predeceased by his wife. This happened to Salim, who found himself in an extremely problematic situation after his wife's death.

Salim had been married to a woman from Koto but he came from a different village. As was customary in Minangkabau society, he moved into the house of his wife's family in Koto after marriage. She came from a large extended family with many female members. Her mother had three sisters each of whom had a number of children who were married themselves. They all lived in a large compound that contained three houses. One of these was the original family home built in the traditional Minangkabau style with many rooms for the married women in the extended family. When the main house could no longer accommodate all of the members who were entitled to live there, the family built two smaller houses on their ancestral land. Salim's wife lived in one of these newer houses with two of her sisters who were also married.

Salim's own village was quite far from Koto and he was not able to visit his family on a daily basis as was also customary in Minangkabau society. It is expected that men spend time working on and managing their mother's land and helping their sisters and their children. Salim was only able to visit his parents' house once a week, usually on Friday when work hours were much shorter because of the communal midday prayer. Because Salim spent most of his time at his wife's house, his sisters were unhappy with his extended absences as he was not present to help them work on the family's land, their main source of income. His parents were also concerned because his absence also meant he could not participate in the upbringing of his sisters' children, one of a man's main responsibilities in Minangkabau society. Salim could feel that, as the years went by, his parents and sisters increasingly resented his lack of involvement in family matters and gradually excluded him from rituals such as family dinners in the month of Ramadan when the whole extended family broke the fast together, family discussions when one of their relatives was getting married, and so forth.

The situation upset Salim as well, but distance did not allow him to do what his family wanted. He felt his parents and sisters were unreasonable so he tried to fit in to his wife's large extended family by working harder on their land. He felt that the family appreciated his help and liked the fact that he was there with them most of the time. This made him feel a little better. After many years, when his six children were older, Salim felt like he was a member of his wife's family. Her brothers and sisters treated him like one of their own siblings, and his wife's parents were fond of him as well.

The sudden death of his wife changed Salim's life instantly. She was killed in a bus accident on the way to Padang to visit one of their daughters who was about to have a baby. Salim had not gone with her because she had told him to stay in the village and join her later closer to the birth. She wanted to go earlier to help their daughter with her housework.

As soon as his wife was buried, it was no longer acceptable for Salim to stay at his wife's house, especially as her sisters and their families also lived there. Salim's children were all grown up. His daughters, both married and unmarried, were entitled to stay after the death of their mother while his married sons were living at their wives' houses. There was no place for Salim at his wife's house, no matter how much her family liked him. He had two children who lived outside the village though. In addition to the one in Padang, another of his daughters lived in Jakarta with her husband who was also from Koto and who had moved there several years before. This son-in-law worked at a government ministry in Jakarta as a mid-level employee, having earned a bachelor's degree in Padang. Salim's daughter was a kindergarten teacher. She was his oldest child whom he felt closest to.

Salim was shocked and confused by his wife's sudden death. Before he had a chance to think about his options, he was already expected to leave the house where he had spent his whole family life and where he was very comfortable. He had often told people that he felt he had been better treated by his wife's family than by his own. His parents and his sisters and their children, some of whom were by now grown up, did not even suggest that he return home to them. He was even told by them that he was not welcome because he had spent years helping his wife's family while neglecting his own. For months, he stayed at various mosques, first in his village until he found that too embarrassing because he knew so many people there, and later in nearby locations. It was terribly shameful if a person's own family would not take them back in this kind of situation. He then moved to other villages and stayed at the mosques there, helping the villagers keep things clean in exchange for them allowing him to stay.

When his two daughters who lived in Padang and Jakarta heard about this, they told him to come and live with them. He chose to go to Jakarta because he had become bitter about the customs and traditions of his community and the way men were treated. He wanted to leave, and Jakarta seemed to be a good choice. It is uncommon in Minangkabau culture for a man to live with a daughter after the death of his wife, again because of tradition, so Salim felt that Jakarta would be far enough away, geographically as well as in terms of customs, that this would not matter. He was grateful that his daughter had invited him to live with her, and he knew her husband and felt quite comfortable living with him as well.

After his initial excitement, however, Salim became depressed in Jakarta. He was treated well by his daughter and his son-in-law, but he felt completely isolated and lonely in the capital city. His two grandchildren, who were in primary school and whom he adored, ignored him. They spoke in the Jakarta dialect of Indonesian at home, and Salim could not understand them, much less speak to them. They did not speak Minang and, when Salim tried to speak Indonesian with them, they could hardly understand the limited and old-fashioned language that he had learned in primary school in West Sumatra. His range of language was small, and the dialect was almost incomprehensible to his grandchildren, so they quickly began to avoid speaking to him. They also found him odd, especially the way he dressed and talked.

Salim's daughter seemed to be too busy to spend much time with him. At least that was how Salim felt. She did not neglect him and provided for all his needs, but this and her work took up all her time. Her husband left the house at 5 every morning because the traffic in Jakarta meant that, if he left any later, he would be late for work. Salim's daughter was already up at 4 a.m. to prepare her husband's breakfast and do housework. Once her husband left, she would make breakfast for the rest of them, get the children ready for school, and dress for work.

Salim spent most of his time alone in the house. When everybody was home, they all seemed to be too busy to talk to him, beyond brief and superficial interaction about what they did during the day. Everyone went to bed early because they were exhausted and had to get up early in the morning. Even on the weekends, they were all busy catching up with chores they could not do during the week. Salim tried to watch television but he could not understand most of the programmes. The type of Indonesian used was unfamiliar to him, and he had few points of reference. It was also often mixed with English and Javanese about which he knew nothing at all. This meant he could only enjoy music or sports programmes that did not rely on language. But he didn't find this too entertaining as he had no one to talk to about the shows who would share the excitement.

Salim tried to talk to the neighbours. They also used language that was unfamiliar to him. Some of them were Javanese speakers, others spoke Sundanese, and still others were speakers of other local languages from other parts of Indonesia. They all spoke some Indonesian, but their dialects were difficult for Salim to understand. Initially, like with everything else, he enjoyed talking to the neighbours, but his pleasure was quickly exhausted as he was unable to talk about much other than superficial daily matters.

Salim became more lonely and depressed by the day. He did not want to go back to West Sumatra because he felt he had no place to go to. He died less than a year after moving to Jakarta.

TECHNOLOGY AND OLDER MINANGKABAU

Like other Indonesians, members of the Minangkabau community have been quick to adopt the technologies made possible by the expansion of the Internet and the availability of smart technology in cellular telephones and other mobile devices. Internet use, and especially the use of social media, is extremely high in Indonesia and has been taken up very rapidly and extends to all social strata of Indonesian society (Puspitasari and Ishii, 2016). For many elderly Minangkabau, the ability to connect online with friends and family members has had significant impacts for language use as well as attitudes and perceptions that relate to language choice, and many, especially those living in the *rantau*, have become avid users of social media

The nature of online networks means that older individuals can locate and communicate with people from the same background, even if they live in different parts of the country and would find it difficult to meet in person. The low cost of Internet and mobile phone service in Indonesia facilitates this and make online communication affordable to large numbers of older people. Not surprisingly, many older Minangkabau use social media, such as Facebook, and mobile applications, like WhatsApp, to stay in contact with relatives and to keep up with the activities of their extended family. However, many of them also participate in online social groups whose members originate in the same geographical area in West Sumatra but currently live in various parts of Indonesia or in groups based on old school ties or other shared experiences, often from decades before. These groups are an important means of social support for the older people who use them and also serve as a forum for the maintenance of language.

Overwhelmingly, online and social media groups that are popular among older Minangkabau use Minang as their medium of interaction. While some members may post to them in Indonesian or in a mixture of Indonesian and Minang, the majority of speakers pride themselves on using Minang exclusively. When a social group is geographically based, the members generally make an effort to use the dialect of Minang they spoke at home and, in this way, maintain and reinforce dialect characteristics, at least among the participants and perhaps their immediate family members. Historically, Minang has been primarily a spoken language without its own writing system or standard orthography. For several hundred years prior to the twentieth century, it was written using an adapted form of Arabic script, although there were always many people who were not able to read the language written in that form.

Members of the Minangkabau community are generally very sensitive to linguistic variation in Minang, and it is not uncommon for speakers to draw attention to their own or another person's dialect use in conversation, where it may be the subject of teasing or amusement. The popularity of online social networks has heightened this sensitivity among older people and has created a new focus on Minang usage as an identifying characteristic of individuals and groups within the wider Minangkabau community. While providing an important social resource with the potential to support emotional well-being and adaptation among members, these groups may have a stressing effect on older people who have reduced ability to use Minang and for whom Indonesian (or another language) has become their primary means of communication. The fact that Minang is not generally a written language further complicates the matter, as speakers have to figure out the best way to render spoken forms in writing. Nonetheless, regardless of language facility, most elderly Minangkabau find participation in these technology-mediated social networks satisfying and see them as a source of resilience.

In form and content, these online social networks replicate the normal patterns of direct interaction in the Minangkabau community. Pre-existing relationships with other individuals are maintained online, so traditional markers of social status, such as economic success, age, level of education, and religious affiliation, remain important. The groups are generally used to spread news deemed to be of interest to the members, which often includes the activities of various individuals, the situation in the places they live, the details of participants' visits to West Sumatra (especially for holidays); discussion of religious issues that are important to the groups; and information about children and grandchildren. This last is significant in direct interactions in the Minangkabau community as well, as most people believe it is necessary and important to ensure that existing social networks and family connections are maintained into the next generations. For older people living in the village, the relationships between younger people from various families across generations tends to be clear and observable. However, those living in the *rantau* have often never met younger relatives of their peers, especially grandchildren who may never have lived in the village themselves.

The BI70 WhatsApp Group

The BI70 WhatsApp group has sixteen members who come from different parts of West Sumatra and who all speak Minang, even though their dialects are different. Four of the members are male and twelve are female. Eleven of the members live in Jakarta and, of these, ten are female. The rest live in different parts of Sumatra. Ilham, a member of the middle generation of the Valley family belongs to the group. Communication among the members of BI70 is extremely intense; sometimes several hundred messages may be sent in a single day.

The number 70 the members use in the group's name refers to the year they began their university study in Padang. The basis for participation in the group is having been at the same university at the same time. Not all of the group members were close friends, however; some knew each other only superficially, others have resumed close friendships they developed as undergraduates. Only five of the members graduated. The rest dropped out of the university for one reason or another. Most of these were the women. In total, three men and two women did get their degree. All the women left the university because they got married, while the one man who did not graduate felt that the university was not for him. When they formed the group, most of the members had lost contact with their university friends and had not seen them for forty years or more. Three of the women continued to be friends over the years because they became related by marriage. It was these three women who started BI70 group.

All the members of the group were in their mid-sixties at the time of this study, and those who had had a professional career had retired. One of the men had worked at the Foreign Ministry since graduating from college and, by the time he retired, had been an ambassador for Indonesia in various parts of the world. Three had been school teachers, and one worked in the Office of Education in one of the provinces of Sumatra. The remaining members, who were women, had come to Jakarta with their husbands, many of whom had become successful in their fields. Most of these women were very well off when they and their husbands retired. In terms of financial security, those who had dropped out of college to get married generally did much better than those who had had jobs, including the ambassador.

It was apparent that all of the members became happier after forming the group. This was evident from their messages to each other and, more importantly, was visible in the way they lived and behaved. They spent a lot of time reminiscing which they greatly enjoyed. They liked to talk about the many things they did together when they were in college, recalling funny events that had happened years before. They talked continuously about their families, children and grandchildren, what they had done since they last saw each other, and discussed other friends they had lost contact with over the years.

What is notable about this group is that they use Minang and informal Indonesian as their language of communication. All of them feel that, because none of them live in West Sumatra, their Minang has become very rusty. Some say they have forgotten words, especially those who are married to people from other ethnic groups and who do not use Minang on a daily basis. They generally speak an informal variety of Indonesian at home and use standard Indonesian at work. Ilham falls into this category. He is a highly educated professional who uses Indonesian every day but, unlike some of the other group members, has retained his original fluency in the Minang dialect of the village and can converse with equal facility in the standard variety of Minang used in the provincial capital of Padang. The women who did not have a career had tried to teach their children Minang, but the children were not interested, especially because their friends did not speak the language. Many of their children understand the language to some degree but certainly cannot engage in conversation.

Members of the group re-established their long discontinued friendship quickly. They often comment about how happy they are to be able to communicate regularly in Minang again and whenever they want to, even if only through social media. They make fun of the members whose Minang is incorrect or who forget words. Many of them also call each other to talk (as opposed to writing). They feel their Minang has improved as a result of all this. They frequently say that they now have more energy to do things that before they felt no desire to do, unless it was absolutely necessary. They visit each other frequently, especially if someone is sick, and celebrate occasions like birthdays and graduations as a group. The ability to interact in their long-disused first language has provided an immense increase in their well-being and has also supplied an additional social network of people who understand their background and share the same cultural basis as them.

LANGUAGE AND ETHNIC IDENTITY

For most Indonesians, identity as a member of an ethnic group is extremely important and, for many people, represents their true persona. This is the case for the older members of the Minangkabau community who often revert to a more Minang identity as they age and especially when they are no longer working. One reason for this is related to the nature of Indonesian identity and ethnic identity in modern Indonesia, a dichotomy that is closely associated with language use. For many people, with the exception of those who work in the informal sector in a community that uses their local language, employment requires the use of Indonesian which people tend to associate with their professional identity. When they are no longer part of the work environment, the need to use and be Indonesian lessens for many older people. At the same time, if they live in West Sumatra, they may take on a more important role in the leadership of their extended family or occupy themselves more with religious or community affairs that are compatible with the social norms for older people. Even for those who reside permanently in the *rantau* and do not have a great deal of contact either with their extended family in West Sumatra or with other Minangkabau, older age is often characterized by behaviour and attitudes that are more associated with their culture of origin than with the culture they live in.

The reason for this is that the Minangkabau community has been, and continues to be, strongly focused on individual origins in an ancestral village. Modernization and urbanization have been relatively recent social forces in Indonesia, and people now aged over sixty generally grew up in very different social and cultural contexts. For example, many parts of West Sumatra began to have access to electricity in the 1970s, but there are still areas of the province that do not (Arditono 2015). Individuals aged over sixty today overwhelmingly experienced a childhood that was fairly consistent with the traditional pattern that had been in place for centuries prior to that. Part of this experience was the observation of people who were elderly at the time, often their own grandparents and other older members of their extended family. The experience of these elders has determined the expectations for many older Minangkabau today who, for example, hoped and expected to live with a daughter and her family in their old age, in a Minangkabau environment where their social position as a senior member of the community and their extended family was clearly defined in the context of *adat*. This kind of experience is mediated by the Minang language which serves as a proxy for the culturally defined experience of ageing. Social change and the resulting challenge to these expectations are increasingly detrimental to the sense of cultural consonance of today's elderly which is often observable through the dynamic of language.

6

Ageing in the Village

THE VILLAGE OF KOTO

The village of Koto is very different today than even twenty years ago, and the comparison with the more distant past is stark. Physically, the village is much more developed than in the past. Many of the houses have been renovated or replaced by better quality, modern homes made of brick. It is not uncommon for residents to have cars or motorcycles which are visible on the road and parked near their homes. Public transportation of various kinds passes the village and can be used by residents to travel to the town of Batusangkar as well as to other villages in the general area. Virtually every house has a satellite dish, and television is the main form of entertainment for village residents. There is an elementary school, a mosque, several *surau* (prayer houses) and other public buildings, and also a few small stores some of the residents run from their homes. Electricity has been available in this area for more than forty years, and many people's standard of living has improved dramatically in the ensuing decades.

However, compared to the past, the village seems very empty. There are many fewer people visible on the roads, and there are not as many children as there used to be. One reason for this is that more people of working age, many of whom are better educated than ever before, have professional jobs, either in Batusangkar and the surrounding region or have moved to other towns to work. The lifestyle of those who have remained in the village has taken on a more modern pattern where they are away from home all day and return in the evening after work. Those engaged in traditional occupations in the agricultural sector are often working in the fields and gardens for much of the day. Even the older people seem to spend more time indoors, as there is less activity in the village during the day than there used to be in the past. In addition, there is evidence that the rate of migration is increasing. *Marantau* remains an attractive option for young people. In 2010, for example, the province of West Sumatra experienced a net loss of more than 800,000 people. In 1990, the comparable figure was 425,000. Most of this movement is from rural parts of the province to urban areas (BPS Sumatera Barat 2016*e*). In Tanah Datar, the region where Koto is located, a reduction in the average size of households has been noted for some years. In 2000, there was an average of 4.4 persons per home; the comparable figure in 2015 was 3.9 (BPS Sumatera Barat 2016*e*). Statistics are not available at the village level, so it is difficult to quantify the loss of population to more urban areas from Koto specifically. However, overall trends in urbanization are discernable. In, 1980, there were about 319,618 people living in the Tanah Datar region, which contains the town of Batusangkar as well as Koto. In the same year, the provincial capital of Padang had a population of 480,607. In 2015, the population of Tanah Datar (including Batusangkar) had reached 344,828. At the same time, there were 902,413 people in Padang (BPS Sumatera Barat 2016*e*).

At one time, the older members of the Minangkabau community who had remained in the village would have lived close to or in the same dwelling as members of their extended family according to the patterns of their matrilineal social structure. In practice, this meant that a household would normally be headed by a senior woman who lived with her husband, any daughters who were living in the village, and their husbands and children. Other relations in the maternal line would likely live nearby on family land. The male members of the family would be expected to reside with their wife's family, although they might spend a great deal of time at the home of their mother and sisters where they might return permanently upon the death of their wife. While it is not possible to ascertain whether this system worked as well as many Minangkabau believe it did, it is the case that an absence of other alternatives in the traditional context did mean that most individuals had to rely on the structures of the matrilineal system, even when they did not get along with certain family members and the situation was strained. Today, however, many members of the middle generation have moved away for better opportunities or are at work outside the home for much of the day. This means that the experience of older people in the village is very different than in the past.

Most Minangkabau do not like to be alone and feel very uncomfortable if there are no other people around. This is an attitude that is instilled in individuals from a very young age, when they are explicitly taught that it is better to be with other people and it is antisocial to engage in certain activities, such as eating, by oneself. Even when dining in a restaurant, people may feel awkward if their food is served, but strangers sitting nearby are still waiting for their own order. There is also a deep-seated idea in Minangkabau culture that plans made in a group are likely to be better than if done alone because good ideas emerge from the process of interaction. In the past there were usually a number of family members at home or in the immediate vicinity at all times, but this is not always the case today. Many older people, who no longer have a job or who are unable to do much agricultural work, often find themselves at home all day with no one to talk to or interact with. This is a problem, not just in Koto, but across West Sumatra, where the issue of loneliness has been recognized as being the main negative impact on well-being for older people, along with financial need (see, for example, Nugroho 2015). The loneliness and isolation of the elderly in their own home is a serious problem in all parts of Indonesia and is a great concern in the context of health and social welfare (Kementerian Sosial 2008). The Ministry of Social Affairs estimates that almost 10 per cent of the elderly in Indonesia live alone (Kementerian Sosial 2016).

Another impact of the presence of fewer people in the village during the day is that it is more difficult for those who live at home to manage all the daily tasks required to keep a household running. This type of work often includes feeding and caring for pets and livestock, boiling water for drinking and other uses, shopping, cooking, washing clothes, and performing routine agricultural tasks that vary with the season. Even though the quality of houses in villages like Koto has improved greatly, there are few conveniences that would make housework less arduous. For example, water for domestic use may still come from an outdoor source and has to be brought inside in containers. Laundry is washed by hand and hung out to dry in the yard. While many people grow fruit and vegetables, many types of food have to be purchased, usually at a market in a major town. For example, the town of Batusangkar has a large traditional market that serves the surrounding region. It is most active on Thursday, the customary market day, but some sellers are present every day, and the permanent shops and stores are open seven days a week. There are a few smaller markets in some of the villages, but they only operate on their traditional market days. The small stores in the village do not sell meat and other perishable items.

Older people living alone or in households that are smaller than would have been usual in the past often have difficulty managing the daily housework required to keep going, and others in the household often have to take on a greater burden. This further occupies their time and increases the isolation of the older family member. It also emphasizes the imbalance of contribution, which is a source of anxiety and concern to many elderly Minangkabau. In many parts of West Sumatra, however, significant numbers of old people are living alone and do not have younger relatives they can rely upon. The long-standing tradition of *marantau* has contributed to this as has the kind of social change within the region noted above. Badan Pusat Statistik, the Indonesian national statistical agency, has found that two-thirds of those living below the poverty line in West Sumatra live in rural areas and a majority of rural residents are elderly (Riau Mandiri 2016). In practice, the impact of this on the older residents of Koto and similar villages is an increase in amount and difficulty of work that must be done combined with a more isolated and potentially lonely social environment.

Ribuik

Like most men of Koto who stayed in the village all their life, Ribuik worked as a farmer. His family had a significant amount of land, consisting mostly of rice fields, that had been sufficient to support them all economically. After he married in his early twenties, Ribuik continued to help his family work on their land. He spent most of his time there, as was customary for and expected of Minangkabau men. His wife's family did not have much land and did not need his help. His wife worked as a labourer, doing various agricultural jobs, such as planting, harvesting and weeding, for other people depending on the season. She would also do other domestic work that people needed help with, such as cleaning, drying and milling rice, and doing laundry. Custom and tradition allowed

Ribuik to use the produce from his mother's land that was allocated to him to support his wife and children but, as time went on, this was much less than he needed. He had several sisters who were also allocated pieces of the land for their own families after they married, and the family's property could no longer support the larger number of people dependent on it. So, when he had time, Ribuik would also work as a labourer in the village like his wife for which they would be paid daily with money, rice, or whatever form of payment both parties agreed upon. This was very hard work, though, and it took a toll on Ribuik.

No matter how physically strong a person is, manual work in the rice fields and agricultural jobs have a serious impact on health. This was the case for Ribuik, who was a large, strong man. From his teenage years, he had been known as a hard worker and would labour from early morning until just before sunset. People who had a lot of land would rather hire him than many others in the village because he could get more work done in a day. But he had no personal assets other than his physical strength. He had never attended school and he was considered unattractive by his peers. His skin was much darker than most people in Koto, and they thought he was odd looking. In the village, people were often cruel to their friends, and they teased Ribuik mercilessly. Some of them thought that this was the reason he spent most of his time working and did not interact much with other people his age.

Ribuik did have other skills though. He was a good eel catcher and fish trapper. Nonetheless, he was not able to marry a desirable woman in the village. In Koto, desirable normally meant a beautiful woman or a woman from a family with a lot of land. Still, Ribuik married earlier than most of his friends. He and his wife earned enough from their work to provide food and clothing for their children but could not afford to send them to school. All four of his sons left the village and only returned for occasional visits on special occasions, such as for the holiday at the end of the fasting month or if there was a death in the family. Their one daughter married early and lived in Koto with Ribuik and his wife at his wife's house.

Because of hard physical work he did, Ribuik aged quickly. By the time he was in his forties, he had become noticeably weaker and could not do as much work as he used to. He complained constantly about aches and pains. By his late fifties, he could no longer use a hoe or an axe or go to the rice fields to catch eels and leave fish traps in the rivers around Koto. Gradually, his wife and her family began to treat him badly. To make matters worse, his daughter hated him; she thought he was lazy and could not accept or understand why he complained about his health all the time. When he reached the point where he had to stay at home most of the time because of his physical condition, she would yell at him and say he was useless. It broke his heart, and he felt miserable. The only consolation was that his mother-in-law still treated him civilly. She was not rude to him and even defended him when his daughter abused him too much.

Ribuik's life became much worse when his mother died, followed by his mother-in-law a year later. His daughter was married at the time and had a child. She did not want him to live in the house anymore, and there was no one to defend him now. She gave her mother an ultimatum to either divorce him or kick him out. By that time, Ribuik could not even do much around the house. His daughter hated the sight of him watching television all day, so he would spend practically all his time confined in his room. Finally, his wife told him to leave, whether he divorced her or not. His family reluctantly accepted him back. Their own house was now too small for everyone entitled to live there as all the women were married and had their own children. They could not afford to build another dwelling.

Ribuik's sisters and nieces accepted him back in the family compound with the understanding that he would live in a bamboo shed behind the house among the banana trees and other plants. Ribuik had no choice. He considered himself unlucky and cursed that he had to live for just over ten years in this way. No one talked to him except during the brief visits of one his sisters or nieces paid to his shed to leave him food and something to drink. He had nothing in the shed except a wooden bed with no mattress. He slept on two layers of pandan mat with a pillow for his head. He did have an old radio that one of his nieces gave him. When the battery ran out, he would not dare ask anyone for a new one but waited for them to offer. He was terribly lonely, isolated, and depressed and had never imagined that he would spend the end of his life in this way.

Ribuik died alone, and one of his sisters found him in the shed a day later.

THE OLDER POPULATION OF
RURAL WEST SUMATRA

At present, West Sumatra is one of eight Indonesian provinces with a higher than average dependency ratio. Most of this figure can be attributed to the presence of large numbers of the elderly. In rural areas, for example, there are, on average, 13.47 older men and 16.84 older women for every 100 people of working age. This contrasts with 11.01 elderly men and 13.49 elderly women per 100 working adults in urban areas. The rural elderly make up 8.9 per cent of the province's total population, a figure that is considerably higher than in neighbouring provinces which are similar in terms of geography and economic potential. For example, in the province of Bengkulu, the rural elderly comprise 6.45 per cent of the total population; in Riau, this group makes up 4.5 per cent of the total population; and in Jambi, elderly people in rural areas make up 6.02 per cent of the province's population. In West Sumatra, 56 per cent of these older people are engaged in some kind of economic activity, mostly in the agricultural sector (BPS 2015).

The living arrangements of the older members of the Minangkabau community who live in rural areas, while different from in the past, still reflect the traditions of the region and the matrilineal social structure dictated by *adat*. Overall, 10 per cent of the elderly in rural areas live alone; 16.56 per cent live with a spouse with no other family members in the household; 25.92 per cent live with their own matrilineal family; and 43.63 per cent live in three-generation families that include children and grandchildren. Only 3.9 per cent live in some other circumstance, which refers to the small but growing number of older people who must be accommodated in the region's old age homes because they cannot live alone for economic or health reasons and do not have relatives they can live with. When these figures are considered by gender, the impact of several trends is visible: 2.67 per cent of elderly men but 13.35 per cent of elderly women live alone; 20.65 per cent of men and 11.43 per cent of women live with a spouse and no other family; 36.51 per cent of men and 22.57 per cent of women live with their own family; 37.13 per cent of men and 46.68 per cent of women live in three-generation households; and 3.05 per cent of men and 3.96 per cent of women live in other circumstances (BPS 2015).

The fact that so many more older women than men live alone and that almost twice as many older men live with spouses than older women reflects the longer life expectancy for women than men that has long been observed in societies around the world (see Barford et al. 2006). By contrast, the larger proportion of elderly men who live with their own matrilineal family than women may reflect the custom prescribed by *adat* that requires a widowed or divorced man to return to his mother's family to live with sisters and other female relatives in the family home. Elderly women expect to live with members of the matrilineal family, regardless of marital status, although increasing numbers of women live in nuclear households, even though this may be in their ancestral village and on family land. As more younger people leave villages to work or attend school in towns and cities, a larger number of older women are left in the village on their family land. These women, who might have been the senior members of a multigeneration household in the past, are increasingly the only members of the maternal line still in the village. This demonstrates the impact of social change on traditional family structure and highlights the gaps in village society which are increasingly left when people of working age move to other locations. Nonetheless, the fairly high proportion of both older men and older women who live in three-generation households reflects the traditional extended family structure in Minangkabau communities. The difference in the figures (somewhat more than a third of men and almost half of women) likely relates to differences in average life expectancy and perhaps other social factors. The fairly low proportion of both older men and older women living in other arrangements is still extremely problematic in West Sumatra but is about average compared to other parts of the country (BPS 2015).

The need for institutionalized care for the elderly is without precedent in the traditional context in West Sumatra and is viewed by many Minangkabau as shameful because it seems to attest to the erosion of traditional values. However, there are indications that the emergence of institutions that provide care for the elderly who have no other alternatives is a modern response to a problem that has always existed but that the community has been reluctant to acknowledge. In the past, older people who did not have family they could live with had few alternatives. This situation arose when a person had no children, when their maternal line had died out because there were no female family members in their generation, or when a person was simply on bad terms with members of their immediate and extended family. Some of the problems of older people who are childless are discussed by Idrizal (2004) and by Kreager and Schröder-Butterfill (2007). These works focus on the economic aspects of childlessness but do consider the need of some older people to rely on other relatives for assistance with daily needs.

In past generations, older people who did not have family to live with in the village might have had to occupy some kind of make-shift dwelling by themselves and live by doing any work that was available. If they were unable to work, they might have had to depend on the charity of people in the village, which could include living in the local mosque or prayer house and perhaps acting as an unofficial caretaker, who might also receive *zakat* (the religious tax required by Islam that is intended to help the poor), *sedekah* (charity donations), and *fitrah* (the annual gift to the poor paid at the end of the fasting month). Others may have been forced to live on the street in one of the larger towns. While this does still occur today, elderly people who are homeless are often taken to one of the old age homes run by the Department of Social Affairs when they attract the attention of the police or local residents. The social workers who staff these institutions make an effort to transfer the old person to an appropriate facility in his or her region of origin when possible. The idea behind this is to accommodate individuals in the geographic area where they will feel most comfortable and where it maximizes the possibility of locating family members who may be able to care for the person at home. In addition, it is hoped that older people will feel more at ease, both culturally and linguistically, in the region they come from. Demand for accommodation is very high, and the public nursing homes in the province are all at capacity. A number of private institutions have opened as well but these require payment and tend to be located in urban centres. At present, fewer than 5 per cent of older Minangkabau living in rural areas receive any type of pension (BPS 2015), and many have no regular income.

For this reason, one of the programmes of the various local administrations in West Sumatra provides cash grants to elderly people classified as "neglected" (*terlantar*). This definition relates to socioeconomic status but also includes those who have no family members they can rely upon for assistance. The number of neglected old people in rural areas is increasing and represents a major social problem in several parts of the province. For example, the region of Lima Puluh Kota, which includes the town of Payakumbuh, has an elderly population of about 28,000 (7.7 per cent of almost 362,000). Of these, 3,100, or 11 per cent, are classified as "neglected" (Rahmat 2016). This region, which is part of the Minangkabau heartland like Tanah Datar where Koto is located, has an institution for the homeless run by the Department of Social Affairs. It is also full, and many of the residents are elderly. The fact that institutions of this kind are needed in the traditional homeland of the Minangkabau, where many people feel that *adat* and traditional family values should be strongest, is the main cause for the shock and outrage felt by many members of the community. This issue is discussed in detail in Chapter 9.

The outrage that many members of the Minangkabau community feel about the increasingly common situation of old people being placed in the care of institutions is one manifestation of a larger concern that the institutions of *adat* and the traditional community are eroding or are no longer able to compete with other concerns and pressures individuals face in modern society. For older people who live in their village of origin, the changes in population make-up that are resulting in a drain of younger people from rural to urban areas are also contributing to the perception that the structures and practices of *adat* are weakening. One important aspect of this relates to land, the major asset of Minangkabau extended families.

The existence of land that can be used for agriculture, and especially in the production of rice, is at the centre of the Minangkabau conceptualization of the living environment. Traditional literature holds that the existence of rice fields, along with dry fields, a place to bathe and get water, a place to bury the dead, and other necessities of community life are the prerequisites for an organized settlement. *Adat* holds that older women, in consultation with the older men in the maternal line, are the custodians of the land which is held in common by extended families. In the premodern era, all the members of the family who lived in the village relied on the land and what could be produced. For this reason, Minangkabau in each generation accepted the importance of their family's land and had a vested interest in maintaining it and increasing its productivity. While still significant to extended families in the village, the concern for family land has declined, as other sources of income have become available and more Minangkabau have become more heavily integrated into the modern context through education, employment, and an increased level of *marantau*. As a result, one of the most noticeable changes in the villages of West Sumatra is that it is now occasionally possible to buy land that in the past would have been needed to support much larger family groups, especially if it was suitable for rice cultivation.

Aminah

Aminah, until her death, controlled a large amount of land, that included both wet rice fields and dry fields, where many coconut trees, clove trees, and fruit trees had been planted generations before. The family also had a rice mill, a facility for producing cooking oil, and fish ponds. The family land was not contiguous, however, and even Aminah was not sure how the family had acquired all of it. Members of the family only recall that their members have always controlled this land, lived on it, and/or cultivated it for as long as anyone can remember.

Five years ago, the family lost a piece of land when another family from the village took them to court over its ownership. It was a small piece of field that was not connected to the main part of the land Aminah had originally inherited. All the family knew about it was that Aminah's uncle had managed this lot. He planted coconut trees, clove trees and orange trees. When he died, the land was neglected, and all the productive trees became overgrown and stopped producing significant crops.

Aminah's third daughter, Erni (Chapter 3), married a man, Muhammad (Chapters 4 and 10) who worked in different places in West Sumatra. They returned to the village when Muhammad got a job in Batusangkar; at that time, they had seven children. Erni's husband offered to take care of the neglected trees on the small piece of land, to which the family agreed. Soon, the trees were productive again, and he built a small hut to rest in while working. This piece of land was located on the outskirts of Koto and was surrounded by rice fields belonging to other people in the village next to a small river. It soon became a favourite place for members of the extended family to visit during the fruit or clove seasons, especially the children. It was also a quiet place to go for anyone in the family to get away from the communal house in the valley.

The caretaker of the land changed again when a son of Aminah's brother, Hisyam, returned from the *rantau* with his family. He was, of course, not a member of Aminah's extended family but the family was his *bako*, the relatives of his father with whom Minangkabau often have a special relationship. Before returning to the village, he asked Aminah if he could live on this piece of land. Because he was a carpenter, he planned to renovate the hut to make it more comfortable, and this would mean that the building would belong to Aminah's family. Aminah agreed after consulting Erni and her husband, who agreed, with the understanding that her husband would continue to take care of the plants and use the produce.

Over several years, Hisyam also planted many productive trees, and disputes often occurred between him and Erni about the trees and what they produced. She sometimes accused Hisyam of harvesting trees that did not belong to him. In the end, Aminah negotiated that Hisyam would pay a certain amount of money to Erni in exchange for full control of everything on the land. Once this was agreed to by everyone involved, Hisyam had full control of the land even though he did not own it.

When Hisyam died ten years ago, his wife had to leave the hut, even though she really wanted to continue living there. The Valley family, however, did not want her to. This resulted in a great deal of bitterness that strained the relationship between her and her late husband's *bako*. The land reverted to the Valley family, even though by that time no one wanted to live on the land, and the family members who lived in the village had their own houses. At first, various people in the family continued to take care of the land and the plants on it, but this did not last long, and the land was neglected again for several years.

It was during this time of neglect that Dirman, the *mamak* of another family in Koto, whose land was adjacent to this piece of land claimed that Aminah's original field belonged to them. Since ancestral land of this kind has never been documented formally despite this being possible at present under Indonesian law, Dirman saw an opportunity. His family had always had an idea that this piece of land was theirs, but no one had dared challenge Aminah's family until Dirman became the head of the extended family. He was further encouraged by the fact that the Valley family had allowed the land to become unproductive, and most of Aminah's adult grandchildren lived in the *rantau*, while their parents had died or were too old to fight the challenge.

When Dirman presented his case, he managed to undermine the credibility of the Valley family through trickery. He approached Hisyam's widow and promised her a large sum of money if she was willing to be part of the scheme. He told her to show support for Aminah's family when he publicly challenged their ownership of land, which she agreed to do. With the Valley family's presence much reduced in the village, Hisyam's widow approached the *mamak* of the family and offered her help. After all, she said, she had been married to the son of a former *mamak* of the family. While she was unhappy when she had been evicted after her husband's death, she understood and had no quarrel with the current members of the family who lived in Koto. She offered to be a witness for the Valley family and to testify in court that the land did indeed belong to them. Her late husband and his father had often told her this, and the fact that she had lived there with her husband for years supported this. The Valley family accepted her offer.

On the day she testified in court, however, Hisyam's widow changed her story completely. She told the court that she and her husband had never really lived on this piece of land, and her husband had said that the land did not belong to Aminah's family. She further told the court that she had heard Dirman's version of the story from her husband many times. She claimed her husband told her that Aminah's great uncle was smarter that Dirman's family *mamak* at the time, and the Valley family had taken the land from the other family.

LAND IN THE VILLAGE

In the past, productive land was the most important source of wealth in the Minangkabau community. A majority of the community earned a living from agriculture in one form or another such that large property holdings made extended families wealthy and powerful at the village level. Because of the way in which the matrilineal social structure required that land be allocated, there was potential for considerable tension within families that had many female members because the available land would have to be allocated among them to provide a living for each woman and her children. For families that were landless or had small holdings, this was a serious issue that resulted in their members having to find other sources of income, such as working in the fields of other people in the village for wages or a share of the produce. In practice, it was not possible for a family or individual to obtain more land in the village context because all arable space had been claimed in the distant past. It was, however, possible for the wealthier members of the community to gain control of additional property by paying a sum of money for the right to use it. The family that owned such mortgaged property could redeem it by paying back an agreed amount to the lien holder when they were able. There is some evidence that this may be changing, at least in some areas. The circumstances where it may be possible for an outsider to buy traditionally held land can occur if the extended family all agrees to sell it. This was not permitted by *adat* in the past, but some families are starting to consider selling land they are not using if they have a pressing need for cash. Land may also sometimes be sold when a family line has died out. Under *adat*, the land should return to the closest relative in the same clan, but families sometimes do not need the land or would have difficulty managing it and may decide to sell instead. It is still unusual for ancestral land to be available to buy, however, and this can only occur if the land has been registered and has a legal deed.

In many villages around West Sumatra today, however, land belonging to extended families is untended and, in some locations, has become severely degraded. In other cases, fields have been taken over by people who are not associated with the extended family that rightfully owns the land. With so many fewer people in the village, some families have surplus land and are perhaps less alert than they would have been in the past because their members' income derives from other sources. Much of the land in West Sumatran villages is undocumented; in past generations, knowledge of the extent and traditional boundaries of family land was important information passed from generation to generation and was needed to oversee the management of family assets. While it is possible to obtain deeds in the name of the extended family for traditional holdings, many people do not do so because the need for such documentation did not exist in the past, and they may not be aware of the risks to their family property. In addition, the family will be liable for property tax on land that has been legally registered, which may be another reason not to obtain legal deeds to ancestral property.

Nonetheless, increasing knowledge of the national legal system as well as a number of high-publicity cases of traditional land being taken over by corporate interests have raised community awareness of land issues, and there has been a commensurate increase in court challenges aimed at resolving conflicts between extended families and clans in their village of origin. The government of the City of Bukittinggi, which is the main town in the Agam Regency, reports having handled 938 disputes of this kind in the ten years up to 2016. Of these, 457 related to disagreement as to ownership; 318 concerned the process for obtaining deeds; and 50 related to the determination of property lines and boundaries. The remaining cases involved other issues. The position of the local government in this is that land disputes are best handled by the community *adat* institutions (Kerapatan Adat Nagari), but there is an awareness that it may be difficult to reinstate traditional consensus-based processes in the modern community (Pemerintah Kota Bukittinggi 2016). The regional government of Pasaman, located in the northernmost part of the province of West Sumatra, also reports a large number of cases relating to land use rights. In this region, however, many of the issues have arisen because corporate interests have been allocated the use of land which is claimed by a local clan. This local government has also stated its preference that such cases be settled outside the courts with recourse to *adat*, rather than the law (Mukhlisun 2013).

While there are a number of social, political, and economic factors that are contributing to the large volume of cases regarding the rights to land held by extended families and clans in West Sumatra, it is also the case that the depopulation of rural areas has played a role in the situation. In the past, those individuals who left their village to live in the *rantau* were usually unable to interact very intensively with family at home. Travel and communication were difficult and expensive, especially for those who did not become successful in other parts of Indonesia. Many Minangkabau who chose to remain in the *rantau* had, in practice, become removed from the environment of the extended family and were not able to participate to any great degree in its management and considerations. To people who remained in the village, including elderly parents, the younger people who left to live elsewhere were very remote and did not figure into their day-to-day affairs. The individuals living in other locations often felt the same way and would not have been able to contribute to the family's activities, even if they wanted to.

Today, however, social change has made it much more attractive for larger numbers of younger people to leave the village to seek better opportunities elsewhere, even if only to Padang or another nearby city. At the same time, advances in technology have made it possible for almost everyone to have a mobile phone. The use of digital technology for communication has reached to the most distant parts of the country, and mobile telephone and Internet service are available everywhere in West Sumatra, including in areas where electricity is new or even absent and there has never been landline access. Among elderly Minangkabau living in rural areas, 78 per cent own a mobile telephone (the comparable figure for urban areas is 91 per cent) (BPS 2015).

Even as villages in West Sumatra are increasingly occupied by the elderly, communication between these older people and their children and other relatives, who live in other places, is increasingly intense. With the access made possible by mobile communications technology, many older Minangkabau living in the village are in daily contact with their children, and these children, who in the past might have been unable to take part in village affairs, are now able to follow all the activities and events of the extended family and make their opinions known. The result is that many of these younger Minangkabau, who live permanently in the *rantau*, can exert influence over property use and other matters in the village and can demand to take part in the decision-making about family assets from a distance. Instead of relinquishing the right to participate in decision-making and the chance to benefit from family holdings as in the past, younger people are increasingly claiming both the right to live outside the village and also to participate in family concerns in the village.

The results of this are twofold. On the one hand, the ability to contact children and other relatives at any time means that older people living in the village have a way of maintaining family networks, despite the fact some members live in other locations. This is an important source of resilience for many of them that allows them to be involved in the lives of their children and grandchildren, albeit from a distance. To some extent, this helps address problems of loneliness and isolation and has given many older people increased understanding of the situation outside the village and West Sumatra. It has, however, also made it more difficult for both the elderly in the village and younger relatives in the *rantau* to conceal problems and portray themselves in the most favourable light, regardless of their actual circumstances.

On the other hand, the ability of people living outside the village to monitor and perhaps participate in village affairs has created greater tension between the village and the *rantau*. The relationship between people who chose to stay at home and those who decided to leave has always been difficult in that people in the village have tended to see those who left as giving up their right to be directly involved in the management of assets and the accompanying decision-making. Those in the *rantau*, however, often feel they retain the right to participate in village affairs, especially because they frequently send money back to relatives who have remained at home, especially ageing parents and siblings whose income is low. This practice has been recognized as contributing significantly to poverty alleviation in the province (Akral 2014), with the funds returned to the region by those living in other locations estimated to exceed the income of the province by a considerable margin (Singgalang 2016). This transfer of funds into West Sumatra is particularly intense in the period leading up to and during the fasting month of Ramadan when very large numbers of Minangkabau return to their village of origin to visit family and show off their success in the *rantau*. One important impact of this yearly event is an enormous increase in the redemption of items pawned for cash during the past year by people living in the province with money given to them by relatives returning from the *rantau* (Makruf 2016).

Limeh

Limeh, one of Aminah's grandsons, comes from a large family. He has three brothers and four sisters. Despite the fact that the family is large even by the standard of Koto in his generation, its members are reasonably well educated. Each of Limeh's siblings at least finished junior high school. Four have undergraduate degrees, including Limeh, himself, who graduated from a hotel school in Bandung, West Java.

By his own account, Limeh had a happy childhood in the village with his brothers and sisters. His father was a high school teacher, and his mother, Nurijah (see Chapter 2), was one of Aminah's daughters and had access to a large amount of land. These fields provided the family with more than enough rice for their needs. Their fish ponds and fruit and coconut trees allowed them to produce most of what they needed to eat. They lived in his mother's extended family house on their ancestral land, so there was no rent to pay either. All this, in addition to his father's salary, meant that Limeh and his siblings enjoyed a reasonably good life. By the time Limeh was born, his mother had built a house of her own on family land and no longer had to share with her married sisters and their children. But they remained very close, and all the children could sleep at any of the family houses as they liked.

All of Limeh's siblings lived in the village at least until finishing junior high school, including Limeh himself. His oldest sister, Marni (Chapter 8) married a man from the village soon after she graduated from senior high school. He had a very good job at the Ministry of Finance in Jakarta and took her with him to the capital right away. Because of her husband's job, unlike many people from the village who chose *marantau*, this sister's life in Jakarta was very good. She lived in the Ministry's housing complex, had a car, and other luxury items people in the village could not afford at the time, such as a television set and refrigerator.

As was often the case with Minangkabau people at the time, this sister became an anchor for her siblings who wanted to move to Jakarta and surrounding areas to work or further their studies. One of Limeh's brothers, Fauzi (Chapter 8), who completed an undergraduate degree in Padang, went to Jakarta to work. Because he had a low-ranking position at a government office, he could not afford to buy or even rent his own place. He stayed with his sister until he was able to earn enough to support himself. Similarly, Limeh was able to study in Bandung because of the support of his sister and her husband. Eventually, all his siblings, with the exception of one brother, moved to Jakarta. The remaining brother, Hamzah (Chapter 3) went to Makassar in South Sulawesi, married a woman from there, and became the only member of the family who was almost completely disconnected from the rest and from the village as a whole. Eventually, only Limeh's parents were left in the village.

After graduating from hotel school, Limeh immediately found a job at a 5-star hotel in Jakarta. The whole village knew about it, and his parents were proud of him and would talk about him constantly. But there was something about Limeh that puzzled many people in the village, including his family. After four or five years working at the hotel, to everyone's surprise, especially his older sister and her husband who had helped him get his position, Limeh told everyone he was not very happy there. There was no reasonable and sensible cause for this as far as his friends and relatives could see. He finally decided to leave Jakarta and work in Padang.

Everyone was astonished and thought that this was a poor decision. The job he was able to get in Padang was at a small hotel that was not doing well. But Limeh pointed out that this was, in fact, a promotion. At the hotel in Padang, he was the food and beverage manager, while in Jakarta he had been a low-level employee in the hotel restaurant. Nonetheless, the whole family felt that his prospects in Jakarta were much better, but Limeh would not listen.

After just a couple of years, Limeh began to complain about his job at the hotel in Padang. He disliked the management which he felt was too provincial and not open to new ideas. He felt that he was not valued. He also said that the fact that he was a manager did not mean much. His supervisors did whatever they wanted without consulting him. Soon, he was saying that he planned to change jobs again. It happened that a new hotel had just opened in Bukittinggi, an upland town in West Sumatra not far from Koto. Even though it was a smaller town than Padang, Bukittinggi is considered more of a tourist location than the provincial capital, even though it does not compare with other tourist destinations in Indonesia, and the hotel in Padang where Limeh had been working was busier.

Limeh applied for a position as food and beverage manager at the hotel in Bukittinggi when it became available and was hired. But to most of his friends in Jakarta and Padang, this was another bad move.

His family, however, began to worry about him. They suspected that he lacked the ability to succeed in a career. When he had been working in Padang, he had often talked about giving up his job entirely and returning to the village to live. This was very odd in the context of Minangkabau tradition. If a person had managed to obtain an education that was not readily available in West Sumatra and then was employed in the field, it was unthinkable to return permanently to the village. The aim of *marantau* is to better oneself and get a good job. It is then expected that a person who has done this will help other family members and other people from the villages to achieve similar success. Returning to the village in the way Limeh was talking about was not common and was considered strange. Even his move to Padang and then to Bukittinggi was viewed as negative.

In Bukittinggi, Limeh talked more and more about giving up his job and how wonderful it would be for him to move back to the village and start a business. He planned to raise chickens and, despite everyone's objections, returned to the village to do so with the money he had saved.

Limeh's wife is also from Koto and works as high school teacher. But she did not have many assets to support the family. Unlike Limeh's mother, his wife did not come from a family with a large amount of land, so they could not rely on family wealth. Instead, Limeh's wife helped him with the chicken business.

Tradition allows men to use the land of their maternal family if the female members agree. Limeh had many female relatives because his mother had several sisters, each of whom had daughters. Some of them were Limeh's age, some were younger, and quite a few were older than him. They did allow him to have the chicken business on family land, but, after just three years, Limeh decided that this was not for him, and the work was too hard with very little profit.

By the time Limeh's chicken business failed, he was the only one of his immediate family left in the village. His father had died and his mother, Nurijah, was paralysed from a stroke she had suffered a few years earlier. She was living in Jakarta with one of Limeh's sisters. She would never allow herself to be taken care of by her son or, even worse, by his wife in the village. Since Limeh lived with his wife, the house his mother had built and where he had grown up was now empty; it had been for three years since Nurijah moved to Jakarta. So, when the chicken business did not work out, Limeh thought he would turn his mother's house into homestay accommodation for any tourists who might visit the area. He thought his hotel background would help him, and there were occasional visitors to Batusangkar because it is only several kilometres from the village of Pagaruyung, the seat of the ancient Minangkabau kingdom and where there is a museum of Minangkabau culture. This, along with some ancient inscriptions and other archaeological sites, are sometimes visited by Malaysian travellers.

So Limeh began to fix up the old and now abandoned family house. But when this news reached his sisters in Jakarta, they were furious, believing he had taken over a house that rightfully belonged to them. It did not matter that the house had been empty for years. When Limeh did not pay attention to their demands, all four sisters returned to the village together and undid the work Limeh had done on the house. They warned him not to try use the house again. Limeh now has no job or business, except what he can do on the land of the extended family. He raises fish in one of the ponds they have and has planted some fruit trees. None of these provide much income, however, so Limeh, now in his mid-sixties, relies on his wife's salary.

THE VILLAGE AND THE RANTAU

Up until the present time, the relationship between the village and the *rantau* has been strong but was limited to certain, very specific types of interaction that centred on remittances from people in the *rantau* to their family members in the village. Beyond this, those who were living in the village tended to feel that they had more right to determine what happened to family assets and how they would be used. Not surprisingly perhaps, Minangkabau who chose to remain in the village became increasingly integrated into the matrilineal social structure and filled in gaps where others had left. People who went to the *rantau* were often gone for years and generally had a much lower level of contact with the village than is now possible with available technological innovations. While many of the people who left the village decided to live permanently in the *rantau*, *adat* reserves a place for everyone within their matrilineal family, especially in older age, and there have always been older people who returned to the village after many years away.

Among the current elderly in West Sumatra, there is a small number of people in this situation. In many cases, they spent their entire productive life in another part of Indonesia. Many experienced only moderate economic success and decided to return to the village because of increasing difficulty making a living associated with their age, because of problems in their immediate family, or for other reasons, such as that they missed the village and wanted to live in a Minangkabau community. It is notable that there have never been large numbers of older people who return to the village from the *rantau*, and those that do are often disappointed by the reception they receive, despite what *adat* suggests should be the case.

Many older people who have been in the *rantau* for years were brought up with the understanding that *adat* guarantees a place for every person within their mother's family. However, they tend to be equally sceptical about the truth of this in actual fact. The tension between the village and the *rantau* can be largely attributed to the fact that people who remained in the village are often wary of those who left, despite benefitting from their financial contributions. In older age especially, people in the village have often achieved social status they are unwilling to have affected by the sudden presence of another relative who might upset the balance and who will likely also be a drain on resources. Older people in the *rantau* are aware of this and will often choose to remain in very difficult circumstances, rather than return to a potentially awkward and unpleasant life within the village context.

Behind this is the problematic position of older men in Minangkabau society. Because men traditionally live at their wife's house while married, they are somewhat removed from the household dynamic of their own family for at least part of their adult life. A man who married in the *rantau* is not likely to have a wife from his own village, even if she is of Minangkabau ethnic origin, and, hence, will not have a place to live in the place where he comes from. For this reason, older men who return to the village are often unmarried, widowed, or divorced, and must live with their sisters or other female relatives in the maternal line. The nature of their welcome by these female relatives is determined by their economic potential and whether, or to what extent, they are capable of contributing to the family's income. There is a tendency for men's value to be measured largely in economic terms in the Minangkabau community, as in the case of Ribuik above, regardless of whether they remain in the village or go to the *rantau*.

The contrast between men who went to the *rantau* and became successful and those who failed to make money is an important element of the traditional Minangkabau view of personal achievement. The expression "be absorbed by the *rantau*" (*laruik di rantau*) is used to describe someone who did not become wealthy in the *rantau* and, as a result, has faded into the community where he was living. This is viewed negatively, as a sign of personal failure as well as failure to help the family. Older men who do return home are expected to bring wealth with them that, in effect, pays for their re-established position among their female relatives. In the past, this wealth was largely in material form, usually money earned in a small business of some kind. Today, however, in addition to such tangible assets, education, social status, and position in the *rantau* may also be important. Even when a man has achieved success in the *rantau*, his return is problematic and may be seen as extremely disruptive by the female relatives who head the household he is returning to.

For this reason, the decision to return to the village is often a last resort for older men. Even when they believe they might prefer to spend their older age in the environment where they grew up and where they are familiar with the language and culture, they may find that life in the home of a sister or other relative is intolerable or that it is better to try to live by themselves in or near their village. This likely explains the fact that the number of men in West Sumatra who require public support, including accommodation in old age homes, is more than double the number of women (see, for example, Nugroho 2013).

Interestingly, even women who have spent their working or married years in the *rantau* are often reluctant to return to the village to live. There are several reasons for this that are quite different from those of men. One of the most basic is a desire to remain near their own children, who, especially if born in the *rantau*, generally do not speak Minang and are not part of the larger Minangkabau community, except through their older relatives. In seeking to maintain cultural norms, women in this position expect, and often do, play an important role in the life of their daughters and grandchildren. Another very significant reason is that women also understand the difficulty of returning to the village after years away. While they cannot be denied access to family assets and ancestral land, they will have to compete with sisters, cousins, and other female relatives for these resources, and the power struggles between Minangkabau women within the context of the extended family can be vicious. Bad feeling and serious quarrels, that are often suppressed for the sake of appearances, are common and can create a very unpleasant living environment. For women who do not have their own home in the village, the prospect of moving in with their female relatives who have spent their entire life there is often unappealing. In addition, the presence of children strengthens the social position and potential power of older women in the village, just as the presence of a husband does for younger women, so a woman who returns home in older age by herself, while her children remain in the *rantau*, may be at a serious disadvantage in terms of supporters for her position in cases of disagreement.

Nonetheless, it is far less common for older women to become homeless in the village than it is for older men. The negative associations of the "betraying child" (*anak durako*) are deeply engrained in Minangkabau culture and reinforced through the folklore of the group. The desire not be to be branded *anak durako* is extremely strong motivation for many Minangkabau in the *rantau* to send money to their mother, to build a house for her in the village, and to generally provide for her needs in a way that shows both the family and other residents of the village that the person involved cares about this extremely important familial tie. When elderly women are not permitted to live in the family home and use its resources, it is often because they have no daughters and have to rely on the daughters and granddaughters of their sisters and cousins. If daughters do not allow an elderly mother to live in the family home, it generally indicates a serious problem exists within the family and becomes the talk of the village. While these multigeneration families are acceptable and expected under *adat*, in practice, this situation is often difficult as older women compete to gain the most favourable access to land and other assets for women of their own line. The difficulty of having to depend on relatives from a collateral line has also been noted by Idrizal (2004) and Kreager and Schröder-Butterfill (2007).

A view exists among the social workers and other authorities who work with the elderly in West Sumatra that the older people in the village who end up under their care are rejected by their children because they were bad parents themselves. One of the main aims of social services that exist to support the rural elderly is to try to bring these issues out in the open by encouraging younger family members to talk about their perceptions with the aged parent and try to resolve their disagreements so that the parent can return home. There is no doubt that this kind of family problem is not new; there have always been serious conflicts between children and older relatives, parents as well as the maternal uncle, the *mamak*, who has a special responsibility for his sister's children. While these kinds of family problems are rarely mentioned openly, they are widely known in the village and are sometimes used as cautionary examples in private. However, in past generations, there were few alternatives for children and elderly parents who did not get along. The individuals who were in conflict would often have to live in the same household or close by because village society and its social norms made any other arrangement impossible. Today, however, the fact that many individuals have a source of income outside of family land frees them from the rigidity of *adat*. Placing an elderly relative in an institution, such as an old age home, which is outside of the village context, will have negative impacts, but for some individuals, these are less severe than the problems of taking care of the older person themselves.

Like the elderly in all societies, many older Minangkabau experience failing health as they age. This presents a special problem for elderly people living in the village. With fewer younger people present than in the past and with those who do live there busier with work and other concerns, many elderly people with chronic illnesses or who experience a catastrophic event, such as a stroke, have no one to care for them. This has given rise to a situation for which there has been no historical precedent in Minangkabau society and which is a serious challenge to the resilience and coping skills of the people involved.

Like Nurijah, whose story is presented in Chapter 2, the very old, who are sick or infirm, are increasingly brought by their children or other relatives who can afford it to live with them in *rantau* in their final years of life. These elderly people would often prefer to live out their lives in the village, where they feel they understand the language and culture and, more important, where they can maintain the connection to their ancestral land and home. However, in the modern context, as more people are living longer and, as a result experiencing more illness and disability in very old age, the possibility of remaining in the village increasingly no longer exists, and an elderly person has to accept moving to the *rantau* to live with younger relatives because he or she can no longer cope without support in the village. At the same time, there is little hope of enticing younger family members to remain in the village as the opportunities available elsewhere are considerable, and the benefits of education and modern employment are generally perceived by Minangkabau of all ages to be more valuable than those achievable in the traditional context.

7

Ageing in Padang

PADANG AND THE TRADITIONAL *RANTAU*

In the traditional Minangkabau conceptualization of place, the city of Padang, which is now the capital of the Indonesian province of West Sumatra, was seen as the *rantau*. Because folklore holds that the Minangkabau originated in the mountainous interior of the region, *marantau* included a spreading out in all directions, first to closer areas outside this heartland and later to more distant locations. The Minangkabau world, then, at least as it in depicted in folklore and traditional conceptualizations, consists of a set of concentric rings with the three original regions (*luhak*) of Tanah Datar (where Koto is located), Agam, and Lima Puluh Kota at the centre. The oldest traces of Minangkabau civilization can be found in these regions, and the traditional home of the royal family was in the village of Pagaruyung in Tanah Datar, not far from the town of Batusangkar and the village of Koto. Conceptually, if not literally, all Minangkabau are said to have had their origins in one of the three original *luhak*, even if they went to other areas in the distant past.

The oldest *rantau* areas were those places closest to this cultural heartland and are located within a few days travel on foot. They include the coastal areas of West Sumatra, where Padang is located, as well as cities and towns in neighbouring provinces. It is believed that Minangkabau going to the *rantau* first reached the Jambi region in the seventh century. These early travellers set themselves up as goldsmiths, a traditional profession in an area of Agam near Bukittinggi (Munoz 2006). Other parts of Sumatra that are farther away were reached by Minangkabau settlers later. By the fourteenth century, there were colonies of Minangkabau living permanently in Sibolga and Natal in North Sumatra, Meulaboh in Aceh, Bengkulu, Lampung, as well as in Negeri Sembilan in Malaysia (Dobbin 1983). In time, people of Minangkabau heritage came to dominate the population in Negeri Sembilan, and Minangkabau cultural elements are still visible in the community, which has become part of the Malay mainstream (Peletz 1994). By the sixteenth century, large numbers of Minangkabau were living in towns on the island of Sulawesi, where, in addition to trading, many became religious leaders and teachers (Mukhlis et al. 1995). In the early twentieth century, a very large number of Minangkabau had settled permanently in Batavia (later Jakarta) and could be found in major cities and towns across Indonesia (Kato 1982).

For this reason, the area of closest *marantau* includes Padang and other locations along the coast and eastern border of West Sumatra. These areas have been settled by Minangkabau for the longest and today are, in practice, fully Minangkabau. The next ring of settlement encompasses the rest of the island of Sumatra, where Minangkabau now dominate the population of many cities and towns. The outermost circle of Minangkabau migration encompasses the island of Java, including Jakarta, other Indonesian islands, and of course Malaysia and beyond. This history has led to a situation where almost the entire population of West Sumatra is of Minangkabau origin. The language used everywhere in the province is Minang, and land is held according to the traditional pattern by extended families who, in practical terms, view themselves as coming from the location in question. This includes the city of Padang, which is officially almost 350 years old, having been founded in 1669. The fact that virtually all available land in and around Padang is held by extended families who have been established there for centuries has greatly impeded development and the expansion of infrastructure for the city's population (see, for example, Kompas 2014*b*; Haluan 2016*b*).

As the provincial capital, Padang is the seat of modern administration in West Sumatra and also the part of the region where the impact of contemporary Indonesian culture, including governance, is most felt. The city has a number of universities and colleges, branch offices of all the national ministries, local affiliates of the national television stations, a number of major newspapers, and an international airport. While people who live in the city are very much part of a Minangkabau community that uses the language and maintains the social customs of the group, they are also part of a city that operates in the ways established by national institutions and practices. Not surprisingly, Padang has a higher proportion of professionals than other parts of the province as well as a much greater number of people who are employed in salaried positions. The average person in Padang has completed 10.34 years of formal education; the comparable figure in Tanah Datar, for example, is 7.34 (BPS Sumatera Barat 2016d). The relationship between formal education and income is very strong in Indonesia and is reflected in household spending. Even allowing for the fact that many people in rural areas do not need to purchase all their daily necessities, the level of disposable income available to households in Padang is on average far greater than in rural areas. For example, 41.4 per cent of households in Padang report spending more than Rp1 million per person per month. In Tanah Datar, where Koto is located, only 14.3 per cent of households have this level of expenditure (BPS 2014).

Despite the fact that modern roads and vehicles have reduced travel time between Padang and the interior of the province, the distance between the two locations seems much greater for many Minangkabau, especially those who live in the heartland. For older people in particular, Padang seems as remote as Jakarta in terms of cultural distance and removal from life in the village. Nonetheless, more so than ever in the past, it is easier to travel between rural areas of West Sumatra and Padang because of a much greater availability of public transportation and also because so many more people have their own car, even in the villages and smaller towns. Nonetheless, provincial roads remain underdeveloped relative to demand and level of use. In fact, the main road that connects Padang to the upland areas was built by the Dutch during the colonial period and is narrow, winding, and very steep and very crowded, especially as it is heavily used by trucks travelling between provinces as well as long-distance buses in addition to private vehicles. As a result, travel between Batusangkar in Tanah Datar and Padang, a distance of about 100 kilometres, can take as long as three hours under normal circumstances. On Sundays and holidays when more people are travelling, the trip can be much longer. Nonetheless, the psychological distance is still much greater than this for many people.

While a significant portion of Padang's current population counts itself as coming from the city, many people retain strong ties to their village and region of origin elsewhere in the province. Many of them did grow up in another part of the region and moved to Padang either to work or attend school or college. Many younger people who were born in Padang have parents or grandparents who came from a rural area but have no first-hand experience of life in the village themselves. While city residents of this kind are living in the *rantau*, it is fairly easy for them to maintain their connection to their village of origin and to their extended family and its assets. In many cases, these individuals take part in decision-making that relates to the family's activities in the place they come from and may also benefit from the income generated by their property. For older women especially, these links are important as it is often very difficult emotionally for them to give up the right to contribute to the management of family assets, even when they have professional jobs and earn a salary. In this, it is possible to see the transitional nature of the city in the spatial conceptualization of the Minangkabau as well as in their cultural outlook. Because the city is a Minangkabau area and is readily accessible to the older, highland settlement regions, it is possible to participate in some, if not all, aspects of life in the village while also having a more modern lifestyle associated with Indonesian national culture. In this way, people in Padang can still play a role in their extended family if they choose to, even if that role is reduced compared to what it would be if they lived in the village. Not all choose to do so, of course, but this situation has to some extent expanded the reach of the traditional social structure in a way that permits, or in some cases requires, people living in Padang to take part in village life.

Rosni

Rosni, sixty-six, is married to Muhsin (Chapter 2), the eldest son of Aminah's third daughter, Erni (Chapter 3). Her village is only a few kilometres from Koto. Rosni and Muhsin have known each other since they were in the seventh grade and met at school in Batusangkar. They also went to the same senior high school and to the same university in Padang where they majored in economics. They were married as soon as they graduated, and Muhsin was appointed as a junior lecturer in the department where they had studied. A few years later, Rosni got the same type of job in the same place.

Rosni is the fourth child, and third daughter, in a family of seven children. In addition to two older sisters and an older brother, she has one younger sister and two younger brothers. From her parents' point of view, there was nothing remarkable about her when she was born, as the family already had two daughters. But Rosni soon showed that she was more academically inclined than any of her siblings and was a very good student. Her parents, and particularly her mother, had always wanted the children to study at a university and become professionals, different from their father, who was then a small-scale trader, like several others in his as well as his wife's family, who sold groceries in Batusangkar. None of Rosni's older siblings had a similar interest in school or any kind of academic success, much to the disappointment of their parents. They followed their father's lead and started in similar businesses before they finished high school. Unlike their father, however, they expanded their trade to include household items.

When Rosni finished high school, her parents and older siblings all encouraged her to continue to university study in Padang. By that time, her two older sisters had become very successful in business in Batusangkar, and they and their parents could easily afford Rosni's tuition and other costs. Rosni became the first person in her extended family, as well as in her father's extended family, to go to college. By the time she graduated, she and Muhsin were very close, and both families approved of their relationship, which remains very important to couples who want to marry in the Minangkabau community. This is especially significant for women because family disapproval, even among the extended family, can affect their role and claim to family assets. This was one of the main reasons Rosni and Muhsin were able to marry soon after they graduated. Without the support of the families, and especially hers, they would not have been able to afford it. The family helped them buy a piece of land in Padang and build a simple house on it.

Even though her career at the university was not as successful as Muhsin's (he rose through the administrative ranks to become Rector while she remained a lecturer), it is apparent that Rosni had an extraordinary opportunity to achieve the best of two worlds. She has remained part of her village but also has benefited from being in the *rantau*, which in her case, is still within the Minangkabau world from where her village is accessible. She has taken advantage of this opportunity with great success.

But her family situation in the broadest sense, both in Padang and the village, is much more important to her than her work at the university.

Rosni has five children, three girls and two boys. She has often expressed her satisfaction with the fact that she has three daughters who will continue the matrilineal line along with the daughters of her sisters. All five children have university degrees, and all are married. She now has eight grandchildren, three of whom, significantly to her because they are daughters of her daughters, are girls. Her sisters and brothers consider Rosni to be in the most fortunate position they can imagine: fifty years ago, no one imagined a member of the family would be able to teach at a university; her husband's success, especially when he was Rector, increased the prestige of the whole family to a level they never imagined; her extended family credits her husband for the fact that all her younger siblings as well as the children of her sisters who are younger than she is went to college as well; and Rosni herself is the most highly regarded member of the family, even though she is not the oldest daughter or the most successful woman in her extended family. However, she is credited with having been the first to lead the family into modern education and the professions.

Rosni is fully aware of her situation and the way others in her family see her. Because she never reached a very high rank at the university, she had to retire when she was sixty while her husband, being a professor, continues to teach and enjoys all the financial and social benefits his status confers. Rosni has not had to worry about their financial situation for a long time, especially as all her children are now employed. She is content to stay at home taking care of her grandchildren while their parents, her children, are at work. Her relationship with her extended family in the village was never negatively affected by the fact that she has not lived there since graduating from high school. If anything, Rosni's achievement and the close proximity of the village to Padang has strengthened her position in the family. They see her as educated and successful outside the village. She has raised her children well, which is very important to people in the village.

Rosni's life exemplifies the possibilities available to a Minangkabau woman in her older age, but, of course, most women will not achieve them in the way Rosni has. Many things can go wrong over the years: a woman's relationship with her husband may not work out; a child might shame the family in some way; people in the extended family might become jealous and undermine her role; and so forth.

THE EXPERIENCE OF OLDER PEOPLE IN PADANG

For many older people who came from a rural area but have spent their whole adult life in Padang, the desire to maintain ties to their village of origin is extremely strong. Among older women, this often centres on the idea that their share of family assets will eventually be taken over by their daughters and that it is vital they compete successfully with their other female relatives to ensure that this can occur. This creates a dilemma, however, as younger people who were born in Padang generally have very little knowledge of day-to-day issues in the village, even when they have visited often and are close to relatives who live there. They almost certainly are unfamiliar with the complications of managing productive land, much less with doing some of the work themselves. In this, younger people in Padang are generally much more like young people in other Indonesian cities than they are like their peers who grew up in the village, even though rural youngsters increasingly have the same interests and access to information that those living in urban areas do. The difference is that younger people who grow up in rural areas of West Sumatra still experience life within the network of extended family and have a much better understanding of the family's status and position in the traditional context.

Many older people in Padang, as well as in other parts of the *rantau*, are concerned about this lack of direct connection that their children and grandchildren have with their village of origin, even when they are aware that their own actions and decisions contributed to this. The difficulty of participating in the mainstream culture and institutions of the nation while also maintaining traditional knowledge and cultural belonging is increasingly difficult for many Minangkabau, even when they live in Padang or another town in West Sumatra that is Minangkabau but that is removed from the village. One such individual, writing about his adult children, described this in a blog post about the family's links to the village:

Ada sesuatu yang agak rumit bagi anak-anak pada awalnya ketika berbicara tentang kampung. Ketika kepada mereka dijelaskan bahwa Koto Tuo – Balai Gurah itu adalah "kampung papa". Mereka agak bingung mendengarnya. "Berarti kampung kita juga, kan?" celetuk mereka. Lalu dijawab, bukan. Itu bukan kampung kalian, tapi itu adalah kampung/rumah bako kalian. "Lho, kampung kita dimana?" tanya mereka lagi setengah tak percaya. Cerita atau obrolan berlanjut tentang sistim kekeluargaan matriakhat yang dipraktekkan oleh orang Minang. Kampung mereka (anak-anakku itu) adalah kampung mamanya, yang adalah kampung nenek (ibu dari mamanya). Sementara rumah saudara-saudara perempuan ayah disebut rumah bako.

"Di mana itu? Kok kita tidak pernah pergi ke sana?" desak mereka.

"Kampung asal kalian di Simawang, di tepi Danau Singkarak. Hanya masalahnya, nenekmu tidak pernah tinggal dan menetap di sana, meskipun saudara-saudara sepersukuannya masih ada di kampung itu. Sesuatu yang sekarang sangat lazim, di mana keturunan orang Minang lahir dan besar di rantau dan tidak mengenal kampung halamannya, tapi tidak begitu biasa beberapa puluh tahun yang lalu," aku mencoba menjelaskan.

Batulimbak namanya di kanagarian Simawang. Melalui jalan mendaki cukup terjal dari Ombilin di pinggir danau Singkarak. Yang bahkan istriku sendiri sepertinya baru sekali itu mengunjunginya. Sayangnya kami tidak berhasil menemukan siapa-siapa, karena tidak mengetahui tempat yang jelas dari rumah pusaka (tapak perumahan) nenek mereka, meski sudah sempat berkonsultasi dengan seorang saudara yang tinggal di Jakarta melalui telepon. Mungkin usaha kami kurang maksimal, tidak bertanya kepada penduduk kampung itu. Dan kami tidak pula tahu apakah masih ada saudara sepersukuan yang masih tinggal di sana saat ini.

Kampung yang ditinggalkan oleh warganya memang sangat lumrah. Di kampungku, dari tujuh buah rumah sepersukuan kami hampir keseluruhannya kosong. Hanya satu rumah yang ditempati oleh seorang saudara laki-laki. Kami mengupah seseorang untuk sekedar menjaga dan membersihkan, menyalakan dan mematikan lampu setiap harinya. Rumah ibuku tempat kami menginap selama kunjungan ini, sehari-hari terkunci. Kadang-kadang saja rumah itu kami datangi bergantian.

[It was quite complicated for my children when we first started talking about our village. When I told them that Koto Tuo – Balai Gurah was "Papa's village", they were confused. "That means it is our village, too, doesn't it?", they asked. Then, I told them no. It was not their village, but the village/home of their *bako*. "So, where is our village?", they asked in disbelief. Stories and discussion followed about the matrilineal system that is used by the Minangkabau. Their village (my children's) was their mother's village, which was their grandmother's (their mother's mother's) village. The place where their father's sisters lived was the home of their *bako*.

"Where is that? Why have we never been there?", they pressed. "Your village is called Simawang, at the edge of Lake Singkarak. The problem is, your grandmother never lived there for any length of time, even though some of her extended family are still there. This situation is extremely common now that young Minangkabau are born and raised in the *rantau* and don't know their own village, but it was not very common a few decades ago," I tried to explain.

The name of the part of Simawang (where their mother came from) is Batulimbak. The road there goes up steeply from Ombilin at the edge of Lake Singkarak. Unfortunately, we didn't succeed in finding anyone because we didn't know exactly where their grandmother's ancestral home was, even though we consulted a relative who lives in Jakarta by phone. Maybe we didn't try as hard as we could have; we didn't ask anyone in the village. And we didn't know whether anyone from the extended family was still living there at the time.

It is extremely common for villages to have lost (many of) their inhabitants. In my village, of the seven houses belonging to our extended family, almost all are empty. There is only one house that is still being used by one of my male relatives. We pay someone to keep an eye on things and clean up, to turn the lights on and off every day. My mother's house, where we stayed on this visit, is kept locked. It is only occasionally that anyone takes a turn to use it.]

(MD Saib's Diary, 4 December 2015
<http://mdsaibsdiary.blogspot.co.id/2015/12/kampung-siapa.html>)

AGEING IN THE MINANGKABAU URBAN ENVIRONMENT

The fact that so many Minangkabau have lived their entire lives in Padang or in locations outside of West Sumatra has had significant implications for Minangkabau culture as well as language that extend beyond the problems of ancestral property and its management. As is the case elsewhere in Indonesia, official communication in the context of governance and the media as well as formal instruction in schools and universities uses Indonesian, but the language of daily interaction and that is heard spoken in all situations except the most formal is Minang. For a city of its size, Padang is extremely homogeneous with respect to the ethnic origin of its citizens and, while the national census has not collected data on ethnicity since the 1930s, it is estimated that at least 98 per cent of the population is of Minangkabau background (see Pemerintah Kota Padang 2016). This has contributed to the emergence of a modern Minangkabau culture that, in many ways, parallels the national mainstream culture but is separate from the traditional context of the village. In other words, the residents of Padang speak Minang, maintain social customs and behaviour associated with the Minangkabau ethnic group, carry on religious and cultural traditions that are part of their ethnic heritage, but, except for those individuals whose ancestral land lies within the city area, do so outside of the spatial constraints and social networks between extended families that govern life in the village.

For the elderly, this situation contributes to a very different experience than ageing in their village of origin would, and there are several distinct groups of older people in Padang whose concerns are quite different. The first of these are older people who come from Padang in the sense that their ancestral home is located within the modern urban area and they do not know of a time when their family may have lived in another location. Many families do possess oral histories that suggest they originally came from other areas in the highlands, but the details of this are sketchy, and it is no longer possible to trace their exact origins. Like many Indonesian cities, Padang spread from a small settlement around the mouth of the Batang Arau River, and eventually grew to encompass a large number of villages that were in existence in the general area. These villages are now urban neighbourhoods, but the land is generally owned communally by extended families in the same pattern as is seen in the highland areas. This is the reason that development of urban infrastructure has been so complicated and fraught with problems as well as being an often-cited impediment to tourism, as much of the land adjacent to the beach is held by extended families native to the area that do not wish to sell their property (see, for example, Padang Ekspres 2015). There is considerable evidence that families whose traditional land is in Padang are under greater pressure to give up land than those in rural areas due to the demand in the capital. In some cases, this process began in the 1930s when the city began to grow rapidly. Nonetheless, the courts have, in some cases, tended to support the claims of families, even against major institutions, such as the recent successful suit by one extended family in Padang against Universitas Bung Hatta, a major private university, that had been granted land by the local government for its new campus (Haluan 2016a).

Elderly people who come from Padang and have family assets there are in some ways similar to older people who live in their own village in any part of West Sumatra. They have rights and responsibilities within the extended family, although, in practice, it may be difficult to claim their place, especially if the family is large. They experience the same kinds of intergenerational conflicts as other older Minangkabau and may also have children living in other places with whom they may have little contact. Generally, although not exclusively, the residents who are native to Padang are of lower socioeconomic status, which means that many older people from this group must continue working for as long as possible. This may be in agriculture (there are parts of the city that contain rice fields and other productive land), fishing, or more urban occupations, such as selling things in the traditional markets. At present, 6 per cent of the city's population (approximately 52,000 people) is aged over sixty, with more than 10,000 of these elderly over seventy-five. The largest demographic is people aged twenty to twenty-four because of the large population of university students and younger people just beginning a career (BPS Kota Padang 2015).

In addition, and in common with many older Minangkabau in other parts of the *rantau*, these lower income elderly are usually under economic pressure to continue to work for as long as possible. In some cases, their children, who may be in Padang or elsewhere, are able to help support them. This may occur in the context of a shared household in the traditional pattern or may take the form of financial contribution only. In many cases, however, everyone in the family may be employed in the informal sector where their earnings are often uncertain and at the subsistence level. Perhaps not surprisingly, the number of families at or below the poverty line is greatest in the parts of Padang that are older and where long-standing extended family networks are present. It is these areas, such as Kuranji, Kototangah, and Padang Selatan, where a significant amount of productive land (rice fields, fruit orchards, dry fields, and so forth) is located (BPS Kota Padang 2015). Kototangah, located north of the city, and Padang Selatan to the south include coastal areas, and a considerable amount of the land is swampy and difficult to cultivate. Kuranji is a large district that extends into the foothills of the mountains to the east of the city and includes areas that are still jungle, in addition to land currently under cultivation.

Older people from these areas often have little interaction with the institutions of modern Indonesia, despite living in a major city. In this sense, their experience replicates that of people in villages in other parts of the province. However, because there is little separation of different types of activity through zoning in Indonesian cities, they must often negotiate major roads with heavy traffic and cope with intensifying development, including the encroachment of industry into areas that were previously open land, and increasing population density. There is some evidence that the stresses of this type of change are increasingly difficult for the part of the community that is native to Padang and that there are direct impacts on the elderly. For example, a growing number of the elderly people living in public old age homes come from Padang, and many of them have been brought there by the police who found them on the street or in a market. The problem of old people without an appropriate level of income and social support is recognized by the city government and has been included in medium- and long-term development planning (see, for example, Pemerintah Kota Padang 2008).

Lundi

Lundi, who died five years ago at the age of about seventy-three (his daughter's estimate), lived in Air Tawar, a northern suburb of Padang, with his daughter and the daughter's family. His wife had been killed twenty years before in a traffic accident. He had two sisters who had moved to Java with their husbands and also a brother who lives in Padang with his wife. The extended family used to control a significant amount of land, but it had been mortgaged since the death of Lundi's mother. Lundi's sisters live reasonably well with their husbands in Java but do not have the resources to redeem the liens. So, when his wife died, Lundi was happy to accept his daughter's offer to continue staying with her and her children.

This daughter, though, no longer has land to work on to support the family because her brother sold it to a university located adjacent to their home. This took place about fifteen years before Lundi died. His daughter agreed because, at the time, it seemed like a lot of money, and her brother agreed to build her a home with a boarding house next to it so she could rent out rooms to students. This was her main source of income. In addition, her husband sold a type of noodle soup from a pushcart he took around the neighbourhood. For Lundi, she had built a small food stall next to the house where he sold snacks, coffee, and tea and where he slept at night.

Lundi enjoyed talking to the students who came from all over West Sumatra and often stopped at his food stall to eat, read the newspaper he subscribed to, or play dominoes until late at night. He would tell them stories about when he was young and worked as a labourer at the port of Teluk Bayur loading and unloading the ships. He had had to give up this job because he broke his leg when he fell while carrying a heavy sack on his back. His wife would not allow him to go back to work, even though he wanted to when his leg healed.

Lundi's favourite topic of conversation, however, was how much things had changed. When he was young, he said, there weren't as many people from outside of Padang in Air Tawar. Once the university began to grow, he noticed there were more people around who were not from the area. He also often talked to people about the difficulties of living in Padang now that the city was expanding rapidly. He was worried about his grandchildren, one or two of whom were about the same age as the students, but none of whom had graduated from high school.

While Lundi did not exactly resent what he saw, namely the fact people from outside the area were overwhelming his neighbourhood and the fact that his own children and grandchildren seemed unable to compete with those people in the modern life of the city, he was worried about their future. He acknowledged that the modern system of governance, trade, and employment allowed him to earn a living in his old age with the support of his daughter and grandchildren. His daughter's boarding house was always full, and she only accepted male students. People felt that the reason for this was that five of her seven children were girls, and she allowed the student renters to interact with her children. Lundi, too, did not mind this and even encouraged it. As it turned out, one of the students, who was from another part of West Sumatra, married one of the girls after he graduated and got a job in Padang.

AGEING IN PADANG AS THE *RANTAU*

In contrast to the older members of the community who are native to Padang in the sense that their ancestral village is located within or adjacent to the urban municipality are those older people who have come to the city from another location in the province. Many of these individuals moved to the city as young adults, often to attend high school or college but frequently to seek employment. By the time they reach older age, many have lived in the city for decades and are well established in their local community as well as in social networks associated with their employment. Some of the people in this position are well educated professionals who are generally university educated and middle class. Many others, however, work in various trades, have small businesses, or participate in the informal sector, selling goods in a market or doing various jobs for pay when such work is available. Not surprisingly, the experience of older people varies considerably, depending on their level of income and education. These two factors are closely related in Indonesia, but level of education is also associated with an individual's ability to participate in the mainstream national culture that uses Indonesian and reflects the social structures of the modern nation.

As the provincial capital, Padang has a large number of government offices that represent the various national ministries and agencies. These provincial branches serve to coordinate the lower level offices associated with their function that serve regencies and smaller municipal areas and are the functional units under regional autonomy (see Holtzappel and Ramstedt 2009). The city also has three major public universities and a large number of private tertiary institutions as well as several major newspapers and the regional affiliates of a number of national television broadcasters. All of these organizations are part of the Indonesian cultural environment, which stands in contrast to the traditional context associated with a specific ethnic group. For this reason, the presence of Indonesian as a second and official language is much stronger in Padang than in other parts of the province and reflects the strength of national structures in the city.

Nonetheless, the social context in Padang is an excellent example where the domains of language that have been discussed in the context of Indonesian sociolinguistics can be observed (see, for example, Sneddon 2003a; Montolalu and Suryadinata 2007; Paauw 2009). The language of formal workplaces (government offices; larger stores and businesses; schools, colleges and universities; institutions within the health care sector; and so forth) is Indonesian, as is the language of instruction in public and private education at all levels. The media uses Indonesian, as do the signs and advertising seen in the public environment. However, due to the fact that the vast majority of the public is of Minangkabau background, the language used by almost everyone in day-to-day interaction is Minang. Even in workplace settings, people generally speak to each other in Minang when they are not engaged in the formal business of the organization, and it is common for employees to use Minang with members of the general public, especially where it appears the customer or client is more comfortable with that language. Even in school, where an important goal of the educational system is to teach the national language, teachers frequently speak Minang with their students when they are not engaged in formal classroom instruction.

The effect of this is that, except for the specific domains where Indonesian is always used (such as in the formal media), Padang represents a modern Minangkabau society where almost everyone is a native speaker of the same language and has the same cultural understanding and cognitive framework. While the traditional structures that govern village life are largely absent, except for the comparatively small number of people whose family originates in Padang, the culture of the city and its social practices are strongly Minangkabau, and there is high level of social consensus about certain issues in the community as a whole as well as social practices that apply to almost everyone. This is the reason, for example, that elected officials often refer to traditional Minangkabau principles, such as *Adaik basandi sarak; sarak basandi Kitabullah* (*Adat* is based on the law; the law is based on the Holy Book [the Quran]) (see Chapter 3 for discussion of this). It is also the basis for local government policy enforcing restaurant closures during the day in the fasting month of Ramadan (see Chapter 4) as well as for the passing of municipal regulations relating to *adat* with the encouragement and support of the Consultative Assembly on Minangkabau Adat (Lembaga Kerapatan Adat Alam Minangkabau (LKAAM)) and the Local Consultative Assembly on Adat (Kerapatan Adat Nagari (KAN)) (see, for example, Mukhlisun 2012). Similarly, shared cultural principles are often used to support various government initiatives, including crime prevention (see Berita Sore 2016).

In practice, this means that people of Minangkabau background who live in Padang experience what can be viewed as the modern manifestation of the traditional environment that is authentic in terms of language and certain social and cultural practices but that lacks the personal traditional dimension that shapes life in the village. While many city residents maintain a close connection with their village of origin, especially if they have family members who still live there, they remain somewhat removed from the often complicated social networks and attendant problems that arise in the traditional context. At the same time, it is frequently possible for individuals living in Padang to participate in the events and decision-making of their extended family in the village, even though they do not live there, because of the much greater degree of connection allowed by modern transportation and communications technology.

This has some serious limitations, however, that often frustrate Minangkabau living outside their village. There is a long-standing custom that, once a person leaves the village, he or she can contribute to its affairs and is, in fact, expected to do so, but the people in the village have the final say about what will be done. Therefore, while the whole community, not just family members, expects people living in other places to support the village in any way possible (money, opportunities, networking, and so forth), those living in the village feel entitled to use these contributions in any way they see fit, which is not necessarily the way the contributors intend, even if their contribution was solicited for a specific purpose. For example, when a village decides to build a mosque, the community will collect contributions from villagers living elsewhere; those in Padang are the easiest to approach and the most likely to be able to contribute because they tend to have better jobs and higher incomes than people who live elsewhere in the province. Once the money has been collected, the village community will spend it on whatever the residents feel is appropriate and resent any complaints or questions about the mosque or how the money was used. Family members of people living elsewhere react in the same way if their relatives want to know what they have done with the money sent to them. A Minangkabau proverb states: *Pitaruah jan diunian* (A claim must be vacated), which refers to the idea that once something is entrusted to another person, it is no longer appropriate to ask about it or monitor how it is managed. In this sense, accountability and transparency are not part of the culture.

This is a common source of friction between the Minangkabau who live in Padang and people in their village of origin. Those who live outside the village are generally employed in some kind of non-traditional workplace, such as owning or working in a business, teaching at a school or university, working in a government office, or working in the service sector. Modern employment in Indonesia increasingly demands greater accountability and transparency because of the mounting concern about endemic corruption and government initiatives to try to reduce it. People who work in these modern types of jobs are very aware of the need to behave in accountable and transparent ways and come to expect such behaviour in all aspects of life, including when they deal with people in their village. The village culture on this has not changed, however, creating a serious mismatch of expectations on the part of those involved.

Rosni and Muhsin

Rosni, who is discussed above and her husband Muhsin, whose situation is described in Chapter 2, exemplify the way many Minangkabau in Padang think about their relationship with the village. They would prefer to remain at arm's length from the village, but, when they can afford it, as Rosni and Muhsin can, they would also like to have as much influence and input into life in the village as possible. They would like this to be on their own terms, and it is this that sets the tone of the relationship between people in Padang and people in their village who want to get as much as they can from those living in Padang without allowing them a say in village affairs.

Rosni and Muhsin contribute a great deal to their villages, as well as to their families specifically. This was especially the case after Muhsin became Dean of his faculty and later Rector of the university. While their families, did not need financial support from them, they did need help putting the younger children through college. This included Rosni and Muhsin allowing these young relatives to live with them in Padang while they were in school. One of Muhsin's six younger siblings, Ilham (Chapters 4 and 5) was only a year below him and hence had graduated from college at about the same time he did before Muhsin and Rosni were even married, but the other five did not enter the university until Muhsin was already a lecturer such that they were able to benefit from his and Rosni's support.

Rosni, too, has a number of younger siblings that went through the university in this manner. The fact that she and Muhsin were low ranking at the time and did not earn much mean that they needed financial support from Rosni's family but were able to balance this by providing a place for her younger siblings to live in Padang. For Rosni's family, the need to support her and her husband was insignificant because, by this time, her older siblings had also become successful business people in Batusangkar. Her parents' desire that the younger children all finish college was much more important to them, and the fact that Rosni and Muhsin made this possible far outweighed the financial cost of contributing to their livelihood. Even some of the children of Rosni's brothers and sisters were able to benefit in this way.

Over the last twenty years, people in the village have also needed their help. When Muhsin became Dean and then Rector, he was able to help young people from his and Rosni's village get into the university. He was also able to help them apply for scholarships that were available from the university itself as well as from the Ministry of Education. During this time, a record number of younger people from their villages went on to college after high school. One of the consequences of this was that more children stayed in high school hoping they, too, might have this chance which they recognized was the best path to a good job in the future.

Despite all of what Rosni and Muhsin did for people in their villages, they still have difficulty taking part in and influencing the decision-making process. People living in the village often have projects they wish to undertake, and Rosni and Muhsin often receive guests who want to talk to them about these initiatives. The holiday at the end of the fasting month is the best time for people in the village to approach those living in the *rantau* for contributions to village projects because so many return home for the holiday. Rosni and Muhsin used to visit their villages at this time as do so many others. They have stopped doing so in the past few years because they increasingly do not like the unwillingness of people there to be open about what the money they contribute is to be used for and what the results of past projects are. They know that the committees that manage the funds often misuse them.

The kind of problems Rosni and Muhsin have encountered when dealing with people in their villages recur all over West Sumatra. This may at least partly explain why those Minangkabau who live elsewhere rarely return to their village when they retire. Rosni and Muhsin are no exception. While Rosni has already retired, Muhsin plans to continue working until he turns seventy in a few more years. They have already decided that they will stay in Padang. While they say that their children and grandchildren are the reason for this, they also admit that they simply do not want to return to the village. Four of their five children live in Padang. All are married and have one or more children. Three of the four living in Padang work at Muhsin's university, two as lecturers and one as an administrator. Rosni proudly says that she enjoys spending time with her grandchildren and also makes sure that her three daughters are familiar with the village and what belongs to them there, but she would never return there to live. After all these years, there are many things in the village that she finds unacceptable and even hates. Muhsin feels the same way about his village.

Recently, they shocked their children and other relatives when they announced they will not be buried on family land in the village. They wanted to be buried on the land they purchased in Padang. Some of their family members took offence at this, but Rosni and Muhsin no longer care. The decision is a manifestation of the dilemma they face and their ambivalence about their relationship to the village and the people there.

SOCIAL STATUS AND AGEING IN PADANG

For older people, who have often spent much of their adult life in Padang but originally came from another location, the ability to participate in the affairs of the village, even if only in a limited way in addition to their activities in Padang, allows them to maintain the ties to their extended family and its assets. In practice, connection with their village of origin is an important aspect of personal identity in Minangkabau society that is never lost. Even those who have spent decades in Padang tend to see themselves as living in the *rantau* but retaining the right to claim a connection to another location. This connection is often largely symbolic as many people in Padang, especially during their working years, do not wish to be heavily involved in village affairs, even if it were possible, but continue to see themselves as part of the village social milieu.

This represents a dilemma for these same individuals once they reach older age, when many are no longer working. Without the structure and social status conferred by employment, many find themselves without a clear identity or social position because often, as is generally the case in Western societies as well, much of this came from their profession and was associated with the modern, mainstream context of Indonesian society. This may be especially pronounced for people who work in the formal sector as a professional. For these individuals, the majority of their work contacts were also people of Minangkabau background, but the important relationships throughout their working life came about as a result of job demands and the structure of the institutions in which they worked. As a result, many individuals find that their social networks erode considerably upon retirement because of their separation from the workplace and because it was, in fact, their employment that created the social bonds in the first place. This stands in contrast to social networks in the village context that are permanent because they are based on birth and position within the extended families of the area in which an individual's place is established by the principles of *adat* and by familial relationships.

The realization, whether conscious or unconscious, that older age, and especially retirement, often results in a loss of social status is frequently a blow to older Minangkabau in Padang. Because they live in an environment that uses the Minang language and, in some ways, reflects the traditional cultural and social outlook, the social context of employment may parallel the traditional social context that a person might be part of in their village of origin. When people are no longer part of this employment-based context, only then do many of them perceive the gap in their experience. The potentially negative effects of retirement on mental health are well known in Western societies (see, for example, Kim and Moen 2002; Dave, Rashad and Spasojevic 2006), however, this issue has not been rigorously studied in Indonesia (see Hugo 2000). Nonetheless, there is evidence that many of the same problems experienced by older people upon and following retirement in Western societies are increasingly experienced in Indonesia. These include loss of social networks, reduction in physical and social activity, loss of income resulting in financial stress, poorer physical health associated with ageing, and a decline in mental health related to adjustment to a new social status. Increasing rates of depression among the elderly have been noted across Indonesia and are the subject of growing concern and attention (see, for example, Kristyaningsih 2011; Astuti 2012; Kusumowardani and Puspitasari 2012).

One of the difficulties of retirement for older Minangkabau in Padang is that they have little to do in their free time, especially as the traditional conceptualization of appropriate activities for older people tends to be quite limited. Living in Padang, which is highly urbanized, most older people do not have much access to the outdoors which limits gardening and similar occupations that might be comparable to opportunities for productive outdoor activity available to the elderly in rural areas. Leisure activities, such as sports or hobbies, are uncommon in Indonesia and have not been part of people's experience in the past. This is compounded by the fact that the retirement age for low- and middle-level public employees, who make up a large part of the professional workforce in Padang is fifty-six despite the significant increase in life expectancy Indonesia has experienced over the last two decades. Once people retire, it is occasionally possible for them to obtain paid work in the private sector, often on a casual basis, and many open small businesses of some kind, as much for something to do as for any income they might generate.

Malik

Living in Padang for a Minangkabau man like Malik, Erni's (Chapter 3) third child, can be quite difficult. He is a trained pharmacist, having received a degree in the field from the one university in Padang that offers this programme. He spent his whole career in the public health care sector, working first at a local department of health in the neighbouring province of Bengkulu and later at the comparable office in Padang Panjang, a town in West Sumatra just 30 kilometres from Koto. Malik is one of Muhsin's younger brothers. He is married to a woman from a village near Batusangkar who is a high school teacher. He retired seven years ago when he was fifty-six because of the mandatory retirement law. At that time, the family had to leave the house he was entitled to use while employed, and they moved to Padang where a relative of his wife's has a house and was willing to let them use it, even though this means that Malik's wife has to commute more than 70 kilometres each way by bus to her teaching job.

Malik has had difficulty providing for his family since he retired. The small pension he receives and the salary his wife earns can barely support the family with three children who are still in school. Living in Padang is expensive, even though they do not have to pay rent. In addition, Malik's wife will also have to retire soon.

Unlike Rosni, Malik's wife does not come from a family that can offer financial support, even though they would likely be happy to help if they could. The best they can do is make the house in Padang available to Malik and his family. Malik and his wife understand, like Muhsin and Rosni, that returning to the village after spending their whole career elsewhere would not be the best thing for them to do. The problems with the extended family they would likely face would not be worth the possibility of being able to use some of the family's land. In addition, this would not benefit their children because, when they died, whatever they had done to improve the land would go back to the extended family, with the possible exception of their daughter who might be able to continue to use it if she lived in the village. So, they have been trying hard to find something to do in Padang.

For Malik, it has turned out to be almost impossible to start a second career. In the last seven years, he has obtained a couple of consulting contracts that provided income for a year or so. The fact that his extended family has a lot of land in the village is of no help to him at all, not even as a location for a business if he wanted to start one. If his wife were to die before him, it would be most unlikely that he would be able to continue living in their current house, even if he still had to support their children. His brother, Muhsin (Chapters 2 and 7), is in a much better position because his job allows him to save a significant amount of money and to retire later. His pension will also be much more substantial, and his children have all graduated from college and have jobs. There are many

Minangkabau men like Malik living in Padang. They come from families with a large amount of land in the village that they cannot use but they do not have enough personal resources to build their own wealth in Padang. In this sense, they have not benefitted fully from the potential offered by modern employment and may still be trapped by the rules of *adat* and custom if their wife dies before them. At the same time, Indonesians are, on average, living longer, and the cost of living has increased greatly in recent years. For men like Malik, who was a professional, later life can be difficult and frustrating in a way they feel it should not be. Despite having been a government employee for many years and being entitled to a small pension, he was not able to accrue significant savings that would either allow him to live comfortably or to start a business from scratch in Padang or elsewhere.

ECONOMIC AND PSYCHOSOCIAL DIMENSIONS OF AGEING IN PADANG

The economic dimension of ageing in Padang is an area where individual experience varies considerably with income and education. While middle-class individuals often find retirement depressing because they have little to do, those with lower socioeconomic status must often continue to work for as long as possible. It has been noted that, in Indonesia, the proportion of older people who are still working out of economic need (as opposed to high-ranking professionals who may be permitted to maintain their employment to the age of seventy by employment regulations) is quite high (Hugo 2000). In West Sumatra, for example, 64 per cent of people aged over sixty state that they are working in an occupation that earns income, and 20 per cent of these individuals report working 35 to 44 hours per week (BPS Sumatera Barat 2016c). For lower income individuals, this work is generally similar to what they did throughout their career, which often centres on some type of trade or retail activity.

Indonesia continues to experience high unemployment, especially among younger workers (see Muhadjir 2015). This means that families are generally dependent on the earnings of all members capable of working, and it may be impossible for any individual to make a decision to stop. Loss of an elderly family member's income if that person's health declines may be a serious problem, especially if combined with an increasing need for other family members to provide care for the older individual. While this pressure exists in rural areas as well, it is much more serious in Padang because many people have no source of income other than what they can earn. Dependence on earned income alone is a serious source of anxiety for many Minangkabau as this situation contradicts the traditional importance of land and other real property as the main source of financial security. The traditional Minangkabau conceptualization of experience does not include the view that it is important to plan for the future. As a result, many individuals have little savings, and only those who were formally employed over a long period have access to a pension. Insurance is new as a vehicle for reducing risk, as is public support for the elderly in need. At present, payments intended to provide for indigent older people in Padang are minimal and do not reach every person who is entitled to them. For example, social support provided by the Ministry of Social Affairs amounts to Rp200,000 (approximately US$16) per month and is payable to people over the age of seventy who are deemed to be indigent. However, in June 2016, Minister for Social Affairs Khofifah Indar Parawansa acknowledged that only a fraction of the people eligible for this aid are currently receiving it and stressed that it was the responsibility of local administrations to ensure the elderly were registered with the programme (Sudradjat 2016).

Nonetheless, some of the older Minangkabau in Padang, and especially those who had professional careers, have considerable assets. Unlike rural areas, it is generally possible to buy property that is outside the traditional system and can be owned on an individual basis. Assets of this kind are subject to Indonesian law, are documented, and may be disposed of by the owner as they see fit. This represents a considerable departure from the traditional system and one which many, more affluent Minangkabau have been able to take advantage of.

This ability to earn a significant amount of money and the corresponding potential to obtain assets through one's own efforts is a significant contrast to the traditional system where real property is held communally by extended families, and the right to use such assets and pass them on to their children belongs to the female members. The modern system, where individuals of both sexes, are able to engage in employment separate from the extended family has especially benefitted men, who traditionally would be bound by obligation to their female relatives and their mother's family and dependent on their wife's family for many day-to-day needs. The potential to accrue personal wealth that can be left to children outside the constraints of the traditional system has been very appealing to many Minangkabau men especially and has freed them from their dependence on the female members of the family, which has often proved problematic, especially once a man retired or was no longer able to work. There can be no doubt that the opportunities afforded to Minangkabau with professional careers are contributing to the decline of the traditional system, and it is not uncommon for older people living in Padang to pay greater attention to their personal assets to the detriment of family land in the village.

It is not only men, however, who have taken to the opportunities afforded by the modern Indonesian system. A large number of Indonesian women work as professionals as well, and this is the case in the Minangkabau community. For them, having an independent income that is not subject to the group decision-making process of the extended family has also freed them from traditional constraints and allowed them to focus on their own interests and those of their nuclear family. Older women who live in Padang usually do not participate in the intense competition among women in the village context for power and influence within the extended family, although this also means that they may not play a major role in the family's affairs. Nonetheless, even in Padang where the majority of Minangkabau live in nuclear families, the mother is generally understood to be the head of the household and is often the main decision-maker for issues relating to children and the household. Despite this, the ability to earn money independent of the extended family has, to some extent, equalized the relationship between men and women, making Minangkabau families in Padang more like those in other parts of Indonesia.

For the elderly, however, this change has important implications for well-being and psychological health. The traditional context provides a place for both older men and older women that is traditionally associated with respect, belonging, and affection, even if these things are sometimes missing in actual practice. Many older people living in Padang, even though they are part of a Minangkabau community, do not have a clear social position like that the extended family could, in theory, provide. Because their self-conception is often based largely on their employment, when they are no longer working they have no replacement and, because of their lifestyle and location, cannot play a larger role in their own extended family. Positions of leadership and respect within the extended family must be built up over years of interaction in the village where each individual has to earn the trust of those in their social network. It is very difficult, if not impossible, for either men or women to return to the village to live once they have retired if they expect to fully reintegrate into the existing social networks, including that of their own extended family. Many older Minangkabau seem to recognize this and choose to remain in Padang, despite the difficulties.

Like other cities in Indonesia, Padang is highly urbanized, with very dense residential and commercial neighbourhoods, large roads, and a great deal of traffic and noise. It is a difficult environment for older people, many of whom are in poor health or suffer from degenerative conditions that affect mobility. By the time they reach the age of sixty, many of the older Minangkabau in Padang have adult children who are living separate from them or who have moved to other parts of Indonesia. Among Padang's middle class, many younger people aspire to attend universities in Java or even overseas and may settle permanently in another part of Indonesia. They may return home to visit their parents comparatively infrequently, and often only at the end of the fasting month. As a result, many older people in Padang live in households that consist of themselves and their spouse with one or two additional relatives, while most of their own children and grandchildren live elsewhere. Even when children have remained in Padang, they often live in other parts of town as the urban environment does not generally support multigenerational living.

This, combined with the nature of the urban environment, proves very difficult physically, as well as psychologically, for many older Minangkabau in Padang. Many spend more and more time at home because they have trouble walking, and the city environment is increasingly hard to manage. It is unusual, for example, for city streets to have sidewalks and, where they do, they are often blocked by people selling things and are used to park motorcycles. Traffic is heavy, with little done to manage the flow, and vehicles generally do not give pedestrians the right of way. Not surprisingly, there are a large number of traffic accidents in the city, and this is considered a major public health issue (Nasution 2016). Urban facilities in Padang remain underdeveloped compared to other Indonesian cities of a similar size, due in large part to widespread problems in obtaining land for development (this issue is discussed in Chapter 6).

These factors, combined with the view that it is appropriate for older people to reduce their activities in accordance with traditional cultural norms, mean that many older people in Padang spend an increasing amount of time at home, often minding grandchildren as their own children start families of their own. This may isolate them from their previous social network, especially as friends and acquaintances made at work often do not live in the same area, and increasingly restricts their patterns of interaction. On the one hand, older people in Padang are living in an environment in which they can interact freely in terms of linguistic and cultural background and where their social inclusion can potentially be high. On the other, however, the physical setting in which they live, combined with the culturally determined expectations for older people, often means that they are unable to participate fully in the life of the community or choose not to because of inconvenience or personal limitations.

The result of this is that many older Minangkabau in Padang live largely within the context of their own home and immediate neighbourhood. It is not uncommon, for example, for older women to increasingly choose to shop at small stores near their own home, rather than go to one of the city's many markets, or to turn the task of food shopping over to a daughter who is prepared to help with this chore. Instead, these women remain near home and busy themselves with children and grandchildren or with light chores that can be done without going out. As discussed in Chapter 4, many older Minangkabau take a greater interest in religion as they age, and television represents the primary form of entertainment for these elderly individuals. Almost 92 per cent report watching television on a regular basis (BPS Sumatera Barat 2016a).

The experience of older Minangkabau men in Padang is similar. When they stop working entirely or reduce the amount of formal work they do, they generally spend an increasing amount of time at home, engaged in the kinds of pursuits that are considered culturally appropriate in the community. These may include religious activities, socializing with other older men at local coffee shops, doing light chores around the house, and watching television. They may also be significantly impacted by declining physical health that has an effect on psychological well-being. It has been noted that Indonesia has the highest rate of stroke in the world, of which the majority of sufferers are older men (Yayasan Stroke Indonesia 2012). In 2015, the Ministry of Health reported that West Sumatra has the highest number of strokes of all Indonesian provinces (Kementerian Kesehatan Republik Indonesia 2015). This has been associated with diet, cultural practices and smoking (see Fanany and Fanany, 2015, for discussion of these issues) and is reflected in the location of a national hospital specializing in the management of stroke in the highland town of Bukittinggi.

Syahril

Syahril, seventy-four, is the second child of Aminah's oldest daughter. He has an older brother and a younger brother and sister. Born before Indonesia's independence, his childhood was coloured by the excitement and chaos of the early years of Indonesia's nationhood. Of Syahril and his siblings, only the youngest graduated from college, having studied at a private university in Jakarta. Nonetheless, all of them had good jobs, especially considering the difficulties of the early years of independence. Syahril's older brother was a policeman, who reached a mid-level rank, and spent most of his years of service on the island of Sulawesi where he died before reaching retirement age. His sister, Inang (Chapter 5) worked as a high school teacher in Batusangkar until her retirement a few years ago and has lived in their village all her life except for a few years in Padang when she was in high school. His younger brother worked in the city planning office of the city of Jakarta but died after just a few years of employment.

Syahril worked at the Ministry of Social Affairs in Jakarta as a low-level administrator and moved to Padang for the last part of his career. His wife, who came from a village near to Koto, died a few years after Syahril retired. Since then, Syahril has lived alone in their house in Padang. His pension alone does not support him, so his children contribute financially, especially his two oldest daughters who have regular jobs. Every now and then his youngest child, an unmarried son, visits him and stays for a few weeks at a time. Otherwise, Syahril spends his time alone and tells anyone who will listen how unhappy he is, but he has no alternatives.

It would not be possible for Syahril to go to his wife's village to live with her relatives, even though one of his sons lives there. It would be seen as strange and inappropriate for a man to live at his wife's house after her death. He could, in theory, return to his mother's village and live with his sister, Inang, who is also widowed. She lives in the village with her unmarried youngest daughter, and the house is big enough to accommodate Syahril as well as the two of them.

Syahril cites several reasons for why he chooses to live alone in Padang rather than go back to Koto. Life in the village no longer appeals to him after having spent his whole career in large cities. He has a house in Padang, on land that he bought that does not belong to the extended family. He can do whatever he wants in and to the house. He likes the freedom that living in Padang provides. His relationship with his neighbours is friendly and courteous, if somewhat distant. He does admit that he wishes he had people to talk to at home and would certainly like to have his grandchildren around, but none of them lives in Padang.

The biggest complaint Syahril has, and what is most difficult for him to cope with, is loneliness. He has practically no social activities of any kind. Even though he has neighbours in the housing complex where he lives, he does not know them well enough to do anything together. When pressed, he admits that living in the village has advantages and, under different circumstances, he would enjoy it, especially since Aminah's other grandchildren (his contemporaries) live there, and some of them are the children of his mother's sisters (close relatives in Minangkabau). In addition, living at his sister's house would be considered very appropriate in the community. Even under the current circumstances, he concedes, he would not mind spending time in the village. But he does not do so.

The main reason for this has to do with the fact that his relationship with Inang is not good. This explains why she and her daughter almost never visit him in Padang, even during the celebration at the end of the fasting month. She feels he never really paid attention to her children, his nieces and nephews, when they were young and needed the influence of their maternal uncle. Syahril was the only uncle who could have supported them and taught them in the way expected as part of this relationship. Her children never got a chance to meet their other two uncles, both of whom lived outside West Sumatra and died young. Syahril's sister resents what she considers to be his lack of attention and has never suggested that he return to the village now that they are both retired.

Syahril understands how his sister feels about him and considers himself lucky that he has a house in Padang and children who sometimes visit him. Although he is in a Minangkabau community, Padang and the people around him seem unfamiliar to him. Life in the city is hard for him in his old age, but he does not have the alternative of returning to Jakarta either because he does not have a house there. Even though two of his daughters live there, their husbands are not Minangkabau. Syahril does not speak their language and is not comfortable with the kind of Indonesian they and his grandchildren use at home, which is a colloquial Jakarta dialect. Most importantly, he knows that his sons-in-law, who come from a different Indonesian ethnic group, would not accept him living with his daughters. He has felt the tension when he has visited them. He used to visit once or twice a year but has not done so for several years as his health makes it difficult for him to travel. Like many older Minangkabau men, Syahril is stuck with limited alternatives, each of which has problems. Nonetheless, he is better off than most because he owns his own home and lives in a Minangkabau community whose social patterns are familiar to him. While he is lonely, he feels that he can cope and his situation is tolerable, especially as he is still able to live independently.

HEALTH AND PSYCHOSOCIAL CHALLENGES AMONG OLDER PEOPLE IN PADANG

In recognition of the problems of isolation and poor health experienced by older people in Padang, as well as in West Sumatra as a whole, the provincial health department, along with the health offices at lower levels of administration, are increasingly active in health promotion activities targeting the elderly. One example of this has been the establishment of health posts for the elderly (*posyandu lansia*). The use of integrated health posts (*pos pelayanan terpadu* = *posyandu*) has long been a feature of the Indonesian public health system. These posts, which are run by and associated with individual public health centres (*pusat kesehatan masyarakat* = *puskesmas*), are intended to provide health monitoring and information that supports health literacy and personal agency at the neighbourhood level. Originally, the activities of the health posts focused on monitoring maternal and child health issues, such as immunization, adequate nutrition, and infectious disease. More recently, the growing number of elderly people in the community has prompted a need for the same type of monitoring of health and well-being issues among this group. There are currently ninety-one such health posts for the elderly in Padang, while 87.5 per cent of public health centres have an associated health post dedicated to the health of older residents (Dinas Kesehatan Kota Padang 2010). In addition to their health monitoring function, these health posts provide supplemental nutrition and run exercise programmes for their users intended to address the sedentary lifestyle of many elderly in Padang. The exercise programmes for older people were established throughout Indonesia to support better physical and mental health among older people, especially in light of rising incidence and prevalence of chronic disease.

The impact of declining health on the experience of elderly Minangkabau in Padang is significant in their experience of ageing, but it is increasingly apparent that depression and other psychosocial conditions are becoming more prevalent as well. While there has been some documentation of this in the literature (see, for example, Yeni 2016), the magnitude of this phenomenon is difficult to evaluate, and much of the concern about the mental health of older people has focused on those individuals who are living in old age homes (for example, Masithoh, Hamid and Sabri 2012; Putri and Heppy 2016). However, there is evidence that one underlying cause of increased depression among the elderly in Padang is related to changes in their social environment that are recent in the context of Indonesia and that represent a major departure from the traditional patterns that individuals who are now over sixty generally experienced when they were younger (Fanany, Fanany and Tasady 2014).

The specific factors that appear to contribute to decreased mental health and well-being in the elderly living in Padang tend to relate to the loss of identity many individuals experience when they stop working which is not balanced by a comparable status within the extended family that *adat* and tradition can provide for older people. The absence of this expected status and the accompanying role for women has been directly associated with depression (Yeni 2016). Many older Minangkabau living in Padang seem to have difficulty reconciling the more modern lifestyle of the city with their expectations of respect, companionship, and activity in older age. The fact that they live in a Minang-speaking community, which might be expected to facilitate social inclusion, seems to exacerbate the mismatch between experience and expectation. One reason for this may be the expected domains for language in Indonesia, where language use is closely associated with cultural expectations. Speakers of Minang living in an environment where their language is the dominant means of communication in a range of social settings may unconsciously expect cultural norms associated with the use of the language to predominate. When they do not, as is the case in Padang where the lifestyle of the majority of the public reflects the contemporary Indonesian mainstream despite high use of Minang, it is likely that these individuals will find that their expectations for non-linguistic social and cultural behaviour are not met. This may be especially significant for older people when they are no longer engaged in activities that are part of the modern context, such as formal employment. While the nuclear family experience is difficult for many people of Minangkabau background, regardless of age, the situation in Padang seems to make adjustment more challenging than might be expected exactly because it reflects a modern Minang community that lacks the traditional social and cultural dimensions structured by the extended family and village networks of the past.

8

Ageing in the *Rantau*

MINANGKABAU IN THE *RANTAU*

There are large communities of Minangkabau living permanently in other parts of Indonesia, outside the regions that customarily use the Minang language and that are associated with long settlement. This represents the outer ring of the Minangkabau world where the individuals involved typically live among and interact with large numbers of people from other linguistic/cultural groups, even if they are part of a significant community of Minangkabau origin. While the proportion of professionals within this *rantau* population is increasing, the Minangkabau are well known among other Indonesians for their business activities all over the country which have traditionally included various kinds of retail and wholesale activity and restaurants. *Restoran Padang* (Padang restaurants), which serve Minang food with a characteristic type of service, are found all over Indonesia as well as in Malaysia, Singapore and Brunei. These restaurants, where all the dishes available are placed on the table and diners pay for what they eat, are often the first places where unskilled newcomers from West Sumatra work when they arrive in the *rantau*. They also serve as important sources of information about the local Minangkabau community or about people newly arrived individuals may know and are looking for.

It is difficult to estimate how many people of Minangkabau origin are living in Jakarta or other parts of Indonesia outside of West Sumatra because information on ethnic background is not collected as part of the national census. However, it has been suggested that as much as 6 per cent of the population of the Jakarta metropolitan area is Minangkabau (Tempo 2012). The approximately 600,000 people this figure represents are the equivalent of 11.5 per cent of the total population of West Sumatra (BPS Sumatera Barat 2016*b*). While Minangkabau are concentrated in the capital and in the larger cities of other Sumatran provinces, smaller communities can be found almost everywhere in Indonesia. Some of these are very long-standing and began to be established many generations ago. During the New Order period of Indonesia's history under President Soeharto (1965–98), national administration was highly centralized, which resulted in a dramatic increase in the importance of the national capital as the centre of governance, business, and cultural activity. The Minangkabau community in this part of the *rantau* increased enormously during this time in response to the perception of enhanced opportunities (Kompas 2013).

Despite the traditional idea that people who leave the village (or West Sumatra more broadly) to work or study in the *rantau* might at some time return to put their skills and knowledge to use in their place of origin, in practice many Minangkabau have always chosen to remain permanently in the *rantau*. Even though such realities are not expressed in folklore or other traditional forms and may be difficult for individuals to elucidate explicitly, most Minangkabau are aware of the complicated social patterns of the village and the kinds of problems that result from competition within the extended family. In some cases, an individual's decision to leave is based on an awareness of the nature of familial power struggles and the person's self-evaluation of his or her position within the group. In other cases, the decision to go to the *rantau* is a direct response to a lack of resources within the extended family that are sufficient to support all its members. In general, as has been the case historically, the modern Minangkabau community views the decision to go to the *rantau* favourably and admires a young person's initiative in attempting to succeed among people outside the Minangkabau world. However, success in the *rantau* is highly prized as well, and those individuals who fail to prove themselves are often regarded with disappointment.

While there are a number of Minangkabau individuals who have been extremely successful outside of West Sumatra and who have contributed to the Indonesian nation in various fields of endeavour at the highest level through their prominence in politics, education, the arts, business, television, and entertainment, the majority of Minangkabau work in average jobs or are self-employed in small businesses. As such, they reflect the large working class and growing middle class of Indonesian society. In this sense, people of Minangkabau origin have demonstrated a strong ability to adapt to life away from their cultural homeland; in the past, this adaptability was seen largely in the business sector and in education, as teachers and religious instructors, while today more Minangkabau are government employees of various kinds, including school teachers, health care professionals, and managers and administrators (Berita Satu 2014*b*).

Minangkabau who leave West Sumatra to live in other parts of Indonesia are in some ways part of the majority in the Indonesian context. They are Muslim, like more than 80 per cent of Indonesia's population, and they are part of the Malay cultural world. The ethnic group has produced prominent national figures in various fields throughout Indonesian history, and a number of Minangkabau have achieved at the highest level in the business sector. In other ways, they represent a significant minority group with distinct cultural practices and a social structure that differs from all of Indonesia's other major cultures. These differences seem to be intensified in the *rantau*, and Minangkabau are viewed as forming cohesive and self-contained communities (Antoni 2012). This perception is supported by the large number of social organizations that operate in the *rantau* and bring together individuals from the same village or region in West Sumatra. This association with a person's place of origin remains the basis on which personal identity rests for many members of the Minangkabau community, although, as is the case for most Indonesians, people's self-conception has many layers that take on greater importance in specific social contexts at certain times of life.

For Minangkabau living in the *rantau*, even more than for those in Padang, the most immediate aspect of their personal identity tends to be associated with their employment and position in the world of work. Their interactions in this environment usually involve people from other ethnic backgrounds and other parts of Indonesia who do not share their first language (Minang) and cultural background. This means that individuals in this situation must be able to use Indonesian at a functional level and have the cultural knowledge to participate in the public environment. However, the nature of the Indonesian used for communication in different settings varies considerably and is closely associated with the professional and educational requirements of employment.

As is the case for Indonesians of all linguistic and cultural backgrounds wherever they are, the members of the Minangkabau community who work in formal employment must use Indonesian on a day-to-day basis. Those who are professionals, which usually means they have a university-level education, are generally extremely fluent in Indonesian and can use a number of different styles and registers of the language. They may need to use formal, standard language, for example, in the context of their work but communicate in less formal settings in a more colloquial style of the national language. They tend to be capable of switching between varieties effortlessly and appropriately for the social context. Others who are employed in less formal contexts may understand more formal Indonesian but can only really communicate directly in one of the very informal, urban varieties of the language. This type of Indonesian, which is often mixed with certain words and expressions from various local languages, acts as a kind of lingua franca among the lower socioeconomic classes of Indonesia's urban areas. This usage does not correspond fully to the grammar and syntax of more standard usage and often incorporates a large number of slang terms (see, for example, Smith-Hefner 2007; Musgrave 2014). Speakers of these informal, urban dialects often have difficulty using more formal language, although they may understand it. A great deal of popular culture, however, uses more informal language, which Indonesian speakers of this type may be able to participate in.

Within the Minangkabau community, ability to interact in Minang is an important marker of identity, and people from this ethnic background usually switch to this language when they talk to others from the same ethnic origin or when they discover a person they have just met comes from their ethnic group. It should be noted that this practice is not unique to the Minangkabau but does represent an important linguistic norm among members of the ethnic group. For people who have lived for years in the *rantau*, and especially for the elderly who are of special interest here, Indonesian may have come to dominate their social interaction and, in some cases, has replaced Minang as the language they are most comfortable with. This is an important factor that distinguishes older Minangkabau living in the *rantau* from those in the village or in Padang. These individuals have been living, often for several decades, among speakers of other languages and have had to use Indonesian, in some form, as their main means of communication outside the home.

While it is the case that Minangkabau people who settle permanently in the *rantau* tend to group themselves in certain cities and certain areas within the city, this does not always mean that facility in their native language can be maintained. There are a number of factors that may influence this, that include the number and density of Minangkabau speakers in the location in question; whether an individual is married to another person of Minangkabau background; what types of social interactions are usual in the place where they live; their workplace; and individual factors such as aptitude for and attitude towards language as well as educational level and the attitudes of other people in the household. As might be expected, older Minangkabau whose spouse comes from the same ethnic background are more likely to use Minang at home, even if their children do not speak the language. By contrast, those who are married to a person from another ethnic background generally use some variety of Indonesian or even another local language within the family. There is considerable variation in this, depending on where the family is living and whether the husband or the wife is the Minang speaker. It is often the case in Indonesia that the wife's local language is preferred in the household when the two parents come from different linguistic backgrounds, especially if the family is living in a location where this language is spoken or in a place where neither the husband's nor the wife's language is used (Sartini 2015; Sari and Luh 2016; Widodo 2016).

The nature of the language context in Indonesia is complex, and language issues tend to affect every type of social interaction, especially when people need to communicate outside of the community that uses their first language. Differential language ability and factors relating to the mastery of the national language have not received a great deal of attention in Indonesia, despite the official assumption that it will serve as a lingua franca among speakers of different local languages (see Spolsky 2004). Language issues among older people, especially those who have lived much of their adult lives outside their native language community, have not been seen as a cause for concern. However, it has been shown that some older bilingual individuals tend to revert to their first language with accompanying attrition of their second language (de Bot and Clyne 1994; Kopke et al. 2007). It has also been suggested that, as people age, first language ability tends to increase in a linear manner, while second language proficiency decreases in a corresponding manner (Keijzer 2011). In the case of elderly Minangkabau in the *rantau*, these natural linguistic and cognitive processes associated with language use in older age are encouraged by social and cultural norms that strongly associate the use of Indonesian with an individual's working life. When a person is no longer working, a corresponding tendency to return to a more culturally specific Minangkabau identity is observable. However, there are individuals whose first language ability is seriously eroded by long exposure to Indonesian in the *rantau*. This phenomenon, sometimes termed "mother tongue shift", has been documented in various populations, especially among indigenous minority groups (Vago 1991), such as Minangkabau living in parts of Indonesia where their language is not used. For members of the Minangkabau community, inability to use Minang naturally and fluently in older age can be a significant social impediment and also a source of anxiety for the person concerned. This represents a situation that mirrors that of older people in the village who cannot speak Indonesian but reflects the opposite circumstances, where a person in the *rantau* has lost the ability to communicate fluently in the language of their childhood. For the elderly in this situation, loss of Minang also means loss of cultural access and a diminished potential for social inclusion at the ethnic level.

Nita

Nita died recently at the age of eighty-six in a small village outside Malang, East Java. She originally came from Koto. While she was not related to Aminah by blood, Nita considered herself part of the Valley family. As a child, she had spent most of her time playing with Aminah's children and the others who gathered at the large family house to spend their time. Her parents did so as well, as did the parents of other village children. One of Aminah's brothers was a respected religious teacher in Koto and held the title *Datuak*, which meant that he was a member of the *adat* council of the village and represented his extended family in various matters relating to traditions and customs. He also taught Quranic reading, translation and interpretation at the family home. These classes were attended by children and adults from the village. It was originally for this reason that Nita started coming to Aminah's house.

As occasionally happened in the village, Nita spent a lot of time at Aminah's house because she was the same age as one of her daughters.

This daughter and Nita were inseparable until Nita married at the age of sixteen. Unfortunately, the marriage did not last very long, and she was divorced soon after the birth of her first child who died in infancy. The two losses made Nita depressed for a long time, and she refused to marry again, even though her family, as well as Aminah's family, found a few men who wanted to marry her.

When she was in her mid-twenties, civil war broke out when a few political leaders and regional military commanders from several provinces on the island of Sumatra rebelled against the central government. West Sumatra was the centre of the rebellion because most of the politicians and military commanders were Minangkabau. The rebellion lasted for three years, but, during that period, there were intense battles that claimed many lives. The central government in Jakarta sent a large number of soldiers, most of whom came from Java, to West Sumatra. One of these men met Nita, and they became involved, which happened quite often at the time. While most encounters of this kind ended when the army withdrew, the soldier asked Nita to return to Java with him, and she agreed despite her family's disapproval. She also did not listen to Aminah's daughter, who was her closest friend, who also thought this was not a good idea.

Nita was taken by the soldier to his village outside Malang where they married in 1961. They had five children, one of whom was a boy. Nita was very happy to have four daughters, thinking that she would have a strong claim to the ancestral property of her extended family in Koto. In reality, she never visited Koto again and died in Java without having returned to the village. Her husband came from a very poor family, who owned little more than a small wooden house with a dirt floor, without electricity or running water, and a small rice field that produced much less than they needed. While she came from a poor family herself, Nita found that her husband and his family were even poorer. Because he had only been a private in the army, he had to retire very young several years after the civil war ended. This was well before even their oldest child finished primary school. The family could barely make ends meet on his small pension. He supplemented this income and what they could get from the rice field by doing whatever work people in the village needed done, such as weeding their gardens, working their rice fields, and so forth.

Nita was unable to contribute to the family income. She did not have any formal education. In addition, she did not speak Javanese, and no one around her spoke Minang. None of them had enough command of Indonesian to be able to communicate satisfactorily. Nita found it almost impossible to learn the language of the community, beyond a few expressions and she was never able to carry on extended conversations with them. She felt completely isolated and alone.

Nita lost contact with her family and the villagers completely until, almost two decades after she left the village, when Ilham (Chapters 4 and 5), a son of Aminah's third daughter Erni (Chapter 3), went to a university in Malang to study. Before he left Koto, his mother had told him about Nita but the only thing she remembered was that her husband had come from a village near Malang, the name of which she didn't know. One of Ilham's aunts thought she remembered the name of the village and told Ilham about it, but it didn't mean much to him, and he forgot about it when he arrived in Malang.

When a letter from his mother reminded him several months later, Ilham went to Nita's village one weekend. At the time, there was no transportation that went directly there so he had to walk from the closest place that a bus from the city would take him. When he reached the edge of the village, he started asking people about Nita, but no one knew that name. Finally, he asked whether anyone knew a woman from Sumatra who had married someone from the village twenty years before. Finally, someone remembered that such a woman lived at the edge of the village near a rice field and not too far from a mosque. The woman told him to ask at a food stall near the mosque. The young girl minding the stall confirmed what the old woman said and told her little sister to show Ilham where to go.

When Ilham arrived at the house, a woman who looked much older than his mother came out accompanied by two girls who were about ten and fifteen years old. He told them that he was looking for a woman from Sumatra named Nita who had married someone from the village a long time before. The older girl explained what he had said in Indonesian to the woman in what sounded to Ilham like a mix of non-standard Indonesian and Javanese. The woman did not seem to understand. She then told the girl to ask him who he was. The girl explained to him that the woman was her mother and she was from Sumatra and that the other girl was her sister. She then asked him who he was. Ilham turned to Nita and spoke in Minang. He told her who his mother was and that he understood she and his mother had been very close.

Nita was overcome. She cried for a long time. When she did try to speak, it was apparent that she was no longer able to communicate easily in any language. She used a mix of Minang, Indonesian and Javanese that took Ilham a while to understand. She had lost so much Minang that they could not converse exclusively in the language. Quite often, one of her children would have to translate if they needed to discuss anything even slightly complex. Nita's vocabulary was very limited in all three languages, and she used them in a way that was difficult for Ilham to understand.

After this first meeting, Ilham visited often, usually on the weekends. Eventually, he learned how to communicate with Nita and could have significant discussions. Nita asked a lot of questions about the village and described how difficult her life was. She wanted badly to go back to Koto but she saw it was not possible. She knew she would never be able to afford it, and her children were all in Java. In addition, her husband was sick and had been for a number of years. He died two years after Ilham found the family.

Nita felt completely isolated because of her inability to communicate with people in the Javanese village where she lived. In addition, she lacked self-confidence and rarely left her house. Her children and housework constituted her entire life. She had hardly ever gone shopping and almost never did once her oldest child could do it for her. She went to the mosque regularly and worked in the family's small rice field, something she knew from her life in Koto.

Ilham was in Malang for only two and half years. When he left, he lost contact with Nita's family again. Almost forty years later, he reconnected with them when his work took him to Malang again, and he had the chance to visit Nita. Many things had changed when he saw her again. Her children were all grown up, and she had many grandchildren. Nita seemed happier to him, largely because some of her children had done well and had built a new house for her where she lived with one of her daughters. She told him that she still missed Koto badly but had decided not go back, even though her children would have been able to pay for her to do so. She said she was certain her family would not welcome her in her old age. She feared she would not be able to talk to them and wouldn't know what to talk about anyway. Worse, she said, her sisters would be suspicious; they would think she had come to claim her rights to the family's property which they had been protecting all these years. She did not want to deal with family problems of this kind at this point in her life. Her assessment of the situation was probably accurate. One of Nita's daughters, accompanied by her own daughter, did go to Koto and met the family. They were disappointed that, during the short visit, the family in the village kept telling them how Nita no longer had a right to their land, since they had divided it up among the women in the family during her long absence. It didn't seem to matter to them that Nita's daughter and granddaughter repeatedly explained that they were not there to claim anything. What Nita's children told her about this visit allowed her to feel more at peace with her decision never to go back to Koto, even though her children could have paid for her to go. She realized that, even though she sometimes felt sad, she would feel worse if she had to face family members whose reaction to her presence was negative.

While she could not go home, Nita remained an outsider in her husband's village for life. Her grandchildren loved her, but they rarely spoke to her. They said that it was difficult to talk to their grandmother, and Nita felt the same way. It was even more difficult for her to talk to them. Their language was odd and incomprehensible to her. But the daughter with whom she lived until her death was very kind to her, and Nita submitted to what she called her fate of never seeing Koto and her family again. Nonetheless, for many years after her first meeting with Ilham, Nita yearned for the past and the village she wished she could return to. These memories made it even more difficult for her to adjust to the world around her which was changing far too quickly for her to comprehend.

LINKS TO THE VILLAGE AND THE PAST

Many Minangkabau living in the *rantau* retain a strong emotional attachment to their village of origin, even though they may have only lived there for a comparatively small portion of their life. The group's cultural narratives stress this association to the Minang homeland and one's immediate family. This is a recurring theme in much Minangkabau folklore as well as in popular culture genres, such as Minang language pop music that often expresses the longings of those in the *rantau* for the village and vice versa (see Barendregt 2002, for discussion of this). Despite the fact that the reality of life in the village and among the extended family is often quite different from the harmonious and loving situation portrayed in such songs, this conceptualization is attractive to many older Minangkabau, and the connection to their village of origin is real. Many older people strive to instil these same feelings in children and grandchildren born in the *rantau*, but this is difficult in practice because younger family members often have no first-hand understanding of the rural environment and have not experienced events and practices that are central to their older relatives' sense of identity. The fact that the children, and especially the grandchildren, usually do not have a command of the Minang language makes this even more difficult.

For many elderly Minangkabau, this feeling of continuing connection to their village of origin is manifested in a willingness to help support family and the village, in general, financially from the *rantau*. The level of this support is significant. The village of Sulit Air, near the town of Solok, is often portrayed as the most extreme example of this support by former residents and their descendants who no longer live in the region, but the same situation can be observed all over West Sumatra. Sulit Air is located in an area with poor agricultural land and, as the name suggests, little available water. A large number of people from the village have traditionally gone to the *rantau* because it was difficult to make a living where they were. The loyalty of these individuals over the years and their willingness to fund the village has allowed the local mosque to be refurbished at a cost of Rp1 billion. The village also has five schools and an Islamic boarding school, a health centre, library, bridge, and irrigation system, all funded by people living in the *rantau*. From the 1970s to 1990s when money was generally sent by money order, the local post office reports handling almost Rp1 billion per month that was remitted to individuals whose relatives had sent it from all over Indonesia (Detik News 2016).

Nonetheless, the financial relationship that exists between people in the *rantau* and people in the village is complicated. There can be no doubt that family in the village often expect financial support from those members who are living in the *rantau*. This is an important measure of success, on the one hand, but also a familial responsibility, on the other. For those who choose to remain in the *rantau* permanently, this financial responsibility is permanent as well, and they typically feel they must help relatives in the village for as long as they are able, especially if money is needed to address situations that affect the whole extended family, such as the redemption of mortgaged rice fields or the repair of the ancestral home. Those in the *rantau* often feel pressure to contribute to village initiatives, like those in Sulit Air, as well. These projects often relate to repair or building of local mosques, road paving or construction, and similar infrastructure projects that will help develop the village.

Despite the level of financial contribution, Minangkabau living in the *rantau* cannot usually participate very much in the affairs of the village. Attempts by them to contribute to discussion, including about how money they have provided is to be used, are often resented by people in the village, who often feel only those who live there have the right to take part in consultation. In this way, older people, especially, who would rightfully be part of the consensus process if they were living in the village, are often excluded from it, even though their financial contribution enabled the initiative in the first place. This perception of interference frequently exists within the family as well as at the village level, such that many older people find they are increasingly removed from the decisions of the group.

This phenomenon is widely understood by older Minangkabau in the *rantau* and is generally accepted as a condition they must live with, unless they are willing to totally sever their relationship with the village. Nonetheless, this situation, which many of the people involved perceive as exclusion, may be very difficult to accept because of the emotional ties many still feel towards family and the village. For older people who are no longer working and hence have lost their position and status in the employment context, the lack of a comparable status in the traditional context is often more strongly felt. In other words, the loss of identity associated with withdrawal from formal employment is rarely balanced by a greater role in the family and village, which is unconsciously sought by many older Minangkabau.

Despite having lived in the *rantau* for decades in many cases and often having children and grandchildren who have never experienced life in the Minangkabau community, many older Minangkabau continue to view themselves through the lens of ethnic identity. Even those who have high levels of education and are fully integrated into the broader *rantau* community express concern and disappointment that their children and grandchildren usually do not speak Minang and tend to be uninterested in the village and its problems and promises as they see them, as well as Minang culture more generally. For example, older Minangkabau often comment that their adult children are not interested in Minang music or traditional forms of cultural expression that are very meaningful to them. Minang music and dance might feature at wedding parties, which are typically oriented towards the hereditary culture of the bride and groom but are strictly ceremonial to younger Minangkabau born and raised in the *rantau*. In fact, these younger family members are often part of a new and growing urban contemporary culture made up of people who speak only Indonesian well and whose experience is more reflective of the modern, globalized context. This is a source of unhappiness for some older people who would like their children and grandchildren to maintain a distinct Minangkabau ethnic identity that includes the very strong feelings of attachment to the extended family and its heritage.

Interestingly, it is only in older age that many of these individuals begin to recognize that some of the choices they made earlier in life contributed directly to the situation they observe in children and grandchildren. For example, many older people who have spent decades in the *rantau* rarely returned to their village to visit, and, as a result, their children have little familiarity with the family and environment there. This decision was often based on financial considerations, and many people did not consider it important, but the impact was also unexpected. Similarly, many older people encouraged their children to use Indonesian at home and spoke the language to them, instead of Minang. This was often a necessity, especially for older Minangkabau who married people from other ethnic groups, but others chose to do so because of the advantage fluency in Indonesian confers in the educational and employment context. They often did not anticipate the importance of language in the perception of Minangkabau identity and the emotional attachment to the village and its community. There is evidence that this issue is of growing concern to members of the Minangkabau community both within and outside of West Sumatra, leading even political figures to call for people in *rantau* to use Minang at home in order to maintain the group's cultural perspective in future generations (see, for example, JPNN 2013; Kaba News 2016).

While the disconnection from their ethnic heritage has most frequently been connected with the inability to speak Minang, some older Minangkabau in the *rantau* are beginning to realize that the characteristics they observe in children and grandchildren are also due to the fact that these younger people lack first-hand experience in the village. Minangkabau culture, including its values, traditional perceptions and ways of understanding the world, and even day-to-day behaviours, are deeply rooted in the physical environment in which the culture emerged. This is very much a rural world, centring on small villages made up of extended families surrounded by mountains, rice fields, and the jungle. These elements appear consistently throughout traditional literature and provide the source imagery for figurative usage in modern speech (see Fanany and Fanany 2003, for a detailed discussion of this). The fact that many older Minangkabau deeply miss this environment that they experienced as children along with the fact that lack of this experience seems to have affected the self-perception of their children and grandchildren epitomizes the lack of cultural consonance that many of the elderly members of the community currently feel. This issue, which affects many older Minangkabau in the *rantau* crosses socioeconomic boundaries and appears to be a cultural phenomenon related to the social and cultural change experienced by everyone of this generation, is discussed in depth in Chapter 10.

Marni

Like so many Minang women of her generation in the *rantau*, Marni went to Jakarta, where she still lives, with her husband, who is also from Koto, as soon as they got married. Marni, who is now sixty-nine, is the first child and the oldest of four daughters of Aminah's second daughter, Nurijah (Chapter 2). She also has four brothers, two of whom live in Jakarta, one in South Sulawesi, and one in Koto. Her husband had a very good job at the Ministry of Finance, so she did not hesitate to give up her high school teaching job in West Sumatra to go to Jakarta with him. She eventually got another teaching job at a high school in Jakarta. Both Marni and her husband are now retired.

Marni has four children, three girls and one boy, who is the youngest. All the children are now adults. They have jobs and are married but they all live near her, and the family often gets together. Marni and her husband live a very comfortable life, in terms of finances. They have their pensions and were able to save a significant amount of money during their employment such that they did not have to change their lifestyle when they were no longer working. They are able to support their children who are still trying to establish their careers and also to help their own siblings, not all of whom have been as successful as them.

Marni likes the kind of life she has in Jakarta where she has a modern house with every convenience. The family has a car and is financially secure. Still, she has never stopped thinking about the village and about her entitlements as one of Aminah's granddaughters. She feels that the Valley house and all the property Aminah controlled is very attractive. Her memories date from the time when she was a child, living in the communal house with her siblings and the children of her mother's three sisters and Aminah herself until her death. The house was not very big, especially for four families, each of whom had several children. Marni fondly recalls every stage of the rice cycle, from plowing and hoeing, flattening the ground before planting, planting, weeding, harvesting. She used to marvel at the amount of land her grandmother controlled and how she managed its distribution for use by each of her four daughters and her son, who played the role of *mamak*. She even allowed other members of the extended family to use some of it if they needed a way to support their families.

Living far away from Koto both geographically and culturally, Marni has retained a very fond impression about life in the village, even though she cannot see herself going back there to live. She has maintained a relationship with the village, with her nieces and nephews, and especially with her aunt, Maryati, who is Nurijah's youngest sister (Chapter 2). She goes back to the village regularly, if only every year or two. Limeh (Chapter 5), her brother who lives in the village, keeps her informed about what is going on there and with the family.

Because Marni has very strong feelings about Koto but feels Jakarta offers the kind of life she now enjoys, she wants to make sure that she is not losing the property she believes she has a right to. She does not want control to fall into the hands of the family members who live in the village, including her brother, who could be allowed to use the property with the consent of his sisters. This includes the house her mother and father built on land belonging to the extended family. A few years ago, she heard that her brother who lives in the village wanted to convert the house into homestay accommodation because no one has lived there since Nurijah had a stroke and became bedridden several years ago. She now lives in Jakarta with one of her daughters. Marni's brother thought this could be a good way to maintain the house. Koto is close to the village of Pagaruyung, the seat of the ancient Minangkabau kingdom where inscriptions and royal tombs can be seen and are often visited by domestic and international tourists especially from Malaysia. Limeh thought there might be a market for some sort of accommodation because Batusangkar, the district town closest to Koto and Pagaruyung, does not have adequate hotel facilities.

Marni was furious when she heard what her brother was planning. She talked to her three sisters in Jakarta and convinced them that the house was theirs and their brother should not be allowed to convert it into a cheap hotel. All four of them went to the village to confront Limeh and told him the house belonged to them, not him, and they did not want a business there.

More recently, Marni bought a small piece of land adjacent to Aminah's extensive holdings. This is an increasingly common phenomenon. Marni, like some Minangkabau who have been successful in the *rantau* and want to maintain a connection to their village and perhaps exert their traditional claim to family property, is not comfortable dealing with members of the extended family who live in the village. Those living in the village always have first choice in which piece of the family's land they want to use. Those living in the *rantau* have very little influence in this, if any at all. The only property women living in the *rantau* can control for certain is anything their grandmother specifically gave to their mother, such as the land where Marni's parents' house stands or a specific rice field that was ceded to their mother. These will remain under their control, even if they live in the *rantau*, and will pass to the control of their daughters, granddaughters, and so on. Marni wants a safe piece of land she can use at any time and where she and her daughters can do whatever they want. She is now building a house on the land she just purchased.

CHALLENGES FACED BY OLDER MINANGKABAU IN THE *RANTAU*

The problems and difficulties experienced by older Minangkabau in the *rantau*, and to a lesser extent in Padang, include a range of psychosocial, economic and linguistic issues whose nature and dimensions are related to the location of residence as well as to a set of individual factors that include attitude, reason for going to the *rantau*, level of education, language facility, ability to integrate into non-Minangkabau society, the nature of the family, and many others. Many of these issues take on greater importance in older age when individuals may no longer be working and have adult children with lives of their own. This re-emergence of their heritage cultural background as the dominating aspect of many older people's personal identity would seem to suggest that returning to the village might be an appealing and desirable prospect for at least some older Minangkabau, but this is overwhelmingly not the case. In fact, most elderly Minangkabau who spend their adult life in the *rantau* choose to stay there in old age, while the much smaller number who do attempt to return to the village are usually deeply disappointed and disillusioned.

As described in Chapter 3, *adat* reserves a place for every Minangkabau in his or her mother's extended family. In theory, a person's maternal relatives must accept any family member in the matrilineal line who wishes to live on the family's land and make use of its assets. The reality of the situation may be very different, however. Once a person leaves the village and settles in the *rantau*, he or she is outside of the village social structure, and others, who do live in the village, take on the social roles that are available. In other words, just as the person who leaves adapts to life outside the village, the people in the village adapt to living without the people who have gone to the *rantau*. At the present time, the rate of out migration from rural areas is high, and it is not uncommon for all members of the younger generations of a family to have left, even if some of them have gone only as far as Padang or another town in West Sumatra. Over time, power in the family shifts to those in the village who are most competent or most capable of influencing others. Not surprisingly, those who have remained are usually reluctant to share their position and assets with a returning family member who has been in the *rantau* for years and has not taken part in the affairs of the family and village. Nonetheless, the situation for men and women is quite different.

Women, as the heads of families and the inheritors of the extended family's communal assets, cannot be denied a place in their mother's home, regardless of how the situation may have changed over time. It should be noted that, historically, participation in *marantau* was usually reserved for men. It was assumed that a woman who left, perhaps because of marriage to a non-Minangkabau man, would generally remain with her husband for life. In the modern context, however, many women leave West Sumatra to work, attend universities, or for other reasons, as men have for generations. If these individuals choose to return in older age, they can expect to be accepted into their maternal family even if this is not under the best of terms. Because power within the extended family in the traditional Minangkabau context lies in the hands of older women, it can be very disruptive to have to accommodate an additional person, especially one who has been absent in the *rantau*. Bitterness among older women in the same family is not uncommon, and quarrels and disputes about family wealth and access to land and other real property are common. Nonetheless, older women do have the right to assistance from younger relatives as well as contemporaries in the maternal line and can, in fact, take advantage of this type of familial support (see, for example, Schröder-Butterfill and Marianti 2006; Schröder-Butterfill and Fithry 2014). Even when an elderly woman has no close matrilineal relatives, more distant relations have a responsibility to assist that has traditionally been difficult to abrogate in the context of the village.

Older men, however, are very much at the mercy of female relatives if they wish to return to the village. This would traditionally only occur if the man was widowed or had not married because a married man is expected to live with his wife and her relatives. For this reason, one very problematic situation is when a Minangkabau man is married to a woman from another ethnic group, as occurs not infrequently among people in the *rantau*. The expected pattern for many Indonesian ethnic groups is for a woman to live with her husband's family; a Minangkabau man cannot bring a wife into his mother's family's home and will have to live outside of the matrilineal context for the duration of the marriage. Any children such a union produces will not be considered Minangkabau by their father's family but may be seen as belonging to that group by their mother's. Children in this position are referred to as *anak pisang* (banana children) in Minang, perhaps because the offshoots of a banana plant grow close to, but are separate from, the original plant. It is possible to transplant them without damaging either the parent plant or the new shoot. Children in this position do not have rights that would make it possible for them to live with their father's family, their *bako*, in his village of origin. Within the Minangkabau community, it has frequently been suggested that the status of these children is a concern because they are not members of a clan (a larger grouping of extended families related through the female line) which is a problem in terms of *adat* but also for members of the community where clan affiliation is an important aspect of the social network (Haluan 2016c).

The willingness to accept men returning from the *rantau* back into the matrilineal family is often dependent on their ability to contribute economically to the household. There is a strong tendency in Minangkabau society to value men based on their ability to support the family, either financially or in the form of work on the land. An older man, who may not be able to do much agricultural labour and does not have considerable personal wealth, may be very unwelcome in the household of his sisters or female cousins. As is the case for older woman, the presence of such an individual may be seen as disruptive but not really beneficial.

The result of this is that many older Minangkabau of both sexes do not consider returning to the village, or even to West Sumatra, to be a viable option after years of living in the *rantau*. When asked about this, it becomes apparent that older members of the Minangkabau community are very much aware of the problems that would emerge if they decided to return to the village. Many of them do not see this as reflecting the traditional social structure but, instead, believe that it is more a problem of their own family. In this, many are very reluctant to consider the possibility that the problems they are aware of result from the precepts of *adat* and hence are inherent to the traditional system. For these elderly individuals, it is generally very difficult to accept that an ideal Minangkabau society structured by *adat* may still have elements that do not function as intended. This idea seems to conflict with their understanding of the nature of *adat* (as discussed in Chapter 3). Instead, many believe that this kind of problem, including the often vicious feuding and competition within families over resources and the right to control them, represents a failure of the community to uphold traditional values and maintain customary institutions and practices. This is a common thread that runs through discussion of a whole range of social issues, including crime, drug abuse, educational problems, intergenerational discord, and many others, in both the formal media as well as on social media platforms (see, for example, Publika News 2012; Chatra 2015). A recent governor of West Sumatra, Irwan Prayitno, has frequently discussed the need to return the values of *adat* to Minangkabau society. Interestingly, Prayitno received an undergraduate degree from a university in Jakarta and holds postgraduate qualifications obtained in Malaysia. He returned from a teaching position at a university in the capital to serve as governor but has maintained his academic post and is still officially employed in the *rantau*. Prayitno's personal website (http://irwan-prayitno.com/) outlines his views on *adat* and society as well as his background and professional training.

Fauzi

Fauzi, sixty-six, one of Marni's (see this chapter) younger brothers, moved to Jakarta as soon as he finished college. He lived with Marni at first, who at the time already had a house there that was bought by her husband who worked at the Ministry of Finance. Fauzi went to the capital hoping that he would be able to find a job. He did not care whether his employment related to the undergraduate degree in education that he received from a university in Padang. After a couple of years living with Marni and her family, he finally got a job at the Ministry of Transmigration, which was an important agency at the time because the government was trying to move as many people as possible from the overpopulated islands of Java and Bali to less dense areas, especially on the large islands of Sumatra, Kalimantan, Sulawesi and Papua. Fauzi's entry-level job paid a low salary, and he could not afford to rent or buy his own home. Soon after, however, Marni arranged a marriage for him to a woman from Koto who had recently moved to Jakarta to live with her brother. She had found employment as a kindergarten teacher. After their marriage, with their combined salary and help from Marni and Fauzi's wife's family, the couple bought a house in a housing complex far from the city centre. At the time, low-cost homes in large developments were becoming common in the many newly established suburbs of the capital. Fauzi now lived very far from his job at the Ministry. He had a motorcycle but had to leave home by 6:00 every morning to arrive at the office by 8:00. This meant he had to get up at around 4:30 a.m., get dressed, and make the commute in extremely heavy traffic. Initially, he now says, he enjoyed it; he was young and liked the freedom a motorcycle gave him. He could weave in and out of traffic and sometimes rode on the sidewalk when traffic was really bad, and there were no police around. Additionally, he learned quickly he didn't have to be physically in the office all the time and could do other things that could earn him some extra money. The motorcycle made this possible. His entrepreneurial spirit and skill gave him an extra income that sometimes exceeded his salary.

Fauzi is personable and gets along with everyone. People generally like him. Several years after he started working, the Ministry needed someone to manage its transmigration programme on site in South Kalimantan. Fauzi managed to get the assignment because he got along with his superiors. In addition to his salary, he received a large relocation bonus for living in the difficult environment of the transmigration site. The newly cleared jungle area had to be developed for the residents: housing, schools, mosques or other places of worship, and agricultural land and technical assistance all had to be put in place. This required management and coordination. Fauzi excelled in his new role and felt satisfied for the first time in his working life. In addition, there were many opportunities for extra income in this new area that was rich in natural resources, like timber and other jungle products. Fauzi made even more money through these side jobs.

Fauzi's wife went with him to Kalimantan. As a civil servant, she was able to get another job at a local kindergarten. After just a few years there, they had saved enough money to add several rooms to their original house on the outskirts of Jakarta. When they went to Kalimantan, they had two small children, a boy and a girl. When they returned to Jakarta after several years, their home was very comfortable and more than big enough for the four of them. They were even able to buy a used car.

As much as they had liked Kalimantan, the family was happy to return to Jakarta. Fauzi's wife returned to her old school. Fauzi, however, did not like his job at the Ministry, where he was now doing office work. In addition, he increasingly disliked the traffic, which got worse from year to year. Travel by car was much slower than by motorcycle, and he spent most of his time in traffic. He had to get up even earlier now than before he went to Kalimantan and he dreaded it every morning. It was so bad, he said, that sometimes he did not get up in the morning and skipped work. He would stay in bed until late but, the next day, he would feel even worse.

Before Fauzi knew it, the children had grown up. His son left home to take a job in Bandung, three hours away by car. His daughter married, worked as a secretary at a hotel, and lived at home with Fauzi and his wife in the Minangkabau tradition. But increasingly, the relationship between Fauzi and his wife and their daughter and her husband became strained. They had not entirely approved of her marriage, and her husband did not have a regular job. By the time their daughter had two young children, Fauzi and his wife had retired and spent most of their time taking care of the babies. They initially enjoyed this but soon found it very difficult and time consuming. They began to resent the imposition on their time, especially as their son-in-law showed little interest in caring for the children. This became a source of argument, and the quarrels between Fauzi's wife and their daughter were intense.

Based on his experience in Kalimantan, Fauzi felt that returning to Koto might be better for him and his wife, especially since she is also from Koto. Fauzi's wife was completely against this idea however. She is the only daughter in her family, and her mother is dead. Her mother's two sisters and their children warned her that, if she returned to the village, she would have to build her own house because the extended family's home was not even big enough for them and their children. In addition, the family's land did not support the family members who had lived in the village all these years, so she should not expect to live on the land if she did decide to return.

Fauzi's wife also knew that her family would make trouble for her even though she had as much right to the land and the house as the other women in the family. She was certain it would not be worth the trouble to return to the village. In addition, Fauzi knew that, while he had a right to use the land in the village that had been given to his mother and that his mother's family has a lot more land than his wife's family, it would be just as difficult for him to negotiate with the relatives who had always lived in the village. Nonetheless, Fauzi increasingly longed to return to Koto.

Luckily he felt, a relative of his wife's offered him a chance to join him in business in the town of Solok, about 40 kilometres from Koto. This relative is a doctor and was building a clinic. He thought Fauzi might be able to manage it. Fauzi was extremely excited, but his wife was much more cautious. She thought getting involved in a relative's business could be risky, but Fauzi was adamant. He tried to convince her that this was the best chance for them to escape the unpleasant situation at home with their daughter and her family. He also reminded his wife how happy they had been in Kalimantan and that this would be similar. It would be better, in fact, because they would not have to live in the jungle far from the facilities and conveniences of a town. He further assured his wife that this would be the best alternative for them; they would be returning to West Sumatra but not to the village.

Eventually, they accepted the relative's offer and decided to try to build a new life in West Sumatra, but not in their own village, hoping for the best. However, the clinic was never built, and it became apparent that the relative had overpromised what could be done. At the time he made his offer to Fauzi, he had not yet secured a construction permit. That permit was eventually denied, and the relative decided to move to East Java. Fauzi ended up with nothing.

To make matters worse, against the advice of everyone he spoke to, including his own wife, Fauzi had sold the house in Jakarta where the family had been living before they returned to West Sumatra. He had bought a house in Solok as well as a piece of land where he hoped to start a business. Nonetheless, Fauzi was paralysed by this bitter experience and what he felt was a betrayal by the relative he had trusted. He did not begin his new venture and now has nothing to do. However, he cannot return to Jakarta, because he no longer has a house there, or to Koto, because of shame and embarrassment.

SOCIAL AND FAMILY NETWORKS

In addition to their awareness of the problems of returning to the village, the wish to be near adult children and grandchildren is an important reason many older Minangkabau choose to remain in the *rantau*. The desire to interact with grandchildren especially is very strong among many of these elderly people, as is the hope that their daughters will be available to help them if they are in need. Unlike older people in the village or even Padang, individuals who have spent years in the *rantau* can generally communicate effectively with grandchildren who are primarily Indonesian speaking and have a good understanding of these young people's experience. For this reason, many older Minangkabau in the *rantau* have very close relationships with their children and grandchildren that they try to structure in ways that are characteristic of Minangkabau society. Many older people, for example, would like to live with, or close to, a daughter and her family if possible and view grandchildren in the female line as members of their mother's family, as is the case in Minangkabau society traditionally. Interethnic marriage is quite common in Indonesia, and older Minangkabau are very much aware that their children may marry non-Minangkabau. In some cases, they themselves did the same thing. The desire of many Minangkabau to marry, and have their children marry, others of the same ethnic background, however, is recognized within the community and is a topic of considerable interest in the blogosphere, where there is often an observable difference in perception, depending on whether the man or the woman is Minangkabau. One blogger describes the situation as follows:

> *Ada kejadian di mana laki-laki Minang dilarang menikah dengan selain perempuan Minang. Alasannya menurut saya karena hukum matrilineal yang berlaku pada adat Minang. Anak akan mewarisi suku ibunya. Jika ibunya non-minang maka anaknya gak punya suku, tidak ada yang meneruskan suku, karena suku bapak gak akan diwariskan ke anak. Jadi menurut adat Minang, jika laki-laki Minang menikah dengan perempuan non-Minang akan mengaburkan silsilah garis keturunan anak di Minangkabau. Secara adat si anak tidak dapat diterima di Minangkabau karena tidak ada garis keturunan Minang. Si anak akan dianggap tidak memiliki darah Minang.*
>
> *Perempuan Minang dengan laki-laki non-Minang ... Dari sisi adat Minang sendiri ini sah-sah saja. Karena anak-anaknya nanti akan tetap mewarisi suku ibunya ... Tapi masalahnya malah di pihak laki-laki yang orang Jawa. Ibunya tidak sreg sama orang Padang. Entah karena alasan apa, saya juga ngga ngerti. Mungkin karena ada omongan buruk tentang orang Padang, bisa jadi. Memang*

kita ngga bisa nyamain semua orang dengan suku yang sama, tapi kita juga ngga bisa membatasi pikiran orang ... Beberapa kali teman saya sharing mengenai hal yang sama, ditolak oleh calon mertua, satu di antaranya karena orang Padang. Tapi akhirnya mereka menikah, karena calon suaminya berhasil meyakinkan keluarganya bahwa tidak semua orang Padang itu seperti yang dikatakan orang-orang.

[It has happened that a Minangkabau man has been forbidden (by family) to marry any woman who is not Minangkabau. The reason, in my opinion, is the matrilineal rules that are part of Minangkabau *adat*. A child will be part of his mother's clan. If the mother is not Minangkabau, then the child will not have a clan, because the father's clan membership cannot be inherited. So, in Minangkabau *adat*, if a Minangkabau man marries a non-Minangkabau woman, it will confuse the child's heritage in the Minangkabau world. Under *adat*, the child will not be accepted in Minangkabau society because he is not part of a Minangkabau lineage. The child will be seen as not having Minangkabau blood.

A Minangkabau woman with a non-Minangkabau man ... in terms of Minangkabau *adat* itself, this is valid because the children will inherit their mother's clan membership ... But the problem has been on the part of the man's family if he is Javanese (for example). His mother wouldn't get along with women from Padang. I don't know what the exact reason for this is. It may be because people say bad things about people from Padang. We can't lump everyone from one background together but we also can't prevent people from thinking what they want to ... Several times, a friend of mine has told me about this. She was rejected by her future in-laws because her family was Minangkabau. But they finally did get married because her future husband succeeded in convincing his family that not all people from Padang were like people say.]

(Listentorica, "Pernikahan Padang vs Jawa
(Minang vs Non-Minang)", blog post, 9 February 2015
<http://listentorica.blogspot.com.au/2015/02/pernikahan-
padang-vs-jawa-minang-vs-non.html>)

While the older Minangkabau of interest here may have encountered this situation in their own youth, many have also experienced the problems of mixed marriage as the parents of the young people involved and, in fact, have their own ideas about people from other ethnic groups as well. In this, they are not unique as the nature of modern Indonesian society facilitates social interaction between members of different ethnic groups, especially in large cities and modern workplaces. However, greater social interaction outside of the Minangkabau community by individuals living in the *rantau* poses dilemmas that may challenge culturally based expectations that are often difficult for older people to accept. In particular, the social behaviour, attitudes and perceptions of children and grandchildren that do not fully fit with Minangkabau norms may be confusing and unexpected to elderly Minangkabau, especially as their own cultural and linguistic background takes on more significance in older age. It is difficult for many individuals to articulate exactly how they perceive grandchildren who seem to them to be "un-Minangkabau" in certain ways, but it is often apparent from their comments that they find them different from their expectations.

What these older people seem to be referring to is the inevitable shift in cultural outlook that has occurred in younger generations who are subject to a wider range of influences than they themselves experienced. These influences come from the national mainstream culture, from other local cultures that may be present in a given region, and the globalized international culture that is increasingly important to Indonesian youth. Older Minangkabau tend to view the social and cultural change they observe in younger people as a loss of traditional values that is detrimental to the larger Minangkabau community. In fact, the changes they recognize and are concerned about in younger people might more accurately be categorized as a move to a more Indonesian identity that reflects the national culture, separate from any one ethnic group's perspective but drawing on elements from a number of them. It also reflects the underlying philosophy of the Indonesian state that seeks to meld the numerous indigenous cultures into a characteristic national culture relevant to all Indonesians. The development of a modern national culture was an objective of the long-lived New Order government that accelerated rapidly as technology improved. Individuals who are over sixty at the present time, however, were born in the first decade of Indonesian independence or earlier and spent their formative years in communities that did not yet reflect current cultural and social patterns. In this, it should be noted that the level of development, especially outside of major cities, at the time Indonesia achieved independence was rather low. This was the motivation for the emphasis on improving the standard of living and providing infrastructure that characterized both the Soekarno and especially the Soeharto governments. For this reason, people who are now over sixty experienced an almost constant level of change that was also marked by politically dynamic periods, such as the rebellion of West Sumatra against the central government that occurred in 1958 and the 1965 coup that led to the establishment of the New Order government of President Soeharto (see Elson 2008, among many others for discussion of these issues).

Many elderly Minangkabau who have spent years in the *rantau* find that they are very lonely in older age and often feel displaced. The natural inclination towards their ancestral culture encourages the formation of social organizations based on village affiliation or other past associations, like the BI70 WhatsApp group described in Chapter 5. However, major urban centres in Indonesia are often very spread out and difficult to navigate, especially for older people who may have health or mobility constraints. This may limit the amount of direct interaction older Minangkabau have with friends and family members, although the availability of social media and mobile communications technology has greatly facilitated indirect interaction. For older people who live in cities where the Minangkabau community is small, such as in parts of central and eastern Indonesia, there may be practical difficulties associated with maintaining a social network of Minangkabau peers that includes direct interaction.

Inevitably, older Minangkabau in the *rantau* live in neighbourhoods where they know many people and are on friendly terms with at least some of their neighbours. However, the very mixed population of large cities in Indonesia means that much of the population of any residential area is likely to come from other ethnic groups. These relationships are satisfactory to many older people but cannot fulfill their desire for greater involvement in their own culture, including the use of its language. In some cases, these older Minangkabau are quite isolated culturally, especially if they live in a location where the Minangkabau community is small and they are married to a person from a local ethnic group. In many situations of this kind, it is the husband who is Minangkabau, and the wife's culture dominates in the household. If there are few Minangkabau in the area, it can be very difficult for the Minangkabau spouse to create a social network of people from the same culture unless it is mediated by technology. Many older Minangkabau do have such networks, even if they include only siblings and other close family members, which are very important for psychological well-being. Interestingly, many older members of the community recognize how involved in and dependent upon these social media groups they are. Many also recognize that older people married to a non-Minangkabau spouse are dependent on that spouse's tolerance of this activity in order to participate and that this is especially important for Minangkabau men married to non-Minangkabau women.

Not surprisingly, relationships with family members are among the most important sources of psychological well-being for older Minangkabau in the *rantau*. For many, their family network has two distinct components that encompass a different set of members. The first of these includes older relatives and those of a similar age (siblings, cousins, parents, aunts and uncles). These individuals generally share the cultural and linguistic background of the older person in question and may have grown up in the same village at the same time or in an overlapping period. This part of the familial network generally interacts in Minang and reflects the social structure of the village in terms of the relative status of those involved. However, for older Minangkabau, this part of their family is shrinking and static. Members tend to be of a comparable age and are reaching the end of their life. The common bond of experience of life in the village is often not shared by younger family members, and those who do remain have a very different life course than that of people who are now elderly. The second component of many older Minangkabau's family network is made up of children, nieces and nephews, and, as children grow up, in-laws and grandchildren. While many older people are very attached to these younger relatives, they also recognize that interacting with them is different, as the experiences of younger family members are often so far from their own. This is especially the case when these younger people have grown up in the *rantau* and are more Indonesian in behaviour than their older relatives. Older Minangkabau frequently observe that their social interactions with younger relatives are satisfying but cannot replace those with people of their own generation who share their experience as well as language. Intergenerational problems are not uncommon because of this difference in outlook, and many older women especially complain that children, with whom they often feel they have little in common, expect them to take care of their children, and this occupies all of the older person's time because of the all-day work hours and long commutes that are the norm for working people in Indonesian cities like Jakarta.

In Minangkabau communities regardless of location, it is customary and part of the usual social practice to find out where friends and acquaintances are from and to identify individuals who are related as well as the nature of the relationship. This is not always straightforward because there is no system of family names, and family structures are often complex. In the village, people are often known in terms of a relationship to another person who serves as the reference point for a given individual. For example, an older person might know younger people as so-and-so's child or grandchild; others might be identified as either a maternal or paternal relative of a reference person; and so on. In the traditional context, this practice served as a reminder of the shape and extent of the social bonds that connected extended families in the village. Older Minangkabau in the *rantau* tend to be very concerned about these kinds of connections among people they know, even though they have often never met the younger individuals involved, and the nature of the relationships is more for interest than for a practical social purpose. Nonetheless, discussion about the children and grandchildren of friends and relatives is a major topic of conversation among older Minangkabau in the *rantau* when they meet as well as in their social media groups. The other topic of great interest is who is ill and what the nature of the illness is as well as who has died.

ILLNESS IN THE AGEING *RANTAU* POPULATION

One of the main concerns of older Minangkabau living in the *rantau* is how they will cope with illness and possible disability. As average life expectancy has grown in Indonesia, the prevalence of chronic disease and other conditions of old age has increased. Almost everyone knows people who have had a stroke, who have diabetes or heart disease, and who have experienced cancer. Stroke and diabetes seem to be especially common within the Minangkabau community and may reflect genetic predisposition as well as lifestyle factors (see Tasa'ady, Fanany and Fanany 2012; Fanany and Fanany 2015). When asked to reflect on this, many older Minangkabau recall there being some very old people in the village in their youth but feel that these old people were in better health than many of those who are currently of a similar age. They believe this represents a change but generally do not connect either the current lifestyle or levels of stress in modern society with increased illness. It is difficult to assess the accuracy of such impressions, but it may, in fact, be correct that more illness is observable in the Minangkabau community today because there are more people who are older and who are living longer on average. Diagnosis of chronic disease was much less intensive in the past as well, so it is likely that much of the prevalence of specific conditions was hidden and any infirmity of an older person viewed as an inevitable result of ageing.

Nonetheless, the current state of the elderly, and especially the growing number of people reaching very old age (over eighty), means that some older Minangkabau are responsible for extremely infirm parents in addition to concerns about their own health and that of a spouse and other close relatives of a similar age. This situation, which is new in Indonesia but is well known in Western countries, is of extreme concern to many older Minangkabau in the *rantau* because their very ill and very old parents are often insistent that they wish to stay in the village, even if a daughter, who is likely to be over sixty herself, lives in the *rantau* and wants her parent to live with her. The difficulties experienced by older people who have been living in the *rantau* in returning permanently to the village often make moving there for the purpose of caring for an elderly parent impossible. As a result, many families have resorted to unusual arrangements, such as leaving an elderly relative in the care of a son and daughter-in-law (generally considered unacceptable in Minangkabau society) or having a more distant relative in the maternal line assist an elderly parent in the village (considered possible but not ideal) (see Schröder-Butterfill 2004), or have insisted that the ailing parent come to the *rantau*. This was the case with Nurijah, one of the oldest members of the Valley family, whose story is presented in Chapter 2.

As would be expected, older Minangkabau living in the *rantau* experience many of the same situations that affect older Indonesians of all ethnic backgrounds. These include economic pressures that may require some form of employment or participation in small business for as long as possible, restricted mobility in physical environments that are not set up to facilitate those who are older or who have health problems, separation from adult children who live in other locations, and so on. However, the impact of being a cultural and linguistic minority is increasingly significant as individuals age and begin to withdraw from the workforce and other forms of interaction that confer an identity in formal social contexts. At this time, when a cultural identity associated with their Minangkabau upbringing and represented by language use and participation in typically Minangkabau social institutions often becomes more important, many older people living in the *rantau* experience serious loneliness, unhappiness, and depression that they have difficulty overcoming. Many recognize that their present situation reflects decisions they made at younger ages, whose long-term consequences they could not have anticipated, but that they must now accept these consequences. Individual resilience and ability to adapt varies, but most older Minangkabau do experience some lack of cultural consonance and the subsequent psychological impacts that they attempt to address in different ways. This is discussed in depth in Chapter 10.

9

Ageing in an Institution

OLDER MINANGKABAU IN INSTITUTIONALIZED CARE

For more than thirty years, the Ministry of Social Affairs has run old age homes around Indonesia that provide room and board for older people who have no family or the means to support themselves independently. Care at one of these institutions is completely free to the residents, and provision is made for the complex health care needs many older people will develop late in life. Generally, however, an individual must be able to care for him or herself at the time of admission. These public institutions are generally referred to as *Panti Sosial Tresna Werdha* (PSTW). The term *tresna werdha* is Javanese and means "love of old people". *Panti sosial* is Indonesian and refers to any type of social facility, such as a nursing home, orphanage, or other similar residential institution. In addition to these public facilities, privately run nursing homes for older people have been established by a number of hospitals and organizations. These facilities require payment, although some do accept residents who cannot pay.

In West Sumatra, the two largest old age facilities are Panti Sosial Tresna Werdha Sabai nan Aluih which is located in the town of Sicincin, not far from Padang, and Panti Sosial Tresna Werdha Kasih Sayang Ibu, in the town of Batusangkar in the highland interior of the province.

The names chosen for the two facilities are interesting in that they have specific connotations that are meaningful in the context of their function. The PSTW located in Sicincin is in the traditional *rantau*. The name Sabai nan Aluih is a reference to a character in a well-known Minangkabau folk tale, who is portrayed as the epitome of a dutiful and loyal daughter who loves and respects her parents. The character represents the exemplary child. By contrast, the facility in Batusangkar, which is in the Minangkabau heartland, uses an Indonesian name that means "mother's love". Both names are intended to convey the idea of affection between family members and refer to an idealized relationship between parents and children. These two facilities can accommodate 110 and 70 people respectively and account for 75 per cent of the accommodation for elderly people in need in the province. Both facilities are currently full to capacity and are approached by individuals with no place to live or families seeking accommodation for an older relative on a weekly basis. To the extent possible, both homes try to give priority to people from the region; individuals from outside of West Sumatra are preferably transferred to a comparable facility in their province of origin. This is not always, possible, however. Similarly, when no space is available, members of the West Sumatran community may need to be sent to another location or even to another province.

Each PSTW has its own campus that consists of apartment-style housing for the residents, accommodating two to ten people per unit with shared living space and bathrooms. A separate building contains office space for the staff, an auditorium, and common rooms. Each complex has its own mosque and basic health care facilities. The grounds are landscaped and professionally maintained. Both the living and public areas, as well as offices and other spaces, are extremely clean and have been set up to accommodate elderly people who may have difficulty walking. The overall impression is pleasant, convenient, and hygienic, but very different from the living environment of West Sumatran villages and the type of homes many old people in the region have lived in for most of their life.

The managers of the PSTW are social workers who are trained to work with the elderly and who have a network of connections with other institutions, such as public health centres and hospitals, as well as among various branches of government. Nurses, who reside on site, are available at all times to help residents, and staff from local health centres visit several times a week to see residents and treat any health concerns. These health care providers are assisted by a changing group of students on clinical placement from the provincial schools of medicine and nursing. Support staff of various kinds are also employed to deal with the non-health needs of the residents, such as food preparation, laundry, and maintenance. The staff, as well as the students who are on assignment at the PSTW, are extremely patient and try to accommodate the residents' needs and desires as much as possible, including facilitating social activities among them and providing counselling as needed. Nonetheless, depression and other psychosocial problems are common among the older people living there, which is an issue of increasing concern that is beginning to attract the attention of local researchers (see, for example, Huraini and Sumarsih 2012; Husna et al. 2015; Sinthania 2015).

These old age homes were originally envisioned as places where older adults who had no other means of support could be accommodated and provided for. It was assumed that this situation could only come about if the individuals in question had no living family and especially no children. In West Sumatra, specifically, an elderly person should always be able to live with his or her maternal relatives (as discussed in Chapter 3), although this has likely always been problematic. When this was not possible, it was assumed to result from one of two possible scenarios. The first might occur if a person had no children, and especially no daughters (see Indrizal 2004, for discussion of this); the second would be if a person's maternal line had died out, meaning that the individual in question might be the last member of his or her branch of the extended family. In a situation where the youngest generation of family has no female members, the branch of the family is considered extinct because any children of male members will belong to their mother's extended family. This is seen as a very unfortunate and concerning situation in the Minangkabau community and one that may cause great distress to those involved.

As has been noted above, the situation for men and women is quite different in terms of *adat* and entitlement to support within the extended family. Women, in theory, cannot be denied a place within the households of members of their maternal line. Ideally, they would live with daughters and nieces, as well as any living female members of their own generation, in old age. If close maternal relatives were not available, they would still be entitled to the use of family assets, even if this meant living with more distant matrilineal relatives. In the past, it was very difficult for an older woman to be denied the right to live within the extended family and benefit from its land and other wealth. This is not to suggest that the relationships between older and younger women in the extended family were always harmonious. They were not, but there were few alternatives available, and younger people had to accept that older relations controlled the family's assets that they, themselves, were also dependent on, and that older women could not be prevented from using them.

The situation of older men has always been more problematic in the Minangkabau community. Their position within the family is subordinate to their sisters and other female relatives. When they marry, they become part of their wife's family with a status that does not confer on them the rights of a member. If their marriage ends due to either death or divorce, men should be able to return to their own maternal family, but, in practice, this depends on the goodwill of the women of the family. As shown in the cases of Mansur (Chapter 3), Salim (Chapter 5), and Ribuik (Chapter 6), men may have to accept living conditions that are extremely unpleasant, stressful, and even humiliating because of the way in which the traditional social system operates. In some cases, it may be impossible for them to live with the family at all, as happened to Salim, and older men may have to stay at a local mosque or sleep on the street. When this occurs today, these individuals will usually be brought to one of the PSTW by the police or the residents of the local area. In the past, they would have had to get by as best they could, often in a situation similar to that of Ribuik (Chapter 6) where maternal relatives might have built a hut or other make-shift structure for the older man to live in, separate from the rest of the family.

The fact that it is so difficult for Minangkabau men if they do not have female relatives or a wife they can live with is an important factor in the long existence of polygamy in the community. As Islam entitles a man to have up to four wives at the same time assuming he can support them and treats them fairly, this possibility has long existed in West Sumatra and is a practice that may have been valuable to older men in maximizing their chances of having a place to live and someone to take care of them if they became ill. However, it is important to note that polygamy of this kind has also been tolerated and participated in by women as a strategy to ensure a marriage that produces children with the best possible heritage. For this reason, in past generations and occasionally in the present, it has not been uncommon for men from wealthy families, families with high social status, or who were themselves well educated or held formal positions of power to have several wives because they were seen as desirable fathers to future children who would be members of their mother's family. The women involved in such a marriage as one of several wives of the same man generally would have preferred a situation where their husband had only one wife but seem to have been willing to tolerate a polygamous marriage because of the potential benefit to their own family in terms of children and because they were not economically dependent on their husband. Aminah, whose situation is discussed in Chapter 2, is an example of this, as is that of Pulai, her oldest daughter (Chapter 2).

In the case of the Minangkabau, the fact that Islam allows men to have up to four wives at the same time happens to be beneficial in light of the traditional social system and may be a reason why the community seems to adhere to religious views that are conservative in the context of Indonesia but also maintains its traditional matrilineal structure. Men who could afford to have more than one household could, in a sense, better their chances of having a comfortable old age which may also have allowed them to remain active in their own maternal family as a *mamak* (maternal uncle) and decision-maker. Because they did not require economic support from the extended family, they may have been able to get along better with their female relatives and play a role in the family's affairs. While not widespread today, there is some evidence that multiple marriages are increasing among men in the Minangkabau community. This may be a return to the older practice that was documented in the 1930 census conducted by the Dutch colonial government that indicated the rate of multiple marriages among Minangkabau men was almost 9.7 per cent, the highest in Indonesia, in contrast to a rate of 1.9 per cent in Java. At the time, almost 20 per cent of Minangkabau men in certain areas, such as Agam Tuo and Maninjau in the highland region of Agam, had more than one wife (Prins 1954).

It is important to note that, while polygamy was at one time routinely accepted, if not liked, by Minangkabau women, such as Aminah the founding member of the Valley family who was one of her husband's three wives, serial marriages were common among them as well. In the past, many women in the Minangkabau community married, divorced, and remarried, often several times. Because of their social position and assets, there was often little inducement for a woman to stay married to a man she did not get along with, especially as a husband's financial contribution was not needed to provide for any children. This aspect of the matrilineal system is often referred to by members of the Minangkabau community as one of its greatest strengths, namely ensuring the support of women and children. Traditionally, women and their families hoped that marriage would produce female children to continue the maternal line. The system provided the means to support these children and ensure the continuity of the family.

These social patterns, polygamy among men and serial marriage among women, are much less frequently observed today than they were in past generations. Nonetheless, it is not uncommon to see such practices among older people, especially those who come from rural areas and have little formal education. The practical value of these strategies is greatly reduced, however, due to the very rapid social change the community as a whole has experienced. For this reason, it is not uncommon to find residents of the PSTW whose experience reflects a past social norm that has since lost its value.

Udin

Udin, seventy-two, a resident of PSTW Kasih Sayang Ibu in Batusangkar, learned about the facility from someone who prayed regularly at the mosque where he was living. Udin had been there for three months since he returned to his village from Jakarta. He had two wives, both of whom are still alive, and several children with each. His wives as well as some of his children live in the village, but none of them were willing to allow Udin to live at their house. He has no sisters, so his mother's share of the family's ancestral land has been taken over by her sisters and their daughters. Udin's mother died long before he returned to the village, and the family's original house is too small for the many children and grandchildren of his aunts. As a result, there is no place for him there.

Udin left the village for Jakarta several years after he finished primary school and did not have any further education. Like many Minangkabau in Jakarta, he was willing to do any work available to support himself. He met some people from his village in Jakarta as well as many from other locations in West Sumatra, and it was through these contacts that he managed to get his first odd jobs in Jakarta, which included washing dishes at Padang restaurants and helping more established Minangkabau traders. After a couple of years, because he was likeable and able to get along with people, a successful businessman in the garment industry offered him a more permanent job based on verbal agreement. This is common among smaller businesses in Indonesia that operate within social networks based on ethnicity. With a regular income and good prospects, he married a young woman from his village who was brought to Jakarta by her family when they heard about Udin's success there. Udin was only in his early twenties at the time and was pleased and flattered by the way people back in the village seemed to view him.

This marriage ended in separation. Udin accepts the blame for this. He does not hesitate to admit now that he always had relationships with other women. He had many girlfriends in Jakarta even after his marriage. Eventually, after having three children, his wife learned about one particular girlfriend, who also came from their village. Udin's wife was furious, not just because her husband had a girlfriend but, because as she came from the same location, everyone there would know about it, and this would reflect extremely badly on Udin's wife and her family. While Udin says he wanted to be with his family and that he loved his wife and children, his wife would no longer allow him to live in their house in Jakarta. She did not want a divorce because she wanted Udin to continue to support her and the children financially, which he did, albeit irregularly and unsatisfactorily.

Udin eventually married his girlfriend from the village with whom he had four children. Because of events in her extended family, she had to return to the village after the birth of their first child and left Udin in Jakarta by himself. He would only see her and the children occasionally when he was able to go back to the village or on special occasions such as the holiday at the end of the fasting month. Several times, Udin tried to persuade his second wife to return to Jakarta, but she refused even though they had more children during this period when they were living apart. Udin had several more girlfriends, but his wife did not seem to care.

In the long term, Udin was not successful at any of his jobs. Even his best employer, the man in the garment business, eventually became fed up with his womanizing. From his employer's point of view, Udin's problems were beginning to affect his work, especially once he was married but still had girlfriends. In addition, Udin now acknowledges regretfully that he was not a very good employee either, partly because of the many women he was involved with. He would steal from his employers to get the extra money he needed to support his girlfriends. He would skip work and lie about the reason in order to get more time to juggle his relationships. Every employer he had eventually found out and fired him.

When he was no longer able to find work because of his age and reputation, Udin returned to his village. It is uncommon for Minangkabau who leave the village to seek their fortune to return home in old age, especially if they have been successful in the *rantau*. But even those who fail in the *rantau* rarely return home; it has always been considered embarrassing to do so. A few of them, however, do return when, like Udin, they have no other alternatives.

Udin was living in his village for five months before he moved into the PSTW. He had been hoping that someone, perhaps from his mother's family, would allow him to live with them or that one of his children, who was married and had a family, would take pity on him and let him stay with them. He never expected one of his wives to take him back, even though he was not divorced. He was right about this. In the end, no one in the village would have him, and he had to sleep at the village mosque and rely on people's sympathy to get food and other things he might need.

After a few months, people in the village decided Udin could not live in the mosque indefinitely. They learned that he had no plans to return to the *rantau* and that he was not likely to find alternative living arrangements in the foreseeable future. They knew about the old age home in their area and suggested that he go there. Udin did not like the idea of living in a place with only other old people for company. In addition, while he admits that he knew nothing about the PSTW, he thought that living in such an institution would not be pleasant. But the villagers finally insisted that he could not live in the mosque and took him to the old age home.

As it turned out, Udin is quite happy at the PSTW, certainly much happier, he says, than during the months immediately preceding his move there. While he still thinks that living among other old people is not the best alternative, he is satisfied with the overall situation. The facilities are good, and the PSTW provides the residents with the things they need, even though he sees differences among them, depending on the extent to which their family members support them. Some people there, for example, have mobile phones, more clothing of better quality, and visitors who come to see them regularly. Udin must make do with what the PSTW provides but is reasonably content and no longer has to worry about food or a place to sleep.

CAUSES OF INSTITUTIONALIZATION AMONG OLDER MINANGKABAU

According to the staff of the PSTW, the need for accommodation for older Minangkabau without family to care for them is increasing rapidly. While the provincial and regional governments are concerned about the number of older people living below the poverty line (see, for example, Rahmat 2016), many of the residents of West Sumatra's PSTW do have family members who can afford to support them. In many cases, there are indications that these older people do not get along with their children or other relatives, and, as a result, their family would prefer that they live elsewhere.

The staff who run the old age homes in West Sumatra generally believe that, based on their knowledge of the older people in question as well as their familiarity with the life of the community, the residents of the PSTW have antagonized their children especially and were not very good parents when these children were younger. One of their main aims is to try to get the residents of their facility to reconcile with relatives so that they can return to the family home, and their method for encouraging this is to get the older people to think about their family relationships and the events that built up over the years that contributed to them coming to live at the PSTW. While it is possible that some, or even a majority, of the current PSTW residents were bad parents, it is also the case that this is very unlikely to be a new situation. Family relationships in every culture and every time period have often been difficult and stressful for those involved. Deep-seated intergenerational conflicts exist everywhere, including in more traditional societies such as Minangkabau (Mabry, Giarrusso and Bengtson 2004; Edmunds and Turner 2005).

For the first time in Minangkabau history, however, a large number of younger people are no longer dependent on the traditional matrilineal system for economic support. As more people have achieved higher levels of formal education and increasingly gained formal employment outside of the traditional context, the ability of older people to control the household and manage its resources has diminished, and, along with this, many of the precepts of *adat* that structured life in the traditional context have weakened to the point where they are no longer relevant to many younger individuals. The ability to earn money and acquire assets outside of the matrilineal system, with its restrictions on use and inheritance, seems to be very appealing to many younger Minangkabau, and success in the modern Indonesian context is more important to many of them than traditional considerations. This issue is frequently discussed in the West Sumatran media (see, for example, Padangtime 2015), as well as in the blogosphere.

These two issues, dramatically decreased dependence on the assets of the extended family and the lessened importance of certain aspects of *adat* to younger people, have meant that possible forms of behaviour that would have been considered unacceptable or impossible in the past are now becoming more viable to many Minangkabau. The type of care for the elderly afforded by the PSTW is one of these new alternatives. To many younger people, the potential social stigma associated with refusing to care for an elderly relative has lessened to the point where the placement of the older person in public care seems reasonable or even desirable. This is especially the case when the younger family member no longer lives in the village. Even for those who have remained in the village, the PSTW are part of the modern Indonesian context and do not fit into the traditional social constructs that still, to a significant extent, shape village life. There are no specific ideas about them, other than the traditional requirement that children respect and care for their elders in accordance with the rules of *adat*, a view which is always presented as being supported by religious values as well. For this reason, even younger people in the village may feel that placing a relative in one of the PSTW is more advantageous, despite the potential reaction of the community, because of the freedom it would afford them.

In some cases, the possibility of placing an elderly relative in institutionalized care represents a way for people living in the village to shift the balance of power within the family and circumvent the traditional structures that place control of family assets in the hands of older women. In the past, it would have been unthinkable for an older woman to be displaced in this way because of her absolute right to live in the family home and use its resources. This is not always the case today, however, and situations that represent extreme violations of *adat* are beginning to be seen. These cases, while still unusual, hint at some of the hidden problems within extended families that have probably always existed in the Minangkabau community. Historically, however, the only avenue available to alleviate such tensions was for the younger family members to leave the village. This was considered a more viable option for men but was sometimes available to younger women as well. At present, however, more of the conflicts that have always been present in life within the extended family are emerging into the open because there are increasingly more options available for all involved.

Amai

Amai is one of the seventy residents of PSTW Kasih Sayang Ibu run by the Department of Social Affairs in the town of Batusangkar and the newest. She had only been there for three months at the time of this writing. She was enjoying the friendships she had developed with other residents, and the room she was given as well as the other available facilities that are much better than her home some 20 kilometres away. She doesn't have to clean or cook. Everyone is friendly and understands her feelings, perhaps because they are in the same situation. The complex has its own mosque so she doesn't have to walk very far to get there, which she did in her village. Nonetheless, she is very unhappy at the old age home.

Despite the conveniences, Amai does not want to be at the PSTW. She had a house on the ancestral land where her family has lived for generations; she does not even know when they first came there because it was so long ago. She had enough land to support herself: rice fields, a vegetable garden, and fruit trees. Her own nuclear family is small. Her husband died some years ago, and all her sons left the village. There was only one daughter who lived with her in the village. Unfortunately, her daughter did not want her at home, which had devastated her. Amai's daughter told her she was a burden and was not contributing to the household. She could no longer do very much housework, sometimes dropped glasses or plates and broke them, and, her daughter said, it would be best if she did not live at home.

Amai's daughter often scolded her. The more the daughter told her to be careful so as not to break things, the more awkward and less able to do things around the house Amai became. Her daughter then scolded her for being lazy and not helping. This culminated in the daughter taking her to the old age home by trickery. Amai's daughter said she needed her mother's help to buy something in Batusangkar. They would usually shop for whatever they needed at a small market near their home. From the time she was young, Amai had rarely gone to Batusangkar because there was no need. She had never been to school and had no real reason to shop there. But she had heard about it, of course, from other people who went there often. She knew it was a much bigger place than her village.

Amai agreed reluctantly, even though she genuinely believed she would be helping her daughter. They went on a public minibus to the larger town. When they got off, Amai's daughter took her to a very large building that was bigger than any she had ever seen before. Her daughter led her into a room, which turned out to be an office. Amai did not know that at the time and waited while her daughter talked to a man who was working there. A few minutes later, before Amai realized what was happening, her daughter said that she was going to the market and Amai had to wait there. Before Amai could ask for an explanation, her daughter was gone. The man her daughter had spoken to earlier told her that the place was an old age home and that her daughter did not want her to live at home anymore. So, from then on, she would live there with other old people.

All Amai could do was cry. After a few days she told the director of the place that she did not like it there and wanted to go home. The director suggested that she consider whether it might not be better for her to stay where she was since her daughter no longer wanted her at home and had gone to great lengths to trick her. He also explained that similar things had happened to many of the people who were living in the facility. Their families no longer wanted to care for them so they had come to the institution. The other residents tried to console Amai and told her their own stories. But none of this made Amai feel better, and her health began to decline from not eating or sleeping.

Every day, Amai told the director that she wanted to go home. She didn't care, she said, what her daughter did to her. She just wanted to die in her own home where she had lived all her life. The director was worried about Amai's health and emotional state so he decided to take her home to the village. Her daughter was at home when they arrived, and the director explained how Amai felt. He felt the daughter reacted well; she was pleasant, friendly and said she understood. She told the director that she was willing to take her mother back. The director left feeling satisfied and relieved.

Amai, too, was happy because her daughter was now much nicer to her. She talked to her politely and no longer ordered her around. She would even ask if her mother needed anything. Amai felt very happy. After about two weeks the daughter said that they should go on an outing with a friend of hers who had a car and that they both needed a break from housework. They had lunch in a restaurant Amai liked. She really thought that her daughter now accepted her and would never try to make her leave home again.

They were out all day, and Amai greatly enjoyed the trip. By the end of the day, Amai was tired and fell asleep in the car. When her daughter woke her up, she thought they were home. She couldn't tell much about her surroundings because it was dark so she got out the car. Her daughter and the friend immediately got back in the car and left without her. The director of the old age home whom she knew well by now greeted her. In tears, she listened to what the director told her: that her daughter had called and said she was bringing Amai back to the home.

Despite feeling slightly more comfortable where she was, Amai could not stop crying as she told her story.

VIEWS ON INSTITUTIONALIZED CARE FOR OLDER PEOPLE IN THE MINANGKABAU COMMUNITY

The Minangkabau community sees itself as compassionate and concerned for the welfare of older people. The importance of these sentiments is embodied in traditional folklore as well as community values associated with ethnic heritage. The proverbs presented in Chapter 3 are examples of the nature of traditional thought on ageing and the elderly. However, as is the case in many societies, traditional values tend to be aspirational in Minangkabau society and reflect an ideal more than the actual behaviour of its members. Nonetheless, the culture's own narrative is extremely significant in people's self-perceived identity and the ways in which they behave and view their own and others' actions.

When asked about the presence of the PSTW in West Sumatra, many individuals who live in Padang and other parts of the province express shock and outrage that such institutions exist, even though they are located on main roads, clearly identified with signs that indicate what the complexes are and that they are run by the Department of Social Affairs, and have been in operation for some thirty years. This perhaps reflects the very deep-seated assumption on the part of many Minangkabau that extended families live in harmony and that children and other relatives are committed to caring for older people at home. This view, which is contradicted by the observable presence of the PSTW and the fact that they are full, can be seen as a form of resistance to the rapid social change that has been felt all over Indonesia for the past several decades, in which it is difficult for many people to accept that community behaviour and the realities of life in modern Indonesia are very different from those that are suggested by traditional cultural norms, especially when the reasons family members place older relatives in the PSTW are considered. It is also the case that many people likely know of situations within their own family or the family of another person where there were serious disagreements or feuds, where decisions were made and acted upon that violated *adat*, or where behaviour generally agreed to be socially unacceptable was tolerated by the relatives of those involved. When such things occurred, however, it has been the practice to keep them within the family as much as possible and try to prevent embarrassing or shameful situations from becoming part of public discussion. This was the case with Hamzah, whose conflict with his maternal uncle is described in Chapter 3 and who was eventually sent away from the village to prevent further shame to the family.

The disbelief that members of the community express when the PSTW are discussed is often accompanied by outrage that the need for such institutions can exist in the Minangkabau world where *adat* should be in force. The basis for their disapproval seems to be that the concept of caring for elderly relatives outside the family is in itself a violation of Minangkabau tradition. One user of the RantauNet newsgroup, an online discussion forum for Minang speakers all over Indonesia and elsewhere, expressed these feelings in a 2013 post:

> *Memasukkan Lansia ka panti sangat memalukan dan merugikan ... kenapa? Karena merawat orang tua sampai ajal menjemput adalah salah satu jalan menuju surga ... Pernah di kampuang kami ado ciek keluarga mamasuakan ortu e ka panti, padahal anak2 e mampu malah yg padusi ndak do karajo kecuali manyulam se di rumah ... yo heboh kampuang n akhirnyo dijapuik baliak ... Kok maleh maurus piti ado tingga sewa suster ... tp tantu suster yg masuak sarugo ndak? Antahlah .... maso di kampuang wak lah ilang raso tu?*

> [Putting an old person into a home is shameful and damaging ... why? Because taking care of an old person until their death is one way to get to Heaven. In our village, there was one family that put their parent in a home, even though the children had money and the daughter didn't even have a job, except doing embroidery from home. There was a commotion in the village and finally they brought the person back home. If they didn't feel like taking care of their relative, they had money to hire a nurse ...

but then it would surely be the nurse who went to Heaven, right? I don't
know ... how can it be that our village has lost its feelings?]

(Reni Sisri Yanti, RantauNet, 30 May 2013
<https://groups.google.com/forum/#!msg/
rantaunet/VlbHc7GPQI4/qcI4BvOI2ikJ>)

The story recounted by this online user indicates that pressure from others
in the village was strong enough to make the family described change
their mind and bring their elderly relative back home. This is also an
aim of the staff of the PSTW, who try to encourage the families of their
residents to come to some sort of agreement so that the old person can be
taken home. These arrangements can rarely be made, however, and most
of the residents of the PSTW remain there until their death. Nonetheless,
it is generally agreed within the community that it would be better if all
older people could remain in their own home with relatives rather than
having to rely on a public institution for care in old age.

The idea that there should be facilities that provide care for older
people is generally viewed as foreign to Minangkabau culture and is seen
by some as an unwanted, outside influence that should be addressed by
a revitalization of traditional values derived from *adat* and religion. One
of the proponents of this view is Governor Irwan Prayitno. Speaking at
one of the PSTW on National Old Age Day in 2015, the West Sumatran
governor's address was reported in the press as follows:

*Gubernur juga menyampaikan, di budaya ketimuran sebenarnya kita tidak
mengenal panti jompo, karena keluarga dan anak memiliki rasa kasih dan sayang
serta tuntunan budaya ketimuran. Sementara di Barat orang-orang lansia
memang berada di panti-panti jompo, karena itu merupakan budaya mereka.*

*Namun karena ini merupakan program terhadap sosial kemanusiaan masih
ada juga masyarakat kita mungkin karena kehidupan yang kurang beruntung,
terpaksa hidup di panti jompo ini. Mudah-mudahan bagi kita yang mampu,
sedapatnya tetap memperhatikan orang tua sebagai sebuah rasa kasih dan sayang
anak kepada orang tuanya.*

[The governor also said, in Eastern cultures, we actually do not have old
age homes because family members and children feel love and affection
[for the elderly] and are guided by Eastern cultural values. In the West,
older people do live in old age facilities because it is their culture.

> But, because this is a social-humanitarian programme, there still are
> people in our community, perhaps because they have been less fortunate
> in life, who are forced to live in old age homes. Hopefully, those of us
> who can afford to will continue to care for older people as a form of love
> and affection toward their parents.] (*Mata Rakyat*, 17 June 2015)

While there is some truth in the view that aged care facilities of various
kinds are an approach to the needs of the elderly that was developed in
the West, it is, of course, inaccurate to view them as an aspect of Western
culture that is accepted as such by communities in other countries. In
the West, very much like West Sumatra today, attitudes towards the
institutionalization of older people tend to be conflicted and complex, but
the longer history of such care facilities has brought a level of acceptance in
the community (see, for example, McAuley and Blieszner 1985; Biedenham
and Normoyle 1991; Sudha and Mutran 1999; Stuart and Weinrich 2001;
My Tse 2007). There are also important differences in the level of political
involvement and empowerment of older people in Indonesia, including
West Sumatra, and in the West.

The kind of lobbies and organizations that exist in many Western
countries to champion the needs of the elderly do not exist in Indonesia.
In fact, one of the most obvious characteristics of the residents of the
PSTW in West Sumatra is their powerlessness to decide what is best for
them. Speaking to residents of these facilities, it becomes apparent that
they are there because it was the wish of their children or other family
members, because the community in which they lived felt it was best for
them, or because they were taken to the facility by the authorities. Older
people who do not live with family tend to be seen as problematic in
the Minangkabau community and are not viewed favourably in terms of
their initiative to support themselves or in using personal agency to affect
their situation. Instead, older individuals themselves expect to defer to
their younger relatives and especially children, as in the case of Nurijah,
described in Chapter 2, who was forced to live with one of her daughters
in Jakarta because of poor health, despite her extremely strong desire to
remain in the village. Younger people expect this as well and assume, at
some point, they will be the ones making decisions for older relatives.

This perception of the appropriate role and position of older people in
Minangkabau society is embodied in traditional literature and is epitomized
by the proverb used as the title of this book. The expression, "The elderly

must endure", refers to the idea that older people are forced to accept the ways in which younger people behave, even if it is unpleasant to them, because that is the socially appropriate role for them. At the same time, the Minangkabau community tends to perceive older people as potentially critical and difficult but essentially passive and increasingly unable to make wise decisions or determine what is best for themselves. This would seem to conflict with the traditional roles for older people, as the decision-makers in extended families, but, in the more modern Minangkabau context, in which the traditional patterns supported by *adat* are less significant, this view seems more relevant. It is also the case that many older people accept this view of themselves in order to smooth relations with their children and remain part of their families.

This perception of older people is very much the norm within the PSTW, where staff tend to be kind to residents but also treat them as if they are incapable of making decisions, even about their daily activities, and do not have much reasoning ability. Like their Western counterparts, the PSTW have a range of activities that residents take part in. Some of these are compatible with the social norms for older people in the Minangkabau community. For example, each PSTW has its own mosque and encourages residents to pray there as well as to take part in Quranic study groups and religious instruction classes. Many of the activities at the PSTW, however, come from outside the Minangkabau context and represent attempts to engage the residents while encouraging them to be physically and mentally active. These include exercise classes (*senam lansia*), traditional dance instruction, and crafts activities. PSTW Sabai nan Aluih has set up a day care programme for the elderly who live in the surrounding community, within which these individuals can take part in the activities offered at the facility and then return home at night. This programme is part of an initiative of the Ministry of Social Affairs to help families where the younger members are at work all day to continue to care for older relatives at home (Hermana 2008).

The public's reaction to these kinds of activities and programmes intended to enhance the well-being of the older people living in old age facilities also indicates the internal conflict many feel about the best way to manage the growing problems of an ageing population. On the one hand, many people accept the need for new approaches in this area, but, on the other, they feel uncomfortable with the initiatives that have been adopted, many of which do come from experience in the West. One user of the RantauNet discussion forum expressed his feelings upon learning about the existence of nursing homes and their activities in West Sumatra as follows:

Baa sabananyo arati "Panti Jompo"? Iko indak istilah di Kampuang Awak doh kan?

MakNgah caliak-caliak di video ko tampak urang gaek-gaek manari dielo-elo dek anak-anak mudo. Ibo awak saroman gaek-gaek tu lansia-lansia tapaso. Nan maraso bahagia tampaknyo batapuak tangan adolah anak-anak mudo tu. Nan gaek-gaek lansia tu tampaknyo tabawo sato-sato lo batapuak tangan karano diajak diojoh-ojohan dek nan mudo-mudo sabagai pamenan ...

[What is the actual meaning of "Panti Jompo" [nursing home]? This term is not something we know in our village, is it?

I saw a video of some old people dancing and being pulled back and forth by some youngsters. It made me sad to see these old people who seemed to be forced [to do this]. The ones who seemed happy and were clapping their hands were the young people. The old people looked like they were just going along with it and clapping their hands because the younger ones teased them into doing so, like in a game ...]

(Sjamsir Sjarif, RantauNet, 30 May 2013
<https://groups.google.com/forum/#!msg/
rantaunet/VlbHc7GPQI4/qcI4BvOI2ikJ>)

Another user, discussing this same situation, noted how unusual it was for there to be no one at home in the village as minding the house was something older people with limited mobility could do while younger people were out working. This individual compared his own feelings of loss after the death of his mother with the practice of institutionalizing older people, stating:

Kalau bantuak itu nan tajadi, iyo anak cilako tu mah.

Sungguahpun ado adiak jo uni ambo tingga dikampuang, namun babeda juo rasono pulang kampuang kutiko rang gaek (Amak) ambo masih iduik. Sapakan sasudah Amak ambo mandahulu, ambo pulang kakampuang baliak, nan tadapek-i. pintu rumah basaok, karano kabatulan adiak jo uni sadang balanjo ka pakan. Kutiko itu iyo badarai aia mato.

[If this is what happens, those children [who place their parents in a home for the aged] are terrible.

Even though I have an older and younger sister in the village, it still felt different when I would go home when my parents (Mother) were still alive. After Mother died and I went to the village again, what I found was that the door was closed because my sisters were shopping at the market. It made me cry.]

(Z. Bandaro, RantauNet, 30 May 2013
<https://groups.google.com/forum/#!msg/
rantaunet/VlbHc7GPQI4/qcI4BvOI2ikJ>)

The metaphor of the door to a house in the village being closed or locked is very strong in Minangkabau culture and represents an undesirable situation when no one is home to receive visitors and manage the home. It also symbolizes the perception that population loss in rural areas is increasing and the loneliness that this connotes in a society that traditionally values group participation and a communal lifestyle. In the past, houses, especially in rural areas, were almost never empty and, even today, many people feel very uneasy if everyone has to be out at the same time.

The existence of PSTW in West Sumatra has also contributed to the appearance of new situations for which there are few precedents. One of these relates to the management of end of life issues for the residents of these facilities. Traditionally, most Minangkabau have died at home, among their family, and have been buried on family land. In the villages, many extended families or clans have maintained burial grounds where family members would be interred. There is no uneasiness about locating family graves adjacent to current living areas. Many Minangkabau feel strongly that they wish to be buried on their family land or near the graves of other family members. This has long been troubling to those living in the *rantau*, and the sorrow associated with dying away from the village is expressed in a number of Minang popular songs, such as *Nasib Kayu Lapuak* [The Fate of a Piece of Rotting Wood] by Harry Parintang that has been recorded by a number of singers. Its lyrics include:

Tangiang sayuik saluang maibo-ibo
Kampuang halaman ranah Minang maimbau
Sadangnyo untuang di rantau balun lai mujua
Susah datang batimpo-timpo ...

Yo ... malang
Bakubua mati di rantau urang

[I can hear the sorrowful echo of the *saluang* [a type of traditional flute],
My home in the Minang lands is calling me.
Good fortune has been hard to find in the *rantau*,
Troubles come one after the other ...

Oh ... how unfortunate it is
To die and be buried in someone else's land.]

As noted, to the extent possible, older Minangkabau who have no option but to rely on public institutions like the PSTW are housed near to their village of origin. The aim of this is to support reconciliation with family but also to allow them to maintain a connection with their home. Most of the residents remain at the PSTW until they die, which, as might be expected, is a common occurrence in these facilities. While the management feels it would be better for the residents to be buried at home near their family, in practice, it falls to the institution to handle the burial arrangements for most of the residents. As a result, one of the major problems facing them is getting enough land adjacent to the premises to use for this purpose. The PSTW are subject to the same constraints in purchasing land that affect business expansion and government infrastructure projects, however, making it difficult to fulfil this need.

The vast majority of residents in West Sumatra's PSTW are from the province and are of Minangkabau background. Within the facilities, they often recreate the social conditions of the villages they come from as much as possible. The same type of age-based hierarchies that exist in the community in general are also observable among the residents of the PSTW. Terms of address used in Minang often indicate age relative to the speaker as well as the social status of the person addressed, and these are used by residents in speaking to each other. The residents of the PSTW generally know each other's background and are aware of the events that led to them coming to live at the facility. Marriages between residents are not uncommon but are not encouraged by the management because they disrupt living arrangements that are segregated by gender, and married couples must be given a room together. Nonetheless, marriages do occur between the residents from time to time.

Minangkabau culture is communal by nature, and most people prefer to be part of a group, to have others to talk to and socialize with, and to avoid being alone. For this reason, the environment of the PSTW, where the residents share living space and participate in a variety of group activities, fits well with the social needs of those involved. While limited, in the sense that the majority of interaction takes place among the elderly residents or with the professional staff of the facility and the students on clinical placement, many of the residents feel that the social environment is as important to them as the fact that their basic needs for food and shelter are met. They are generally on good terms with each other and willing to try to get along with others. The social desirability of suppressing quarrels and managing one's emotions for the good of the group has been noted in other contexts for Minangkabau society (see, for example, Heider 2006). Despite their rivalries and competition, the fact that the residents of the PSTW generally come from the same background facilitates their ability and willingness to live together.

For this reason, the PSTW environment may be especially difficult for any resident who does not come from a Minangkabau background and, for whatever reason, cannot be placed in a facility closer to their place of origin. In situations of this kind, the nature of the residents' community may magnify cultural and linguistic differences that exist in Indonesian society in general and makes it essential that staff have sufficient understanding of the local cultural and linguistic context which tends to be more important to older people than it may have been at younger ages.

Suharni

When Suharni was taken to the PSTW in Sicincin more than six years ago, the staff estimated she was about seventy years old and was suffering from serious memory impairment related to senile dementia. She does not know when exactly she was born but is unusual among the residents of the facility because she is not Minangkabau. Suharni knows she came from Java but no longer remembers the name of the town she comes from or how exactly she came to be in this part of the country.

Suharni was taken to the PSTW by a police officer who had been watching her for several days as she wandered around a restaurant in the town of Padang Panjang, about 30 kilometres from Sicincin. The officer was concerned because the old woman seemed to be homeless and was clearly confused and unable to communicate. He made the decision to take her to the facility in Sicincin one night when he found her sleeping outside a store. He discovered she was unable to answer even the simplest questions about who she was, where she came from, and how she got to Padang Panjang. She knew her name and told him she was from Java but was unable to provide much more information. When questioned further, Suharni said she thought she came from Central Java but did not know the town. She said that she used to live in Padang but did not know how she got to Padang Panjang. The police officer was convinced that the best and safest place for her would be the PSTW in Sicincin and took her there himself.

While the facility is generally intended for people from the area, the director did not hesitate to accept Suharni, hoping that it might be possible to locate her family. While she was physically capable of taking care of herself, she could not live independently because of her mental and psychological state. One of her difficulties was the inability to communicate fully in a single language; she used a mixture of Minang, Indonesian, and Javanese that was very hard for people to understand.

When asked about her life after having been at the PSTW for several years, Suharni still could not say much more, even though she now had some stability in her daily life and was viewed as doing better cognitively. She did remember a few details although they remained vague. She had come to West Sumatra to work, she said, but could not say when and under what circumstances. She said she worked in Padang but did not know where. Her job involved washing dishes on occasion and doing laundry at other times, but Suharni could not say whether this was at a restaurant, in someone's home, or at a hotel or some other type of business. She did not know how long she had been in West Sumatra. The director of the PSTW thought Suharni might have been a servant brought to West Sumatra from Java by her employer. Java has a traditional servant class, and many young women from rural areas work as household maids.

Suharni is not the only resident of the PSTW in Sicincin who is suffering from dementia and was found in a public place by the police or members of the public. In fact, there were six such individuals at this facility. When an older person who cannot recall where they are from is brought to the PSTW, the director tries to locate relatives in the surrounding community. In three of the other five cases, family members were located, but they chose to have their older relative remain at the PSTW, and, in all cases, the management agreed. In the remaining two cases, the director could not locate the families in this way, so all available information about the individuals in question along with a picture was put on Facebook. The families had been looking for the missing individuals, recognized the pictures, and came to take these two old people back home. They had apparently left home and become confused and were unable to tell anyone where they lived or the name of their relatives.

The director of the PSTW in Sicincin tried to find Suharni's family through Facebook but failed. He concludes that her family may have lost contact with her years ago and hence is not looking for her.

THE NEED FOR INSTITUTIONALIZED CARE IN WEST SUMATRA

The PSTW in West Sumatra, while now well established, have grown from facilities housing a handful of older people, who genuinely had no family or means of support, to large institutions with numerous staff members that cannot accommodate all of the elderly who need support. There is no doubt that they symbolize a growing need that is characteristic of modern life in West Sumatra. At present, in addition to the PSTW, a number of indigent elderly people are housed in other public institutions intended to serve people with disabilities or individuals who are homeless of all ages. These institutions lack the specialized support required by many older people as they age and are not set up to provide the necessary level of health care.

The rapid growth of the PSTW in West Sumatra is notable and concerning for the regional and provincial governments, as well as for political leaders. In 2008, Deputy Head of the Provincial Department of Social Affairs, Ahmad Charisma, was quoted as saying that there were only two to five residents in PSTW in 2002, but, by 2008, the figure had risen to fifty people. Today, PSTW Sabai nan Aluih and PSTW Kasih Sayang Ibu, as well as PSTW Syekh Burhanuddin in the town of Pariaman and PSTW Kasih Ibu in the town of Payakumbuh, are over-full. The two smaller PSTW in Pariaman and Payakumbuh have a capacity of 30 people each, while, as noted, PSTW Sabai nan Aluih can accommodate 110 residents, and PSTW Kasih Sayang Ibu can house 70 more. The situation is most serious in the Lima Puluh Kota region where the town of Payakumbuh is located, as there are known to be a large number of neglected elderly (*lansia terlantar*) living there who require support (Nanda 2016). This situation has even gained some attention on national television (see Viva News 2016).

There can be no doubt that the need for facilities to provide care for elderly Minangkabau whose families cannot do so will continue to increase in the future. It is also likely that the current discussion of the appropriateness of public institutions playing a role in this in West Sumatra will remain unresolved. This conflict is a reflection of changing social and cultural norms in response to the national social and cultural context that all Minangkabau are part of to some degree and which is increasingly significant in shaping the experience of members of the community, especially those who have benefited from more formal education, work in the formal sector, and are increasingly coming into the responsibility of ensuring the welfare of older relatives.

10

Ageing and Cultural Consonance

CULTURAL CONSONANCE

Cultural consonance relates to expectations an individual has for his or her own experience. Specifically, the concept refers to the degree to which a person's situation conforms to what he or she anticipated. This anticipation is often unconscious and relates to cultural norms and practices that were absorbed and learned from infancy. This understanding of cultural practices is closely associated with language (a means by which culture is transmitted) and allows a person to fit into and participate in his or her native society. Often people are not aware of their cultural expectations or how the fact of these expectations not being met might affect them, but they are very much aware of the impact of the lack of consonance, especially when it begins to affect physical or mental health.

The concept of cultural consonance was introduced by Dressler and colleagues (Dressler et al. 2005*a*; Dressler et al. 2005*b*) which they define as the extent to which the beliefs, perceptions and behaviour of individuals accord with prototypes that exist within their culture. The underlying assumption is that individuals wish to act in ways established by their culture of origin but may be unable to do so because of the context in which they live. This creates a source of stress that may manifest in physical disease or psychological distress. Dressler (2005), for example, found that higher levels of cultural consonance were associated with lower blood pressure and greater well-being in a number of studies. Similar results were obtained when cultural consonance was considered for various populations in several different locations (see, for example, Dressler and Bindon 2000).

The meaning of culture applied in the study of cultural consonance is of a body of knowledge that is learned and shared by individuals but that also has a location in a specific group of interest. In this, culture is assumed to be "distributed" (Sperber 1985) and to represent the body of shared learning that is required to function effectively within the social group (Goodenough 1996). Dressler et al. (2007) note that the distribution of cultural knowledge within a given group may vary, with culture potentially being shared by most members or by only a few, concentrated in one or several sub-groups, or widely distributed across society such that there exists a high level of both sharing and agreement. In practice, this means that some individuals may not possess a very detailed conscious knowledge of culture but nonetheless have a very clear sense of the collective aspects of culturally accepted behaviour (D'Andrade 1984; Searle 1995). This exemplifies the distributed nature of culture, which is an aggregate of characteristics of a particular group while also residing within individual members (Jaskyte and Dressler 2004; Atran, Medin and Ross 2005).

Every group then is assumed to have a cultural model that denotes the shared information that defines the characteristic perspective of members in terms of various elements and their relationships to each other (see, for example, D'Andrade 1992; Strauss and Quinn 1997; Romney and Moore 1998). The degree of sharing of this cultural framework by members of a society can be evaluated using the cultural consensus model developed by Romney, Weller and Batchelder (1986), which allows cultural interpretations of individual members of society to be compared with a cultural model for the group to determine the degree of fit with the aggregate model. This approach has a number of advantages that include the ability to evaluate the extent of sharing of cultural knowledge among members of a group of interest; the level of consensus can be quantified, and high-consensus and low-consensus domains can be identified; intragroup diversity can be measured using a calculated cultural competence coefficient; and the level of reliability and generalizability of specific aspects of the culture can be determined (see Handwerker 2001). However, cultural consonance is often most significant in its absence. Dressler and colleagues have suggested that a lack of cultural consonance may represent a chronically stressful situation in which an individual may experience psychological dissonance because he or she is aware that his or her actions do not accord with accepted cultural norms and/or because he or she may experience social sanctions in the course of interaction with other members of the group (see Dressler et al. 2007). This situation, in turn, may result in poorer health that manifests in both physical and psychological symptoms.

A difficulty with this way of describing the nature and effects of cultural consonance is that it implies that the individual may have, in some way, chosen to behave in ways that do not accord with the shared cultural norms for his or her society. While this does not preclude the existence of various constraints that may dictate individual behaviour in certain social contexts, it is important to note that social and cultural behaviours may be dictated by a context that eliminates certain possible behaviours such that "choice" is restricted or nonexistent. In other words, an individual who would prefer to act in a way that is more consistent with the cultural model of his or her group may be unable to because of the nature of the social context in which he or she lives. In this way, behaviour may be limited by forces and circumstances the individual is unable to alter, forcing a loss of cultural consonance that is unintentional and unexpected from the point of view of the person involved. In considering cultural consonance issues among older members of the Minangkabau community, this dimension is central and has resulted from rapid social change in Indonesia over the past several decades that was outside the ability of any individual or group to anticipate or stem.

The cultural consonance model presumes that a lack of consonance, as perceived by individuals in the context of their native culture, represents a prolonged source of stress that is distinct from the types of acute stress associated with specific events or experiences. This, as discussed by Dressler and colleagues (2000, 2005a, 2005b, 2007), may result in clinical symptoms that can be measured empirically and that link cultural experience to physical and psychological health. While this study of older Minangkabau did not include the measurement of blood pressure or other clinical variables, it did focus on the perceptions of the people involved and the experiential dimension of ageing in modern Indonesian society. The increasing prevalence of depression as a concern among the elderly population in Indonesia and West Sumatra is noted above and suggests that a replication of the methodology of Dressler and colleagues might further elucidate the contribution of cultural consonance to the often cited incidence of chronic illness among older Minangkabau in addition to lifestyle factors, such as diet, exercise and smoking behaviour, that are better understood.

THE MINANGKABAU CULTURAL MODEL

The cultural model of the Minangkabau community has been discussed by several authors. Navis (1984), for example, considers several major domains of Minangkabau culture that include the extended family, religion, and *adat*. A more complete discussion focusing on the precepts of *adat* can be found in Hakimy (1984, 1988, 1991). A different approach to elucidating the Minangkabau cultural model was taken by Fanany and Fanany (2003) who use the body of proverbs current in the modern community to elaborate networks of meaning as well as the predominant values that structure interpretation. The specific cultural model relating to health is discussed by Tas'ady, Fanany and Fanany (2012), Fanany and Fanany (2015) and was extended to include cultural consonance issues among older people by Fanany, Fanany and Tas'ady (2014).

Across the Minangkabau community, wherever its members are, there are a number of shared elements that are widely agreed to characterize the culture of the group. Several of these elements are generally known in Indonesia and are seen as identifying Minangkabau individuals and the group as a whole among the nation's hundreds of local cultures. Several of these shared aspects of culture have been discussed above and include the matrilineal social structure of the group with its many sub-elements; the practice of *marantau* and its potential value to the community; and use of the Minang language. Minangkabau culture is also felt by its members to be intimately associated with Islam. In this, however, the Minangkabau are part of Indonesia's religious majority and do not have specific beliefs that are significantly different from those of other groups whose members are also Muslim. In other words, while adherence to Islam is an aspect of a shared Minangkabau culture, the way in which the religion is understood and practised is not distinctive, except in that the community is viewed as being among the more religious of Indonesia's ethnic groups. By contrast, their matrilineal social structure is unique. This is agreed upon by all Minangkabau to be the central element of their shared culture and the one that is most fundamental to their self- perception as a member of the ethnic group.

As discussed in Chapter 3, Minangkabau *adat* that outlines the structures of their matrilineal social structure is ancient and deeply rooted in the community. Nonetheless, despite an idea that *adat* is eternal and applies to all times and generations, there are aspects of the traditional conceptualization of culture that are less significant today than in the past and others that are fading as the existence of alternatives deriving from the modern Indonesian nation becomes more apparent and present, even at the village level. Examples of these include a decreasing role for the maternal uncle (*mamak*) in the life of his nieces and nephews and the willingness of some extended families to mortgage family land for a variety of reasons beyond those considered traditionally acceptable or even to sell it. In addition, a number of social practices that were highly desirable in the past are increasingly uncommon, such as marriage between first cousins to solidify relationships between extended families.

Nonetheless, there are also principles of *adat* that are seen by Minangkabau as immutable. These principles form the basis of the community's shared culture and represent the salient features of group experience. These include membership in the family of one's mother and the position of women as the heads of families; an enduring bond between each individual and a village where the extended family's land is located; communal ownership of family land at the level of the extended family; and the different rights of men and women in the use of family property. In addition, the Minangkabau community shares a very strong food and dress culture, as well as a set of values that reflect the ways in which members wish to see themselves and their community.

Values are less tangible than other forms of shared culture and are also subject to change over time. The most dominant shared values of the Minangkabau community are described by Fanany and Fanany (2003), who discuss their often aspirational nature in detail. Among the most deeply held values in the current community are respect for the dictates of *adat* and the matrilineal system, the primacy of the family above all other kinds of relationships, the requirement for children to respect and support parents, and real property as the most valuable asset an individual or family might have. Respect for the elderly and their placement in a position of seniority and honour within society and the family is seen as deriving from *adat*, and for parents specifically from religion, and representing an important value that supports the functioning of the community. The corollary view is that failure to do this is a sign of betrayal on the part of children (*anak durako*, see Chapter 6) and, by metaphorical extension, of society. This is the basis for the public concern and outcry over the need for institutions to care for the elderly and, especially, the demand for such institutions in the Minangkabau community.

From the point of view of the elderly themselves, this shared culture forms the comparison by which their current experience is measured. Needless to say, this applies to every member of Minangkabau society but may be more significant among older people because their introduction to the culture of the community occurred in their childhood which took place prior to the period of rapid social change that has shaped modern Indonesian society. The changes related to modernization implemented by the New Order government (1965–98), coupled with increasing urbanization nationwide and increased exposure to globalized social and cultural influences, especially since 2001 when regional autonomy was put into place, have contributed to shifting values and changed experience relative to the past, especially for younger people born during these times. For people now aged over sixty, their observations of older relatives during their own childhood and youth no longer fit with their current experiences and perceptions, and it is this gap that reflects a widely observed lack of cultural consonance.

Numerous examples of how this shift occurred can be observed in West Sumatra and the Minangkabau community in general. Many of these relate to the agricultural cycle which is one of the basic elements of the culture in traditional form. Fifty years ago, rice was harvested once a year in West Sumatra, and the harvest period was a major event that required the participation of everyone at the village level and also people who might have been living in Padang or other parts of the province. Extended families that had a great deal of land needed a lot of people who could help with the work of harvesting, and this was an especially exciting time for children, who would be allowed to help and take part in the festivities. Relatives who were living in Padang would be expected to visit during this time and take part in some of the work. The Valley family, whose members are described throughout this book, was one of the families in Koto that owned a large amount of productive land. At harvest time, the Valley would be full of people doing various kinds of work. Some of them were hired hands who would be paid a wage. Others were distant relatives and members of the same clan who worked on the family's land in exchange for help on their own land when the time came. This type of agreement, which is not limited to members of the extended family, is called *julo-julo* in Minang and is one of many traditional agricultural practices that have largely died out (see Uker and Fanany 2011). The harvest was a period of great activity that could last for up to two months and involved harvesting the rice, winnowing, drying, and storage of the grain. The quality and quantity of the harvest would set the family's economic position for the coming year. This event served to strengthen ties between branches of the extended family and among people living in the village and reinforced the importance of productive land in the cultural model that governed life in the village.

Beginning in the 1970s, however, as part of national development initiatives across sectors, West Sumatra took part in a programme to increase the rice harvest and make multiple plantings possible through the use of modern fertilizers and pesticides. The aim of this programme was to increase rice production with the aim of Indonesia becoming self-sufficient, a goal that was achieved by the New Order government in 1984 (Pratomo 2015). Once it became possible to achieve two harvests a year, the importance of the event began to decline and, with it, the social significance of this period began to fade. At present, three or even four harvests are felt to be possible (Dinas Pertanian dan Perkebunan 2014). While the agricultural cycle, whose work is done in a labour-intensive, low-technology manner in West Sumatra, remains important, it no longer has the significance it did in the past when it was an annual event. At present, the rice harvest is still important to the members of the Valley family in that ownership of land and having one's own supply of rice is still an important element of cultural understanding, but the harvest itself is barely remarked upon, and the family members in the village hire people to do much of the work under the supervision of the older women who head the family.

For people who are now over sixty and took part in village events like the rice harvest, the social change described above is very noticeable upon reflection, even though it occurred gradually over a number of years. Without the event the annual rice harvest created, there is much less need to maintain the complex social networks within and between extended families that supported the type of work-for-work systems of the past and also greatly reduced the need for social and cultural practices intended to ensure courteous relationships between those involved. A comparable decline has occurred in relation to other social and cultural events, such as the customary and mandatory visits to family on one's father's side towards the end of the fasting month of Ramadan, also intended to maintain a good relationship between extended families in the village. While changes in social practices of this kind are easily observable, it is important to note that they are the surface manifestation of changes in *adat* that are more fundamental. The willingness to allow certain elements of *adat* to vanish suggests that the alternatives afforded by the modern context are more attractive to many Minangkabau and that some aspects of *adat* are no longer relevant in their daily life. This represents a dilemma for many older people who have difficulty reconciling this fact with the reality of their own experience. On the one hand, they generally believe strongly that *adat* in its more traditional form should be maintained along with its complex set of values and behaviours, but, on the other, acknowledge that their personal situation would not allow them to participate fully, and they benefit more from modern employment and lifestyle than they would from a more traditional existence in the village.

Muhammad

Muhammad, the husband of Aminah's third daughter Erni (Chapter 3), who died in 2011 at the age of eighty, spent a significant amount of his time at his mother's house, even though he did not have any sisters. His mother did have sisters with children, including daughters, with whom Muhammad had a very good relationship. He would make sure that his children knew what custom and tradition required of them in relation to his extended family, the children's *bako*. *Bako*, the extended family of one's father, have a special place in various traditional activities, such as rituals relating to marriage and religious practices such as fasting. Muhammad wanted his children to maintain these customs and practise them as was traditional in Koto. When the children were little, he would take them to his mother's house as well as her sisters' homes when such visits were socially appropriate, often on religious holidays. When the children were old enough to go there themselves, he would encourage them to do so. He would remind them on the eve of the celebration and check the next day to make sure they had done what they were supposed to.

Because of Muhammad's efforts, his children had a good relationship with his relatives, as was the case with most families in the village at the time. Some of his children, particularly the boys, would spend some nights at his mother's house together with the children of his brother (Muhammad had only the one brother and no sisters) and the children of his mother's sisters. When his children reached junior high school, they spent more time at his mother's house with the other children. Muhammad's parents enjoyed this greatly because there were only the two of them in the house. As a result, Muhammad's children became very close to his extended family. At some point, the family contemplated that at least one of Muhammad's sons should marry a daughter of one of his mother's sisters. A marriage of this type is considered desirable in Minangkabau. As it turned out, all five of Muhammad's sons earned at least an undergraduate degree, and four of them had postgraduate degrees as well. None of the daughters of Muhammad's cousins went to college however. These cousins pressed Muhammad to persuade one of his sons to marry one of their daughters, but none were willing to. This caused some bad feeling in the families that has persisted up to the present time.

While this type of marriage was common in Minangkabau society and still does occur today, it has become increasingly rare. In the Valley family itself, for example, one of Aminah's brothers married a daughter of one of their father's sisters, and this had taken place in every previous generation of the extended family. Similarly, one of Aminah's sons married a daughter of one of her brothers. But there were no unions of this kind in subsequent generations. None of the children of her daughters married a child of her sons. So it was not entirely surprising that none of Muhammad's sons wanted to marry one of their cousins, but, in this case, Muhammad's family felt his sons rejected their daughters because they were not as well educated as their prospective husbands. This was the root of the problems between the families.

By the time Muhammad's children were all married and had children of their own, the tradition of visiting one's father's family had changed. While it was still expected and practised, these visits no longer had the kind of significance they did in the past. In those old days, Muhammad and his extended family would keep bringing it up for months if one of the children failed to visit. These social consequences had largely disappeared by the time Muhammad's grandchildren were born. As a result, such visits became less frequent, not just among the Valley family but in the whole village of Koto. This did not mean, however, that the expectation no longer existed.

After Muhammad's parents died, he visited his extended family much less because no one lived in his parents' house anymore. He might go there every now and then to care for their graves which were near the house and would stop at his cousins' houses, but their relationship was not as close as it was when their children were little and played and studied together. Their connection had become much shallower, more superficial and formal, and less intimate.

When his wife died, Muhammad's life changed dramatically as described in Chapter 4. There is little doubt that one of the reasons he did not return to his extended family was because of the changing nature of his relationship with them. If one of his sons had married one of his cousins' daughters, the situation would almost certainly have been different, and he could have returned to them when his wife died. Staying at his wife's house after her death was unusual at the time and still is, especially if a man lives in his own village and has female relatives. This caused Muhammad considerable stress and unhappiness, even though he found a way to adjust to his situation.

CHANGES TO THE PERCEPTION OF
THE EXTENDED FAMILY

Older members of the Minangkabau community generally grew up in close proximity to members of their extended family, often in the context of the village. From a very young age, they were introduced to the social practices of the village that reflected the nature of their relationship to others and long-standing connections between extended families. An understanding of these conventions and participation in the social network was vital because, sixty or more years ago, family land was the main source of income and support in the Minangkabau community, and opportunities associated with modern education were few and out of reach for the majority of individuals. It was common for young men, especially, to leave the community to work in another location, but travel was difficult, time consuming, and expensive. For this reason, leaving the village was a more serious choice than it is today as well as one that attracted greater interest.

Because the role of extended families in the village was generally much greater when today's older people were children, the position of the older people they knew (grandparents, great aunts and uncles, and so forth) was much more significant in the extended family. As in the case of

Aminah and Kamil, whose stories are told in Chapter 2, *adat* outlined a role for older people of both sexes that the elderly often did play because younger people had very few alternatives than to participate in village society as a member of their mother's extended family. Their livelihood often depended on family assets, so they had little choice but to uphold the traditional social structures if they wanted to benefit from them. If they chose not to, the implications might be very severe, as in the case of Hamzah (Chapter 3) who was banished from the village because of his defiance of his maternal uncle.

As a result, most older Minangkabau grew up in close proximity to their older relatives and were expected to maintain close relationships with them, especially those in their mother's line. Having been part of this type of family as children, most of today's older people expected to experience a similar situation in their later years. In other words, the majority of older Minangkabau hope and would greatly prefer to live with or near their children and grandchildren and be an integral part of their lives. Even those individuals, such as Muhsin (Chapter 7), who themselves have enjoyed a modern career away from the village and have considerable personal assets accrued outside the traditional system wish to be surrounded by children and grandchildren. Rosni, Muhsin's wife (Chapter 7), for example, has very much recreated a more typical form of Minangkabau family in Padang with herself as its head. Now that she is retired, she spends much of her time managing her daughters and their children and has provided most of the day-to-day care her grandchildren have needed since their birth.

Many older Minangkabau, however, are not in this position. It is very common for young people in Indonesia today to move away from their parents to attend college or to take a job. This reflects the mobility that has accompanied rising income and higher levels of education but is also a result of regional autonomy that has created opportunities across the nation. Under the highly centralized New Order government, Jakarta was very much the centre of opportunity and the location most aspired to by those with more ambition, skill, and training. Today, despite the continuing problem of high unemployment, social and political change associated with regional autonomy has resulted in an increased number of people working in wage-earning positions across Indonesia, with an accompanying decrease in informal sector employment, as well as a greater distribution of jobs, especially in regions outside of Java (Allen

2016). In West Sumatra, it has not been uncommon, since the inception of regional autonomy, for prominent Minangkabau who have been successful elsewhere to return to the province to enter regional politics. Many of these individuals do not give up their position and residence in the *rantau* but do try to take advantage of the new opportunities available under regional autonomy and the edge people from a region have in the political environment.

This shift in employment opportunities as well as the increasing importance of further education means that many older Minangkabau do not live in the same general location as their adult children, regardless of whether those elderly people are in the village, in Padang, or elsewhere in the *rantau*. This is by no means a situation unique to the Minangkabau but instead reflects a characteristic of the modern Indonesian context. Even those who do live with or near their children and grandchildren typically have a much smaller circle of family members they are in direct contact than was the norm in the past. While a certain amount of interaction with members of the extended family can be maintained through the use of technology, increasing numbers of older people are living in nuclear families, often with only a spouse.

The traditional role for older people, in its ideal form, places elderly men and women in a position of respect and authority within the extended family. Typically, this provides a source of identity as well as a sense of purpose for older people, and traditional values as well as customary social practices suggest that older people are an important influence on children and youth in their formative years. Without this, many older Minangkabau feel the later part of their life has little social value to their family and they do not have the status they associate with the experience of their own grandparents and other elderly relatives they knew. This is particularly significant to those who are now retired and who, for many years, were part of the formal workforce and whose identity derived in large part from this source. Even older women, who lived their whole life in the village, may find that the position of authority they often expected to occupy in older age is not available to them because their extended family in the village is much smaller than in the past, and those members who do live there have other options that have reduced their dependence on the traditional social structure. This may result in a failure of younger people to recognize the traditional status of the older person, and, in the most extreme circumstance, lead to a forced removal of the elder from the village context. This is what happened in the case of Amai (Chapter 9), who was placed in an old age home by her daughter who was living on family land in the village. Identity issues among older people have been recognized in many communities (see, for example, Gubrium and Holstein 2008) but have not been studied in Indonesia, despite indications that this may be an important factor in the rising incidence of depression among older people.

The lack of an identity as an elder in the traditional context is a serious challenge to cultural consonance for many older Minangkabau. Traditionally, older people were expected to help guide the younger generation in making decisions beneficial to themselves as well as to the extended family and also to contribute significantly to decision-making at the family level. Whether or not an older individual feels that he or she benefitted from the advice of older relatives, most Minangkabau do expect to play this role at some time in their life and feel very strongly if they are unable to influence the actions of children and grandchildren. A common complaint from older Minangkabau, wherever they are and regardless of the relationship they have with children and grandchildren, is that these younger relatives do not ask for or value their advice. Many older people are resigned to this situation but generally do not accept that their views may seem irrelevant to their children or that they do not fully understand the problems of the next generation. Because of a strong desire to transmit their cultural values to younger relatives and for their children to share their views on the importance of the family and traditional context, this can be especially distressing to older Minangkabau. Without the support of the extended family and the reinforcement provided by traditional social structures, however, there is typically little they can do to influence the actions of their younger family members.

Malik and Hasanah

Malik (Chapter 7) and Hasanah are grandchildren of Aminah. Malik is the third son of Aminah's third daughter and now lives in Padang with his wife and children. Hasanah is the second daughter of Aminah's youngest daughter and now lives in Singosari, East Java. Both Malik and Hasanah are now retired, he from a position in the regional health department and she from a career as a low-ranking army officer. They are both in their early sixties. Malik is married to a woman from a village near Batusangkar, while Hasanah is married to a Javanese man.

Malik is one of Aminah's many grandsons. There is nothing remarkable about him in terms of his relationship with the extended family. Because his wife is also Minangkabau and comes from a nearby village means that his extended family knows a lot about him and especially about his wife. The two families interact regularly, even though this contact is limited to rituals associated with *adat* and events such as weddings, circumcisions, celebrations at the end of the fasting month, and funerals. Malik's family views his children as part of his wife's family and has limited contact with them.

Hasanah, however, has remained in close contact with the extended family in Koto, even though she lives outside the Minangkabau world and rarely returns to the village because of distance and cost and also because her husband comes from another ethnic group. As a result, the extended family feels emotionally and culturally closer to her and her children. She has two sisters in Jakarta and one in the village with their mother, Maryati (Chapter 1), who is now the only one of Aminah's daughters still living in the village.

There is little doubt that the reason Hasanah is in much closer contact with the extended family in Koto is because she is a woman and will contribute to the continuation of Aminah's family line and its claim to the property in the village, especially as she has a daughter. Since her husband is from East Java and she and her daughter can only visit the village occasionally, Hasanah wants to make sure that her daughter understands her role, rights and responsibilities in Koto. Since her retirement, Hasanah has strengthened her ties with the village, demanded access to the property in the village, and made her presence felt there. At the beginning of 2016, Hasanah and her oldest sister who lives in Jakarta bought a small piece of land in the village adjacent to the land of the extended family and built a house on it. The sister does not have any children but was happy to contribute to the purchase. The two of them hope that Hasanah's daughter will understand the importance of this in the future and benefit from having a place in the village that is a reflection of *adat* and tradition. At the moment, having been born in and grown up in East Java in a culture and tradition completely different from that of her mother, Hasanah's daughter has no interest in the village, Minangkabau culture, or rural life. She recently married a Javanese man and moved to Jakarta where she intends to live for the foreseeable future.

As for the house in the village, Hasanah and her sister deliberately built it on a land they were able to buy, rather than on family land. From years of experience living and working outside Minangkabau, they have had the opportunity to observe their own culture and traditions from a distance and have come to the conclusion that controlling ancestral property inherited and passed on through the female line has advantages for women. At the same time, they also understand the complexities and rigidity of this inheritance system that lacks specific principles about how land should be allocated among female family members and their children and male relatives. In addition, they know that bitter disputes among female relatives, especially between sisters when their mother dies, are very serious and can harm the future interests of the family. In their case, it would be almost impossible to deal with this as they live far from the village. They are worried about what would happen to the land when or if the family has no more female members to continue the extended family line, either because the next generation has no daughters or because female members of the family live outside the village and no longer care about the land.

For the time being, they feel that the best solution is to remain close to the village and the family property but to own their own land. They think they might be able to buy land that has been allocated to a female member of their own family in the future if someone no longer wants it or needs money or has no female descendants. While in theory ancestral land is not supposed to be sold, in practice this is happening more and more often. There are several reasons for this. In a family with many women, the land available for each of them becomes smaller in each generation and eventually does not provide enough to support a family. Selling it might give them a large amount of money that they could use to start a business. More women have good careers in the modern context and see no significant benefits in holding on to ancestral land. Some women have no daughters to inherit family property.

Malik's position in the extended family is not as complex as Hasanah's. Even though he often visits the village, especially on holidays because he has two sisters living in the village, he knows his children cannot benefit from the land his mother and grandmother had and part of which is now controlled by his sisters. In theory, he could use the land for a business whose income he could use to support his children when and if the female members of the family, not just his sisters, gave him permission to do so. When he died, however, the business would return to his sisters, not to his wife or children. So, there is little incentive for a man like Malik to invest in a business on land belonging to his extended family especially since, because of his education (he is a pharmacist), he could start a business on land he could buy or on his wife's land, both of which could benefit his children.

Unlike Hasanah, since his retirement, Malik has been concentrating on developing some kind of business outside the village, specifically in Padang. He has found part-time work at various institutions and started a drugstore at the house he and his family live in in Padang. What is interesting in his case is that this house belongs to his wife's maternal uncle. It makes a lot more sense economically and in terms of the family for the uncle to let them live in the house and for Malik to run his business there, rather than on his family's land. Malik has three brothers who live in Padang and his connection to the village amounts to not much more than visiting his sisters from time to time.

Malik and Hasanah, and others like them, contribute significantly to life in the village. This contribution can be financial but it can also be in the form of support for the precepts of *adat* that they reinforce through their behaviour and relationship to the village. At the same time, their situation may suggest to people living in the village that there are alternative resources that may be available, other than ancestral property. Women like Hasanah represent a new model of female success that combines traditional resources and the benefits of a modern profession.

LONELINESS AND CULTURAL CONSONANCE

A significant side effect of the shift in living arrangements from the extended family to the nuclear family is that many older people spend a great deal of time alone. Where even fairly recently it was unusual for any individual to be at home alone, for houses to be left empty during the day or for longer periods of time, or for older people to live more or less permanently by themselves, this is now the norm in many parts of West Sumatra, as well as in Indonesia as a whole. This trend is likely to continue as more people move into the formal work force and a great majority of children attend school. At the same time, life expectancy is increasing, and the number of the young old as well as oldest old continues to grow.

Minangkabau culture traditionally puts great emphasis on the desirability of being among other people, whether family members, friends, or even the general public. A proverb expresses this metaphorically as "When you sit alone, it feels cramped; when you sit among other people, there is plenty of room" (*Duduak surang basampik-sampik, duduak basamo balapang-lapang*). Being alone can be viewed as antisocial — on the assumption that the person involved does not want to interact with others — and also quickly comes to be frightening or distressing for children who often grow up with a strong preference for group membership. As adults, a majority of Minangkabau retain this desire to have other people around, even if they are not interacting directly with them, and may find it very difficult to eat, relax, and sleep if no one else is present. Most have a strong preference for their companion to be a family member but having a friend or even a maid present is usually seen as better than being alone. It should be noted that the Minangkabau do not traditionally have a servant culture; housework is done by the family itself. However, many middle-class Minangkabau living in the *rantau*, especially in Java and Jakarta where maids are commonly employed by a large part of the population that can afford to, do have servants.

Being alone is a very serious challenge to cultural consonance for older Minangkabau, regardless of where they live. For those in the village, the difficulty of being at home alone is often compounded by the fact that there are many fewer people living in many rural areas than in the past and those that do live there often work outside the home in either traditional or modern occupations, and children attend school. There are many fewer people who are around their house during the day who might serve as someone to talk to for an elderly person in the village. In Padang as well as in the *rantau*, a larger number of younger people work in formal employment and are away from home during the day. Increasing urbanization and road congestion mean that commutes are long, and many people must leave very early and return home late from jobs in another part of the city. Children increasingly participate in Western-style extracurricular activities and also spend more time at school than in the past. In the *rantau*, an additional challenge for older people who are at home alone is that neighbours who might be a source of companionship may well come from a different ethnic background, making communication and socializing difficult or awkward.

The distress caused by loneliness is a very significant psychological issue for older Minangkabau, and for elderly Indonesians in general. While beginning to be recognized in the psychological and social work literature (see, for example, Septiningsih and Na'imah 2012; Narulita 2016; Makki 2016), there has been little work on what might be done to address this. Interestingly, one of the circumstances in which older Minangkabau feel most alone and suffer the most from loneliness is in the context of institutional living in the PSTW, despite the fact that they are part of a community, and there are always other people around. The loneliness they experience in this setting seems to stem from the separation from their family and home and to the fact that, other than living in the institution, many of the older people at the PSTW have little in common, come from different social classes, and originate in different parts of West Sumatra. Sensitivity to differentiating social characteristics is high in Indonesia in general as well as in Minangkabau society and is reflected in patterns of behaviour and also communication.

As Western models of education and work continue to develop in Indonesia, it is likely that loneliness will become a greater problem among the elderly, regardless of their ethnic background. The traditional cultures of Indonesia, including that of the Minangkabau, tend to be communal by necessity. In the traditional context, where people in a particular social group were much more dependent on the goodwill of others for mutual benefit, as in the rice harvesting described above, it was highly desirable, and in fact vital, to have a large number of people available to assist. For this reason, part of the cultural tradition of child raising was to ensure that young people knew how to interact with the people in their social circle and understood the hierarchy in this environment. Minangkabau children, for example, are taught from a very young age to address older people using an appropriate familial term of address, which applies to actual family members as well as other adults who have a close social connection to the family, and to shake hands. In fact, these terms of address are so important that children often do not know the actual names of members of their own family and of other people in the village because they have been socialized from birth to only ever address them by an appropriate term of address. Recently, young children in West Sumatra are being increasingly trained to ritually kiss the hand of an adult by taking their hand and then lowering their head to touch their clasped hands with their forehead. This reflects a renewed concern for the traditional value of respect for one's elders.

This perception that respect may be lacking among the young is another manifestation of the social change that is affecting the nature of interpersonal interaction and is leading to a more solitary experience for many people in certain contexts. For older people, a combination of forces, that include the nature of work, a shift to the nuclear family, and increased life expectancy, often creates a situation where the person is alone. This occurred in the case of Syahril (Chapter 7). However, because of the way in which today's older Minangkabau were brought up, most do not have emotional resources that support adaptation to conditions that increasingly require self-reliance and the ability to structure one's time without input from other people. Most older Minangkabau do not, for example, have hobbies or interests that can serve as a solitary pastime and find it very difficult to carry out their normal activities if there are no other people present.

The result of this may be fear, loneliness, and depression. In many cases, it is not possible to change the situation in ways that can address these feelings, even if the older person as well as his or her family is willing to do so. Limited flexibility is accepted in the formal work environments in which increasing numbers of younger people are employed, and school also occupies much of the time of children and teenagers. Most older Minangkabau will not tolerate a servant as a companion, even if the family can afford this and a suitable person is available. Their strong preference is for a family member, even if the person's role is largely companionship and not care. In the past, it was often possible to have a more distant family member, who was unemployed or worked informally, move into the household, but, in practice, there are many fewer people in this situation, and it may be impossible to find a suitable relative who is willing and available to play this role for an elderly family member.

Having to be alone, and the attendant feelings many older Minang-kabau experience, is extremely serious in terms of the perception of cultural consonance. Invariably, these elderly would prefer to live in a busy household that includes their children and grandchildren. Most grew up in environments where they were part of a multi-family social network where there were numerous individuals in each generation who were related in the maternal line, and they, as young people, interacted regularly with grandparents, aunts and uncles, and cousins, as well as with their own parents and siblings. Their expectation was that they would have this same sort of experience as older people. Many of them did not recognize this need until they stopped working and no longer had structured activities to fill the day. After retiring, however, many older Minangkabau feel the gap between their often unarticulated expectations and their actual experience much more strongly and suffer considerable stress that, in some cases, makes it difficult for them to eat, sleep, or engage in other activities. Their very strong desire to be part of a group and have others to talk contributes to the popularity of social media networks, such as the BI70 WhatsApp group described in Chapter 5. Members of this group, and a similar organization of people who come from Koto, exchange hundreds of messages a day, often in real time, which is one way for members, many of whom live in what to them seem to be very small households, to feel they are associating with other people and engaging in a more satisfactory type of social interaction.

Yunus

When Yunus' wife answered the door, she saw two women she did not know. They asked her if this was Yunus' house and explained that they were his classmates in college more than forty years before. She hurried to the living room calling to her husband that he had visitors and who they were. He eagerly told his wife to bring the women to the living room where he was watching television.

Yunus began to cry when he saw his two old friends, and so did they. He had suffered a stroke eight years before when he and his family lived in Jakarta. Yunus considered himself unsuccessful compared to many of his friends, including those he knew had moved to Jakarta like himself. He had not graduated from college because he could not do the work even though he persisted for several years after all his classmates had either graduated or dropped out. When he realized that he was not likely to graduate, he went to Jakarta to live with a relative and soon after married a woman of Minangkabau background who had grown up in the capital. Her family owned an inexpensive hotel and wanted Yunus to manage it. They felt his background in English would be useful, even though he had not received his degree. Yunus was happy to have what he considered a very good job, especially as the low-cost hotel was reasonably successful.

His marriage and position in his in-law's business gave Yunus back some of the self-confidence he had lost when he dropped out of school while many of his friends succeeded. Nonetheless, he still could not bring himself to contact his circle of college friends in Jakarta. He often heard from a friend of a friend that his friends had had a reunion but he never tried to reach them. For more than forty years, he isolated himself from the people he knew as a student until his two old friends appeared at his house.

The friends told him they had formed the BI70 WhatsApp group (Chapter 5) some time before and had been trying to find their classmates. They learned he was living in Bandung and got his address from a friend of one of their daughters. Yunus was moved and explained why he had never contacted them, even though he had friends who knew they were in Jakarta. He said he had always wanted to see his old friends again but just hadn't had the courage to contact them and was very pleased that they found him.

Yunus' friends were moved to tears when he told them how lonely he had been since suffering a stroke eight years before that paralysed one side of his body and slurred his speech. He could not run the business anymore, and his wife's family was allowing them to live in a house they owned in Bandung. He had three adult children who were, in his words, as successful in school as he was and who have small retail businesses in the Tanah Abang area of Jakarta. His friends understood from what Yunus said that he felt embarrassed because he thinks he was not a good father.

Yunus used a wheelchair to move around and rarely left the house. His wife often went to Jakarta to see the children and grandchildren as well as to help manage the family business. Sometimes she would stay for a few days at a time, leaving Yunus with a maid. Yunus told his friends that he had been thinking more and more about Koto and his childhood and college years, and he longed for the village and a return of those good times. He knew, however, that he would never return to the village. His wife feels that she is from Jakarta and very rarely visited West Sumatra when she was young. In the years they had been married, she had never wanted to go there and had always resisted Yunus' suggestions that they visit the village.

From that time, Yunus' friends visited him often, sometimes four or five of them at a time. Yunus told them how much happier this made him, and his wife was very pleased that his old friends could cheer him up, especially since she knows she often has to leave him in Bandung while she is in Jakarta. The one thing that upset Yunus was his inability to send messages to his friends, even though he decided to join BI70 anyway. He cannot send message himself because of his impaired ability but he enjoys reading messages his friends send to each other. In addition, friends now call him frequently using WhatsApp, and he can talk to them, even when they cannot visit.

THE IMPACT OF TECHNOLOGY

The changes in the social, cultural, and political contexts in Indonesia have included an enormous increase in access to technology, especially the mobile applications that allow individuals to contact friends and family in other areas at very low cost. As discussed in Chapter 5, the introduction of mobile telephones and the take-up of this technology by the public has been extremely rapid in Indonesia. The ability to buy low-cost mobile devices and telephone service that is among the cheapest in the world (Infoasaid 2012) means that even people with very limited earnings can participate in modern communication. This enhanced ability to stay in contact with family and friends has meant that Minangkabau who are living outside of their village of origin can learn about and potentially contribute to life in the village in ways that were not possible in the past. Some of the issues that arise in this context are discussed in Chapters 6 and 8.

The ability of modern digital communications to keep people connected to their village and to be in more or less continuous contact with family members living there has maintained an image of the village in the minds of older Minangkabau living elsewhere that seems current and immediate. This stands in clear contrast to the past when direct communication was not possible and much of the interaction between those in the *rantau* and those in the village occurred by mail or in messages sent with friends and acquaintances who were returning to the village to visit. Before the advent of mobile telephones, very few people in Indonesia had landlines, and the number of such fixed installations remains very low. In comparison, there are 97.7 mobile telephones in use in Indonesia for every 100 individuals in the population (Infoasaid 2012).

In the past, because contact largely took the form of written communication and occasional visits, the importance of the village to people in the *rantau* tended to remain in the background of their day-to-day affairs because they knew less about what was going on there, and what they did know was generally selective and often restricted to the key aspects of any event. Today, however, many people in the *rantau* are in daily contact with various family members in the village by telephone, SMS and through social media. They generally know almost as much about what goes on there as they would if they were physically present, especially since they have the ability to contact a number of different people at any time.

For many older Minangkabau living in the *rantau*, this means that they have a renewed and dynamic connection to the village and to relatives living there. Because their financial contributions are often sought and they feel they are a part of things that go on there, even if only peripherally, they often see the village as more relevant to them than in the past. For some, the continued reminders of village life also recall the possibility of returning there to live in old age that is acceptable in *adat* as part of the matrilineal social structure of Minangkabau society. Many of these older individuals have the means to return to the village if they wished, especially as transportation and other forms of development have made such a move more possible.

Nonetheless, many older Minangkabau are consciously aware that life in the village would be unpleasant and difficult if they were to return. This view often proves very hard to reconcile with their nostalgic feelings about the place they grew up and their right to use the assets of their extended family, which are very difficult to give up for many, as the story of Hasanah above illustrates. The degree of contact it is now possible to have with relatives in the village seems to intensify this conflict and lead to mixed feelings about whether it is possible or desirable to remain a part of the village environment.

While it is no doubt the case that past generations of Minangkabau living in the *rantau* had to come to terms with the fact that they would not be able to participate in the life of the village from afar, older Minangkabau today have generally not had to do this. The ambivalence caused by the resulting status where they are neither part of the village nor fully separate from it represents a significant challenge to cultural consonance for many individuals. The confusion they feel typically has several elements that include an often inaccurate understanding of the way of thinking of people who have lived their whole life in the village, a lack of awareness of the fact that they themselves as well as the people and context of the village have changed in the years they have been away, and a failure to realize that many of their own views of the village were formed at a young age before they were fully a part of adult society. Taken together, these elements often lead to very unsatisfactory interaction with people in the village from the point of view of those in the *rantau*. At the heart of this is the issue of the extent to which people who do not live in the village can influence life there, particularly when they have contributed financially to the well-being of the community. Many older Minangkabau are troubled by this dilemma, which causes them considerable unhappiness and also intensifies the ambiguity they feel about the village and their own attachment to it.

In particular, it proves extremely difficult for many older Minangkabau to abandon the traditional view that productive land in the village is the most important asset a person, and their extended family, can have. Even though people who do not live in the village generally do not benefit from family land and the income such land might generate is much less than can be obtained in other ways, older people especially are often very reluctant for the family to give up land (even if it is not being used) or for productive fields to be mortgaged. The conflict caused by the deeply ingrained cultural model that places land as the single most important asset in the Minangkabau world, alongside the realization that land in the village does not have practical significance for a person living in another location, represents another source of stress that impacts on the psychological well-being of many older individuals.

The Koto WhatsApp Group

People from Koto who are living in the *rantau* formed a WhatsApp group several years ago. The initiative came from a retired couple living in Jakarta, Marni of the Valley family who is discussed in Chapter 8 and her husband. Marni, who is Limeh's (Chapter 6) older sister, and her husband, Marjan, retired about ten years ago, and they are now sixty-nine years old. Marjan worked at the Ministry of Finance, and Marni was a school teacher. They earned and were able to save a great deal of money before their retirement and, as a result, have been able to maintain a high standard of living. In addition, they established a very successful business after retiring so, if anything, their wealth has increased.

The WhatsApp group idea was really Marjan's idea. He not only wanted to use the social media to form a virtual Koto community to stay in touch with people in the *rantau* as well as in the village in order for members to support one another in times of need such as in illness or when a death occurred but also to facilitate charitable activity to support Koto in various ways. Marjan believes that this approach has the potential to support important change in the village. So far, the group has created a scholarship fund for the children of Koto, a cattle business that provides work and income for some people in the village, and a contingency fund to be used in the case of disaster, such as occurred recently when a house in Koto burned down.

But perhaps the most ambitious initiative Marjan has introduced in two years the group has been in operation has been to redeem all the rice fields that belong to people in Koto but that have been mortgaged over the years to people from outside the village. Marjan believes in the traditional value of the land, for individuals as well as for the village as a whole. He and Marni contributed a large amount of money to this mortgage buy-out project. The idea is that the group will pay back the mortgage and hence will become the new lienholder. When land has been controlled by people from outside the village, the lienholder has often refused the traditional owner the right to cultivate it in exchange for a portion of the income generated, as is the usual arrangement. When the group holds the mortgage, they allow the original owner to use the land and keep a portion of the produce with the group receiving the rest. In this way, Marjan thinks, land that belongs to people in the village can now directly benefit them.

The villagers themselves, as well as members of the group, thought this was a great idea, and the first land they redeemed was a large field that produces a very significant amount of rice every harvest, which is now twice in each calendar year. The group allocated most of their funds to this hoping that they would get their money back quickly, which they did. However, the mutual benefit did not last long. After the fourth harvest, the group had recouped its investment and should have begun to earn a profit which they intended to use to redeem more land. The owner of the field refused to give them the portion of the last harvest they were entitled to. The reasoning, on the part of the owners, was that the group had gotten its money back and hence should have no more claim to the income from the redeemed land, even though they had previously agreed that the group will continue to receive a portion of the income until such time as the family can redeem the lien from the group.

The group was not able to get the family to honour their agreement, and the case has now gone to court.

CULTURAL CONSONANCE IN THE *RANTAU*

The majority of elderly Minangkabau today have some direct link to West Sumatra, even when they have spent most of their adult life in the *rantau*. Migration out of the province increased dramatically during the years of the New Order and has continued up to the present time (Kompas 2013). Many of the Minangkabau who are now over sixty have spent decades outside of West Sumatra and have adult children and grandchildren who were born and raised there, often with little contact with West Sumatra or their Minangkabau parent's village of origin. At the time their children were young, many of these older Minangkabau believed it would be best for them to speak Indonesian as much as possible because of the social as well as economic benefits associated with fluency in the national language. More practically, many Minangkabau living in the *rantau* are married to people from other ethnic groups. Even those whose spouse is Minangkabau as well usually live in mixed urban neighbourhoods where they interact with people from all over the country and where there is no dominant cultural community, whether Minangkabau or another, of which they are part.

Participation in the Indonesian cultural mainstream is often acceptable and desirable to members of the Minangkabau community in the *rantau*, especially when children are in school and stand to obtain maximum benefit from full integration into the Indonesian environment. The ability of the Minangkabau to do this is attested to by the large number of government figures, successful business people, academics, and celebrities who are important at the national level. However, in older age, especially if they are no longer working, many Minangkabau find they would prefer their children and grandchildren to be more Minang. Marriage to people from other ethnic backgrounds is common, however, and a reality of life in the *rantau* for all generations. However, it does have the effect of integrating subsequent generations more completely into the national cultural domain and loosening the ties to the Minangkabau world. While not unexpected, many older Minangkabau do not realize that this may result from the choices they made early in life and are unprepared to deal with their own feelings about the Indonesianization of children and grandchildren when they arise. These feelings of disappointment and distance are even stronger among older Minangkabau who lived in the village or in Padang their whole life but have adult children who went to the *rantau* and are raising their own family there.

The language issues that can arise in this context are discussed in detail in Chapter 5 and reflect a situation that is likely to be experienced by members of any of Indonesia's local cultures in the face of increasing urbanization and domestic migration. However, while Indonesians, including members of the Minangkabau community, tend to believe strongly in the value of Indonesian as the national language and support its use in various social contexts, it is unusual for people to think about the fact that mastery of any language brings with it a cognitive framework that is unique to the language in question. For older Minangkabau, this often becomes apparent only through interaction with grandchildren whom they often feel are very different from their expectations.

Specifically, many older Minangkabau expect that their children and grandchildren will share their views about the village and the importance of the maternal family and its assets. They often feel that they have tried to teach them these things, but, in practice, for young people living in a large city, for example, the complications of managing rice fields and other types of agricultural assets, as well as the nature of the extended family networks, are hard to grasp without first-hand experience of life in the village context. Even younger people in Padang, whose parents may interact more directly with their village of origin, the traditional practices outlined by *adat* tend to be vague and irrelevant in the context of their day-to-day experiences. For those living in Jakarta or another part of Indonesia outside of West Sumatra, their parents' experiences have little correspondence to anything they are familiar with and have often been transmitted to them in Indonesian, rather than Minang which contains specific terms and expressions for cultural phenomena.

One of the ways that this gap in perception between the generations manifests is in the inability of younger family members to understand why an older relative insists on staying in the village, even if he or she is miserable and lonely there, or why a parent, who has been living in the *rantau* for decades, takes an increasing interest in life in the village or in Minangkabau culture more generally as he or she ages. These younger relatives often express surprise that their parents seem unable to be content in the *rantau*, even when they themselves grew up in the village. This can lead to conflict and disappointment, especially when an older person requires the assistance and support of younger family members who live in the *rantau*. In some cases, like that of Nurijah (Chapter 2) and Salim (Chapter 5), the older person has no alternative but to accept that he or she will have to live in the *rantau* where family members can provide care. In other cases, the older person may insist on remaining in the village, even if that means living alone or in a socially unusual situation, like Muhammad (Chapter 4).

The lack of a common view of the village and its importance among older Minangkabau and their children and grandchildren can contribute to the psychological pressure the older person feels as well as to a lack of cultural consonance. The inability to transmit to children and grandchildren the central principles of the Minangkabau cultural model that relate to the importance of matrilineal social structures and their relationship to the assets of the extended family may represent a personal failure to the older person in that he or she has not been able to ensure the family's continued existence into the next generations. Even if children born in the *rantau* marry other people of Minangkabau heritage, such that their offspring have a clan identification within the traditional system, they will not be able to participate in Minangkabau society without the detailed cultural knowledge associated with *adat* and, to a large extent, ability to use the Minang language.

For older women, especially, this may be a major concern because of the widely accepted view that preparing daughters to play a significant role in the affairs of the extended family in Minangkabau society is one of the most important duties of a mother. Daughters are especially prized in traditional society where it assumed they will become the next generation of family decision-makers and will become responsible for the management of family assets when their mothers can no longer do so. As younger women become increasingly more concerned with their own career and nuclear family in line with the norms of mainstream Indonesian culture, they often possess a corresponding reduction in interest in matters relating to the traditional context and *adat*. This tends to be especially pronounced when these women have grown up in Padang or elsewhere in the *rantau* and do not have first-hand experience of life in the village context. This is often bewildering as well as distressing to older Minangkabau women, even if they understand how their daughters feel. On the one hand, they recognize that their daughter's prospects are far greater in a modern career and have often been the ones to stress the importance of higher education and professional training to their children. On the other, they may not fully comprehend why their daughter does not see the village and the concerns of the extended family in the same way they do when *adat* considers that a young woman in this position is an appropriate heir to the assets of her mother's family.

There seem to be two aspects of this situation that are troubling to many older Minangkabau women. The first of these relates to the cultural expectation that a mother will prepare her daughters to play a central role in the extended family. When this is not possible, often because the family does not live in the village and the daughters have not interacted extensively with the extended family, an older woman may feel she has abrogated an important, culturally determined duty as a mother and, as a result, has failed to support the continuity of the extended family into the next generation. The second seems to result from the competition between women within extended families. Many older women, even if they understand why their own daughters are unwilling or unable to play a role in the extended family, are concerned that the daughters of sister or cousin will gain control of the family's assets. Even when the potential benefit from land in the village is very small, Minangkabau women are typically very reluctant to give up what they feel should be their share, even if they do not, in fact, make use of it. This is exemplified by the conflict between Limeh and his sisters described in Chapter 6, although the details of that incident were somewhat different. Nonetheless, the desire to maintain control of family property is extremely strong among today's older Minangkabau women, and the inability to do so, either through their own actions or their daughters', often results in conflicted feelings relative to their cultural model.

THE HEALTH OF OLDER PEOPLE

Indonesians are living longer than ever in the past as the result of improvements in nutrition, housing, and general health. Average life expectancy has now reached seventy-one years and is likely to increase further (WHO 2013). As a result, there are noticeably more elderly people in many communities, and the number of the oldest old is also increasing. As might be expected, this expanding population of older people tends to have a variety of health problems that are beginning to attract more attention as a matter requiring an integrated management approach.

In fact, Indonesia is at a turning point, or epidemiological transition, where chronic diseases of a non-communicable nature are beginning to overtake infectious disease as the main health concerns of the population (see Hussain, Huxley and Mamun 2015). Many older Minangkabau are aware of this in an informal way based on their own observations and experiences and also because of aggressive health promotion and advertising about diabetes, heart disease, and other chronic conditions. Stroke is very common in the Minangkabau community, and most older people have a friend or relative who has been affected. Interestingly, there is evidence that strokes were observed in the past as well because a non-technical term for the condition exists in Minang that refers to the characteristic type of impairment that may result (*mati sabalah* = "dead on one side") but was less widespread than it is today. This apparent change in prevalence may reflect the fact that people are living longer on average or a change in lifestyle factors that may be related to the condition or a combination of both. Diabetes and heart disease are very common as well but do not generally evoke the same level of concern that strokes do among older Minangkabau.

As a result, many older Minangkabau are afraid for their own health as well as for the health of family members and friends and feel a kind of helplessness and confusion about the high level of chronic disease among people they know. Many also feel, whether accurate or not, that their own parents and grandparents were healthier than older people are now. This perception is difficult to assess because, in the past, many conditions were not diagnosed and, if a person did not have any characteristic symptoms, any illness was likely to be seen as an expected part of old age. In addition, it is usually not possible to know with certainty how old the parents or grandparents of people now aged over sixty were at the time an illness occurred or at their death, as records of this kind do not exist. Many older people note, however, that their older relatives were able to go to the rice fields and do various kinds of work in the village when they were older than the speaker is presently and did not seem to have the aches and pains he or she does, much less a serious illness. As a result of this perception, poor or declining health represents for many a serious detractor from their psychological well-being, especially when, in other ways, many older Minangkabau are better off than their parents and grandparents were.

In addition to concern about their own health and that of a spouse, a significant number of older Minangkabau must also support a seriously ill parent who has reached a very old age. This situation is well known in Western societies but is recent in Indonesia, where life expectancy increased from sixty-two in 1990 to its present level in only twenty years (WHO 2013). In 1950, around the time many of today's older people were born, average life expectancy was only 37.5 years (UN, 2011). This suggests that there were likely to have been many fewer elderly people in the communities today's older people grew up in but also that they may have been healthier on average. The need to care for elderly relatives who were also very sick was certainly much smaller, and also the ability to do so successfully was lower. Today, however, the support required by the oldest old, like Nurijah described in Chapter 2, represents a significant source of stress for the younger old, for which there are few cultural precedents. In fact, the cultural model of health of most Minangkabau does not include this type of scenario (see Tas'ady, Fanany and Fanany 2012), and the stress and emotional burden care for a very elderly parent causes usually comes as a surprise to the carer and other family members.

Kincuang

Muhammad (Chapter 4), the husband of one of Aminah's daughters, had an uncle named Kincuang. When Kincuang died in 1995, Koto lost its oldest resident. Everyone in Koto knew that Kincuang was by far the oldest person in the village, even though no one knew his exact age, including Kincuang himself. Estimates varied from 100 to 120, but everyone agreed he was over 100. His fully grey hair and extremely wrinkled skin attested to his extreme old age. His death was the talk of the village.

The reason for this was not because this very old man had died but because of the circumstances surrounding its occurrence. People in Koto believed that Kincuang's family had killed him. As recently as three months before his death, Kincuang showed no signs of being sick or any indication that he might soon die. He was not only known as the oldest person in the village, but he was understood to be a model of excellent health. Remarkably, he still had most of his teeth, which was very rare among the elderly in Koto at the time. In addition, his vision was almost perfect, and he did not need glasses. He was physically capable enough to get around on his own and did not need to use a cane.

His routine included going to the mosque before sunrise for the morning prayer, having breakfast of coffee and fried bananas and sticky rice at his favourite coffee shop in Koto, and then walking through his family's rice fields to enjoy the fresh air and morning sun, as he put it. He would then go to the mosque again after lunch and sometimes took a nap there after the afternoon prayer. He would then walk back home and work around the house, sweeping the yard or managing the ponds. Once a week on market day in a nearby town, he would walk from Koto to the market. This was one of his favourite activities, and he would buy food or toys for his grandchildren and grandnieces and grandnephews. People in the village admired his youthful spirit and energy, even though some of them wondered why he wanted to go places by himself at such an old age and why his family allowed him to.

It is true that in Koto it was, and to a large extent still is, the case that an old person is expected not to spend too much time outside the house and certainly should not do all the things Kincuang did. In a way, he was an embarrassment to his children, nieces and nephews, but Kincuang would not listen. After a while, most villagers came to see his unusual health and spirit as refreshing and admired him. But the family finally decided Kincuang should stop adventuring around the village after he fell one day while walking around the rice fields which had just been ploughed. Somebody who happened to be passing by helped him home. Kincuang had been stuck in the mud for about half an hour, unable to free himself until someone came by who was able to help him. He was not hurt but was shaken. His family told him that the next time something like this happened, it might be very serious and could even kill him.

Kincuang was upset but he could not go against his family in this. They told him it would embarrass the family if he got into a serious accident. Kincuang realized that this might happen, and he did not want his family to be ashamed. Initially, they still allowed him to have breakfast at his favourite coffee shop because it was very close to their house. He was also permitted to go to the mosque but had to be accompanied by a family member. He was no longer allowed to go to the market on market day. Even though he now did what his family told him to and did not do the things they forbade him to, Kincuang was very unhappy. Every morning at the coffee shop, he would complain to the other men eating there. He changed dramatically. Where he used to be very cheerful, he was now always gloomy and sad.

Less than a month after he changed his routine, he began to complain about aches and pains. His legs, back, neck, or all of these, were bothering him, he said. A few days later, he stopped having breakfast at the coffee shop. The villagers wondered what had happened to him. The family told everyone he was fine, just tired and resting at home. But rumours in the village said that Kincuang was seriously ill and was having difficulty walking. Some people felt he had become sick because he was not allowed to do the things he wanted to that he had been doing for years. They blamed the family for being too harsh on him because of the one accident.

The whole village attended Kincuang's funeral, and, for a long time afterwards, the villagers talked about how his family had killed him.

CHANGE AND CURRENT EXPERIENCE

There can be no doubt that the experience of older Minangkabau today is extremely different from that of their parents and grandparents. Their experiences are also very different from those of their own children and grandchildren who, even if they live in the village, are more integrated into the modern Indonesian social and cultural context than ever before. In this sense, today's older Minangkabau represent a transitional generation, during the course of whose life Indonesia experienced unprecedented social, cultural, political, and economic change that altered some of the basic aspects of the collective experience. While it is likely the case that most older people are sensitive to differences in the world around them when compared to earlier periods of their life, in the case of the Minangkabau, and more generally all older people in Indonesia, the pace of change has been unusually rapid and far reaching because of specific aspects of the national context since independence. The introduction and uptake of technology is an important aspect of this, as are economic, political, and social shifts at the national, regional, and local levels.

There can be no doubt that many of these older people have benefited from the process of change in a number of ways, not the least of which economically, with many being considerably better off financially than previous generations. At the same time, however, this generation has experienced a significant reduction in the importance of *adat* and its precepts, as well as changes in daily practices that derive from the traditional culture of the group. When asked to reflect on this, most older Minangkabau can list numerous social, cultural, and religious practices that no longer exist in their community that they view favourably in that they feel had benefit for the community or represented significant elements of *adat* and traditional culture. The basis for this assessment is the characteristically Minangkabau cultural model they developed in childhood that derived on their own experiences and the collective knowledge of the community, which at the time had been much less affected by outside elements.

This process of change has been gradual and has occurred over the life course of these older individuals. Many of them have adapted well and have been able to take advantage of new and increased opportunities, especially in the domains of education and work. Nonetheless, in older age, many rely on a cultural model of ageing and end of life concerns that derives from the traditional context and reflects the nature of the village and the extended family as it may have existed in the past. In many cases, this model does not fully fit with the experience of these older Minangkabau or with their interests and desires as a member of the larger Indonesian community. As a result, many experience a serious problem with cultural consonance where the gap between their expectations for their own older age and the reality of their situation is significant and tangible.

Neither Minang nor Indonesian contain the concept of cultural consonance or the terminology to express its principles. Nonetheless, issues of cultural consonance can be observed when many older Minangkabau talk about the issues described here and their perceptions of them using terms that recall the typical definers of depression and other negative psychological states. For example, many individuals mention feeling lonely (*maraso tapancia*), sad (*sadiah*), uneasy (*rusuah, kusuik pangana*), anxious (*cameh*), or ashamed (*malu*). Others report being unable to sleep or complain of having no social role and that their life is empty (*ampo*) (see Syukra 2012; Fanany, Fanany and Tas'ady 2014). Feelings of this kind are common among the residents of the PSTW but are also echoed by older Minangkabau living in the village, in Padang, and also in the *rantau*, suggesting that gaps in cultural consonance are widely experienced, regardless of the environment and situation of the person involved.

At present, there has been little attention paid to the growing problem of depression and mental health problems among older people in Indonesia, although their existence has been noted in many locations. While it is possible that these conditions characterize the current generation of older people, exacerbated perhaps by the dynamic nature of the social and cultural contexts over the course of their lives, it is perhaps more likely that Indonesia's ageing population will continue to experience mental health problems, some of which may relate directly to issues of cultural consonance. For older Minangkabau, the current situation suggests that this is a certainty, at least for the foreseeable future, until a new cultural model comes into being among members of the community that provides precedents and meaning for old age in the modern context.

11

The Elderly Must Endure

Five-year-old Ananda is the youngest member of the Valley family still living in Koto. When she is not in kindergarten, she spends most of her time with her grandmother, Maryati, the oldest member of the family in the village, her single mother, and a number of other members of the family who live on their ancestral land and are her mother's cousins. Ananda, her mother and grandmother have just moved into a new house built for them by her three aunts who live in the *rantau*. They have all achieved some measure of success in their professions and recently bought a piece of land across the road from the family's traditional holdings that was put up for sale by another extended family in the village (see Hasanah's story in Chapter 10). In addition to providing a place for their mother and sister to live, these women wanted to maintain a stake in the village that they owned themselves. While they could, in theory, have built a house on the family's communal property across the road from where their new house is located, this would have meant negotiating with other family members and also that they would not own the property outright. The current situation means that they own the house as well as the land on which it is located and can do whatever they like with it in the future.

Other changes have taken place in Koto that mark a break with tradition. About 90 metres down the road from Ananda's house, a woman from a nearby village has opened a small, roadside stand selling coffee and light meals. The owner, her adult daughter and several grandchildren are all living on the premises which they built on a plot of land leased to them by the village family that owns the adjacent fields. While it is unclear whether such a venture can be successful in Koto, it is concerning to a number of the members of the Valley family, who are increasingly worried about people from outside the village gaining control of land and assets that rightfully belong to the extended families that originate in Koto (see the story of Marni and Marjan in Chapter 10). Nonetheless, the family has been slow to document their own land and obtain deeds to their hereditary assets as it is now possible to do within the Indonesian legal system. This reflects a reluctance to engage in potentially contentious discussion within the family and to do the complicated paperwork, perhaps because the matter of documentation does not yet seem pressing and because several members of the family in the village have stable careers in the formal context.

To the members of the Valley family, as well as to any observer who visited Koto in the past, it is obvious that there are fewer people around than there once were and that those who are living there are, on average, older than in the past. As recently as ten years ago, a child of Ananda's age would have been part of a large group of young children who spent their free time playing in the road and near each other's houses. Now she spends much of her time with adults. Similarly, there are very few young men visible at the village's one intersection where they used to congregate and spend much of the day talking and smoking and very few children in school uniforms on the road. Even the middle-aged and older residents of the village are much less visible, either in the fields or around their homes, and may be spending more time indoors.

This situation can be seen as the result of several converging forces that characterize life in modern Indonesia. One is the very strong trend towards urbanization that is drawing people from rural areas to towns and cities. Many younger people have left the village in search of better employment or to attend school or college in Padang or another town. Even Batusangkar, the closest major town to Koto, has become a centre of education for the surrounding areas. Its public Islamic college has recently been upgraded to an Institute of Islamic Studies, and staff are hopeful the school will soon qualify to become a full-fledged university. A wide range of subjects and degrees are offered, as is the case at all public

Islamic colleges in Indonesia, and the school is a very popular destination for high school graduates from around the region. However, for many younger people from rural parts of West Sumatra, Padang is the obvious choice if they wish to leave their village to continue their education. As the provincial capital, the opportunities to attend college and eventually obtain employment are much higher than in other parts of the province.

At the same time, *marantau* in its more traditional form has become much easier, both emotionally and in practical terms. The availability of online messaging and social media platforms that can be accessed using mobile devices has conceptually brought the *rantau* much closer and allows those living elsewhere to be in constant communication with family in West Sumatra. In this way, it has become possible for Minangkabau in other parts of the country to maintain a more significant relationship with their extended family, albeit at a distance, than was possible in the past and also to have a presence of sorts among people in the village. At the same time, transportation has become much more developed as well as cheaper, and it is now possible for many Indonesians to travel regularly, including by air. In people's thoughts and feelings, this is very different from the past when a person who went to the *rantau* seemed extremely far away in both distance and emotion, and even Padang felt very remote to those who remained behind in the village. It was difficult and expensive for those in the *rantau* to return even to visit, with many seeing relatives in West Sumatra at intervals of years.

The opportunities offered by the formal, national context are also increasingly attractive to younger people who can use Indonesian fluently and have completed higher levels of education. For them, modern jobs that pay a salary and offer opportunities for advancement commensurate with a person's abilities are more appealing and more lucrative than anything the traditional context can offer. It has always been difficult to make an adequate living from traditional agricultural occupations, and interest in this type of work is decreasing among young people across Indonesia (see Mutajali 2015; Jahansyahtono 2016). For men in particular, but for women as well, work in the formal sector is one way to escape the limitations of the traditional system, including the competition for access to assets that occurs within extended families.

The existence of competing opportunities within the formal sector is not new. This situation emerged during the New Order period (1965–98) as a result of political, social, and cultural change across Indonesia and a very strong emphasis on regional and national development that was a major focus of the Soeharto government. Regional autonomy that was established in 2001 brought a wide range of new responsibilities to local governments and also created many more opportunities for employment in the formal sector in regional areas. At the same time, changes in the business context created opportunities in the private sector as well that provided new potentials for many young people.

For older Minangkabau, regardless of where they live, these changes which occurred over a period of only a few decades represent a major societal shift that encompasses the political, social, and cultural domains but has also changed the priorities and outlook of younger people who increasingly do not share the traditional outlook of their parents and grandparents now aged over sixty. It is this aspect of the experience of older Minangkabau that is reflected in the title of this book, the elderly must endure. This statement is the second part of a proverb that, as discussed in Chapter 1, compares the feelings of the young to those of the old. The full expression is: The young must bear their longing; the elderly must endure (*Adaik mudo manangguang rindu; adaik tuo manahan ragam*). At the present time, younger Minangkabau very much long to be part of the wider Indonesian cultural context and participate in the institutions of the nation; this is what motivates their move to cities, their choice of occupation, and their decision to leave West Sumatra, especially for locations that are closer to the political, social and cultural centre. Older Minangkabau, by contrast, must find a way to adapt to this change and cope with the shifting priorities of the young, even as those priorities are increasingly seen to threaten the traditional system and the roots of Minangkabau *adat* and tradition.

For older Minangkabau, whether living in the village, Padang, PSTW or in the *rantau*, this change has come very quickly and demands accommodations that were not necessary in the past. The personal adjustment required seems to be easier for some people than for others and is clearly related to income as well as education as these are the main factors that contribute to individual success in the modern Indonesian environment. Education, it should be recalled, is also closely associated with the ability to use the national language which, in itself, is an important resource in the ability to adapt to change and participate fully in the public sphere. Nonetheless, even those older individuals who are most integrated into the modern context have generally been forced to change their outlook and let go of some of the aspects of *adat* and tradition that are widely considered by members of the Minangkabau community to underlie their traditional social structure, albeit not to the extent Muhsin and Rosni have (Chapters 2 and 7).

One of the conclusions that can be drawn from this study relates to the nature of Minangkabau *adat* itself. As discussed in Chapter 3, members of the Minangkabau community tend to see *adat* as being universally applicable at all times and under all circumstances and believe strongly that adherence to *adat* will result in a more harmonious, better functioning society that is free of some of the currently observed social problems (see, for example, Sumbar Satu 2015). It is also generally believed that, at some time in the past, adherence to *adat* allowed for an ideal community structure that has deteriorated to reach its present form (see Salleh, Ramza and Abdul Kadir 2015). While there can be no doubt that many of the problems with the traditional matrilineal system that are discussed above have always been present and have affected the relationships between members of extended families, it is also the case that the system likely worked much better in the past when there were few alternatives for individuals that could provide a source of livelihood with the exception of *marantau*, which was much more difficult, in practical terms as well as emotionally, in the past. In a relatively closed system where most individuals were dependent on family assets and on each other to survive, the benefits of cooperation, of participating in the forming of consensus, and of supporting the precepts of *adat* were great, and most individuals would have had more to gain from upholding traditional social structures than from going against them.

Nonetheless, it is equally clear that there have always been cases of older people who were denied the rights and status *adat* in theory conferred to them. In many cases, this type of treatment, such as that experienced by Ribuik, whose story is presented in Chapter 6, was widely known to people in the village, but there was an unspoken agreement that such things were not discussed openly or acknowledged by those not directly involved. Older men, especially if they were unmarried or their wife had died, were always problematic in the traditional system, which no doubt accounts for historical precedent for not returning from the *rantau* as well as the modern concern about coming back to the village in old age. While it was always harder to deny women access to family assets in the traditional context, competition between women of the same generation was always vicious, and many women, such as Erni in Chapter 3, had to accept bullying and unfairness within the context of the family.

At present, the widely observed deterioration of traditional social structures and roles for older people, such as the *mamak* (maternal uncle), is directly related to the availability of opportunities outside the traditional system. In other words, there are now alternatives for members of the Minangkabau community that are increasingly allowing them to break the ties to the land that formed the basis for traditional society. This accounts for the changing priorities of younger members of the community in relation to formal education and modern occupations and also contributes to intergenerational disagreement on the importance of the extended family, connection to the village, and the use or disuse of ancestral property. For many older people, including those who have lived most of their adult life in the *rantau*, it is proving very difficult to change their perception of the significance of family land, even when they do not depend on it and do not wish to live in the village.

For many of the older people in this study, this issue is at the centre of their feelings of cultural consonance. Regardless of where they live, most Minangkabau over the age of sixty regard the traditional system as beneficial and important and would like to see it function in the way it did in the past, even if they do not want to be part of it directly. Those living in the village, for example, are typically most concerned that younger people will be unable or unwilling to manage family land in the way past generations have and are increasingly aware of the potential loss to people from outside the extended family or outside the community, including from developers. Many older people in Padang retain an interest in the village and live within easy reach of their ancestral home. However, a significant number, especially if they have been professionally successful, choose to separate themselves from village intrigue, participating in family affairs only when they wish to. For those in the *rantau*, the village is now closer than in the past because of the instantaneous communication new technology allows and because transportation has improved greatly over the past two decades. Like older people living in Padang, many elderly Minangkabau in the *rantau* believe the traditional system is important but expect family assets to be managed by the people who are in the village. In other words, those who live elsewhere have an expectation that family members in the village will maintain the traditional system in the way they feel it has operated in the past. Many expect the village environment to remain stable and see it as a constant in their understanding of their own experience. This desire by those outside the village for the traditional system to remain in place and to maintain their personal position within this system is exemplified by the behaviour of Limeh's sisters (discussed in Chapter 5), when he proposed using family land for a new business venture.

It is increasingly clear to many older Minangkabau, however, that their view, even though very closely held, is unrealistic in the context of current Indonesian society. The outside world has come to the village, and young people who live there are exposed to the same range of outside influences that young people in Padang and the *rantau* experience. This is often discussed by members of the public as well as professionals in the health, education, and social services sectors and often appears in the traditional as well as social media. Beginning with the widespread availability of television in the late 1970s and early 1980s and continuing today with digital media and the Internet, young people in rural areas have much the same knowledge and aspirations as those living in urban areas, both in and outside of West Sumatra. It is increasingly difficult for older people to generate in younger people the same sense of importance and urgency about family property they feel because of the alternatives now available and the observation of many that it is possible to have a better career in the formal sector, even if a person lives in the village. Inang, whose story is contained in Chapter 5, is an example of this, as are two other women of the Valley family who are now in their fifties. One of these women is a lecturer at the Islamic College in Batusangkar, and the other is principal of a high school in a nearby village. Both women earn a great deal more money from these jobs than the family land can provide and have also had a number of opportunities to travel within Indonesia and internationally because of their work. While they live in the village and do manage the rice fields and other assets allotted to their branch of the family, they do not feel the same pressure to maximize its output that previous generations did and rely on hired hands to do the work.

In short, the limited potential of communally owned property cannot compete with the possibility of individual ownership and initiative that is allowed by the modern context and that is much more appealing to many younger people and especially to men, who do not have traditional rights to family wealth in the ways that women do. This perception on the part of many Minangkabau has led to an observed trend in selling property belonging to extended families to developers for various purposes. While it has been noted that such sales are often in violation of *adat* and have been criticized by community leaders (see, for example, Abidin 2016), it appears that many members of the Minangkabau community are more strongly motivated by personal benefit and the possibility of providing for their nuclear family as opposed to improving the situation of their maternal extended family. Under these circumstances, it is likely that, in some areas at least, the traditional system of land management will be increasingly dismantled in the future. Without the strong ties to ancestral property, a number of aspects of Minangkabau *adat* will likely continue to fade, as younger people become increasingly integrated into the Indonesian mainstream.

A second conclusion of this study is that, while older Minangkabau tend to experience gaps in cultural consonance regardless of where they live, the social and cultural context of Padang seems to offer the greatest advantage in terms of supporting the development of resilience and effective adjustment. As has been demonstrated extensively in the literature, there is a social gradient in terms of mental and physical health such that individuals with higher income and more resources tend to experience better health and that this gradient appears to exist in societies of many kinds around the world (see, for example, Wilkinson and Marmot 2003; Marmot et al. 2008). This seems to apply in the Minangkabau community as well in regard to resilience and coping ability, and it is clear that individuals with greater means often, but not always, are able to adjust more effectively. Since people with higher income are often better educated and more integrated into the formal context, the personal benefit they have gained outside the traditional environment is often greater than that achieved by people with lower levels of income and education, which often makes the traditional context less important to them. Even so, many older women begin to be concerned about their family property in their place of origin after their mother's death, even if they have never taken an interest in such assets in the past.

There are several reasons that older people in Padang may adapt best to the rapid and pervasive culture change that has characterized life in the Minangkabau community in recent decades. The first of these is that the social environment of the city draws strongly on the customs of traditional Minangkabau society, and the Minang language is the main vehicle for communication in ordinary interaction. This has meant that the social patterns of people living there are familiar to older people, even though they represent an accommodation to the demands of the modern context separate from the traditional institutions of *adat*. In other words, life in Padang retains a distinctly Minangkabau nature — food, clothing, language, religion and its expression, daily practices, and so forth are all characteristic — but does not require that individuals play set social roles determined by *adat* and tradition. To some extent, a similar situation exists in certain parts of the *rantau* where there are large, long-established Minangkabau communities. However, especially under the present system of regional autonomy, it is more likely for a Minangkabau individual to achieve professionally in Padang than in other locations because of the social environment that supports cultural identity.

The second reason is that Padang allows easy access to the rural parts of West Sumatra, and people living there can readily visit their village of origin if they wish to. In practice, this allows an older person to avoid some of the problems of the village while still interacting with family there in some way. For many older people, this intermediate position is important and allows them to retain a tangible connection to their extended family and ancestral land. At the same time, it is possible for them to avoid becoming involved in some of the internal conflict of the village and the extended family, even though the financial and other demands from relatives in the village may be significant.

A third reason is that Padang is the most developed part of West Sumatra and offers facilities and services that are not available in other towns, although this situation has improved in recent years. While the physical environment is no more supportive of the needs of older people, access to health care and other services is better, and such facilities are concentrated in the provincial capital. For example, a majority of public health centres in Padang have programmes specifically for older people; similar services are much less frequent in other parts of the province, despite the number of elderly people living there. Other kinds of services, including banking, shopping and public facilities, are also concentrated in the city and reflect several decades of increasing urbanization in Indonesia in general.

Finally, one of the most interesting conclusions of this study is the nature of older peoples' feelings about the assets of their extended family and their perspective on what the future might be like for the traditional system. Not surprisingly, for many Minangkabau, who are close to or who are already considered older in the Indonesian context, the nature of the village and the way in which the assets of the extended family are managed forms a backdrop for their experience and sense of self. This understanding of the family and its relationships, as well as the things that are important to the group (such as management of agricultural land) was generally set in childhood and youth and reflects a period when families were larger, more people lived in the village, and there were fewer alternatives to the traditional system prescribed by *adat* for those who stayed there. Many of today's older people left the village at a time when it appeared the existing system was stable and assumed that the people who remained would continue the traditions that had been in place in previous generations. It was not possible for them to anticipate the pace of change or that outside influences would be as intense, extensive, and pervasive as they have become today. It is worth noting that ideas and views from outside the Minangkabau world have always reached even the remotest areas because of the connection between individual villages and the *rantau*, but the intensity was much less even in the recent past and has increased dramatically due to developments in technology.

Thinking about their own feelings as an older member of the community, many Minangkabau hope that the traditional context of the village will remain intact and will continue to function in the ways they are familiar with into the future. Nonetheless, those who do not live in the village generally do not wish to be involved in this directly; they hope that those left behind will ensure that *adat* is maintained and family assets are protected. Many are unaware of the extent of change in the village and react with shock when presented with the realities of life in the rural parts of West Sumatra that, in their recollection, were much more traditional in the past. For this reason, the presence of PSTW in the province is deeply concerning and even unimaginable to some. They see these changes, not surprisingly, as evidence of a serious deterioration of *adat* and religious values that they genuinely believed were the foundation for the life that they recalled from youth.

These older people, when asked about their feelings, also tend to be aware that their children and grandchildren have no interest in or knowledge of the village context. However, most have not fully considered the implications of this to the traditional system and are only beginning to realize that, without the support and participation of these younger people, the traditional context will change irrevocably, relative to their experience at a younger age. This often signals to them the dysfunctional nature of *adat* in the modern era and is generally viewed as a negative transformation of what they often perceive to have been a better, more ideal social context. This shift, whether recognized explicitly or only in terms of its visible impacts in the community around them, is troubling to many and a source of concern that feeds their own perception of loss of cultural consonance.

Nonetheless, there are numerous ways of adapting and a whole range of behaviours and attitudes to the current context that are observable among older Minangkabau. For this reason, it is difficult to generalize about the situation of older people beyond the broad themes discussed above, and each person has a unique story that provides its own insights into the lives of older people in Indonesia today. The members of the Valley family alone exemplify many different older age experiences, but it is interesting to note that, other than Aminah, the founding member of the family who is discussed in Chapter 2, none of the men and women descended from her had the kind of experience *adat* and tradition suggest is ideal for Minangkabau elders. This stresses the fact that the process of social change that began with Indonesian independence in 1945 and has continued to the present time is an ongoing force that is shaping the life course in ways people born at the beginning of this period of change could not anticipate.

The confluence of social trends that has resulted in such fundamental change in the Minangkabau community is being experienced around Indonesia by members of other ethnic groups with their own traditional social structures, language and culture. Among Indonesia's numerous local cultures, the Minangkabau community are at the forefront of the transition from a more traditional, *adat*-based identity and experience to one that incorporates many elements and patterns associated with mainstream Indonesian culture and institutions. It is likely that the custom of *marantau* that now accounts for a net loss of population in West Sumatra (BPS 2016*b*) as well as intense cultural input from outside the region is hastening this change among the Minangkabau but may be slower in some parts of Indonesia or perhaps more rapid in others. In this, the experience of older Minangkabau can be seen as an indication of the experience of people of similar age from other areas and different cultural backgrounds, and, as such, reflects a situation that will inevitably occur across the nation. How other groups will adjust and adapt will certainly depend upon the nature of their local culture, the extent to which they are integrated into the Indonesian environment, and the attitudes and outlook of the members of their community.

In the Minangkabau world, however, the result of the rapid social change that occurred over the last several decades is that many older people have resigned themselves to the fact that the shift can no longer be resisted by the community as *adat* no longer seems sufficient to stem the tide. For the youngest members of the community, like Ananda of the Valley family, their childhood is already extremely different from that of their parents and even more different from the experience of their grandparents. It is likely that Ananda will grow up as a member of a much smaller social network in which the extended family plays a much more minor role than in the past. At the same time, she will almost certainly be more thoroughly integrated into the modern Indonesian social context than her mother and grandmother and will likely have the same interests and exposures as young people in other parts of the province and across Indonesia. Even if she remains in the village and lives and works there for her whole life, Ananda's experiences will almost certainly continue to shift in ways that reflect the culture and structures of the modern nation. Even living in the village, it seems clear that the meaning of being Minangkabau will be different to her than to her older relatives, even though that identity may well be stronger than many older people now fear, and will contain even more elements associated with the Indonesian mainstream.

AFTERWORD

During the final stages of writing this book, Nurijah, whose profile appears in Chapter 2, died. The circumstances surrounding her death were remarkable and illustrate the very significant role cultural consonance, which is discussed in some depth in Chapter 10, plays in the experience of older Minangkabau.

One day a few months ago, Nurijah fell ill. This in itself was not unusual; she had often felt unwell since suffering a stroke in Koto many years before and becoming paralysed as a result of it. This intensified after her children brought her to Jakarta to live. She hated the city and repeatedly asked her daughters why one of them could not return to Koto with her. All four of her daughters live and work in Jakarta and cannot leave, especially for an extended period of time. Finally, Nurijah had to agree to leave Koto and her home there as there was no one who could take care of her in the village. She did not want to live with her son and his wife even though they are also in Koto.

While Nurijah's complaints about her health would not normally alarm her children, this time was different. She began to deteriorate quickly. Within hours, her breathing became irregular, and she was in and out of consciousness, which had never happened before. The daughter, whose turn it was to take care of Nurijah, immediately contacted her three sisters and one brother who live in Jakarta, and they all arrived within a few hours. Everyone agreed that Nurijah's situation was very serious, particularly as, whenever she was conscious, she insisted that she wanted to go back to Koto immediately. The children were all stunned and confused and tried to persuade Nurijah that she was in no condition to travel. They promised to take her back to Koto when she felt better, if that was really what she wanted. Conveying this took hours because of Nurijah's condition and because her speech was even harder to understand than usual.

Finally, Nurijah told her children that she did not want to die in Jakarta. More importantly, she wanted to be buried in Koto next to her husband. Nurijah's husband, who had died many years ago long before she had the stroke, had been buried in the Valley family's burial ground because most of his family was in Malaysia, and those who still lived in his village were all distant relatives with whom he had no contact. When Nurijah was conscious, all she wanted to talk about was when, not if, she would leave. It was apparent to all the children that this was no ordinary wish but an order. They were upset, confused and frantic but tried to find a way to make it possible for their mother to return to Koto. No airline was willing to transport a person who was so ill, and travel by sea would be complicated and difficult. Ships did not sail between Jakarta and Padang every day, and Nurijah was not willing to wait. Travel by land would take as much time as by sea, but they could leave much more quickly. So, the children decided to call the hospitals and arrange to have Nurijah taken by ambulance from Jakarta to Koto as soon as possible, the next day if they could! One hospital agreed. Luckily, money was not a problem, especially for the oldest daughter, Marni (Chapter 8).

Other family members in the village and elsewhere were very concerned by this news. Nurijah's son, Hamzah (Chapter 3), who lives in Makassar, immediately said he would fly to Jakarta that evening and join the others on the trip. In addition to the ambulance, they would use two sports utility vehicles (SUVs) so that everyone could go and they would also be able to bring all the supplies they would need. It was decided that Marni would stay with Nurijah in the village until they could make other arrangements because Marni was retired, even though she and her husband had a business in Jakarta. Marni, who was unable to leave home immediately, would fly to Padang later and get to the village at about the same time as the ambulance arrived. In the end, Marni's three sisters and two of their children, the brother who lived in Jakarta, and the brother who lived in Makassar travelled in the SUVs along with the ambulance.

As Nurijah was put into the ambulance, her children were struck by a change in her mood. All of a sudden, she seemed calmer. The tension left her face and, for the first time in years, she seemed relaxed. The hospital assigned a nurse to accompany Nurijah in the ambulance. There was room for one other person, so the children took turns riding with their mother and the nurse.

Nurijah seemed to be much more alert than when she first fell ill. She was able tell them when she needed to change position or when she was hungry. Most of the time, however, she slept. Once they had crossed the Sunda Strait on the ferry, however, she woke up more often and would immediately ask whether they were in Koto yet. She seemed better and was looking forward to going back to her house in the village. The closer they got to Koto, the more often she woke up and asked if they had arrived. Suddenly, when they were still some distance from the village, after having travelled hundreds of kilometres in the ambulance, Nurijah weakened again. She was asleep when they arrived and did not awaken when they carried her into the house on a stretcher.

Every relative living in the village and many neighbours were at Nurijah's house when she arrived. But because of her condition, only immediate family members were allowed to be in the bedroom when she was brought in. As soon as Nurijah was put into bed, she opened her eyes but didn't speak. The family tried to speak to her, but she did not respond. Nurijah looked around. Finally, as tears rolled down her cheeks, she said softly, "I'm home, I'm home!". Everyone present began to cry. Soon after, Nurijah turned towards her sister, Maryati (Chapter 1) and called her name. She then looked at her son who lived in the village and said his name. She recognized and addressed each of the others who were present in the same way. She remembered every one of them, even though she hadn't seen several of those present since she was taken to Jakarta many years before.

Nurijah began to deteriorate rapidly. She was no longer able to respond when her relatives spoke to her or tried to offer her something to eat or drink. She died less than two hours after she arrived and was buried in Koto near her husband and other members of the Valley family who had preceded her.

REFERENCES

Abidin, Masoed. "Membangun Fisik Pariwisata dalam Tatanan Adat Minangkabau". *Sumbar Satu*, 16 May 2016 <http://www.sumbarsatu.com/berita/12908-membangun-fisik-pariwisata-dalam-tatanan-adat-minangkabau>.

Adelaar, Alexander and Nikolaus P. Himmelmann, eds. *The Austronesian Languages of Asia and Madagascar*. London and New York: Routledge, 2005.

Adioetomo, Sri Moertiningsih and Ghazy Mujahid. *Indonesia on the Threshold of Population Ageing*. UNFPA Indonesia Monograph Serties No. 1. Jakarta: United Nations Population Fund, 2014.

Afrianti, Desi. "Mengintip Tradisi Lansia Sumatera Barat di Bulan Ramadan". *VivaNews*, 24 July 2013 <http://nasional.news.viva.co.id/news/read/431870-mengintip-tradisi-lansia-minangkabau-di-bulan-ramadan>.

Ahmad, Taufik. *Schools and Politics: The Kaum Muda Movement in West Sumatra (1927–1933)*. Singapore: Equinox Publishing, 2009.

Ajrouch, Kristine. "Muslim Faith Communities: Links with the Past, Bridges to the Future". *Generations* 32, no. 2 (2008): 47–50.

Akral. "Orang Minangkabau Merantau Guna Mengentaskan Kemiskinan". Kementerian Pekerjaan Umum dan Perumahan Rakyat, 2014 <http://p2kp.org/wartadetil.asp?mid=7132&catid=2&> (accessed 30 July 2016).

Al-Heeti, Roaa M. "Why Nursing Homes Will Not Work: Caring for the Needs of the Aging Muslim American Population". *Elder LJ* 15 (2007): 205–31.

Ali, A. Mukti. "Islam in Indonesia". *Handbook of Oriental Studies. Section 3 Southeast Asia, Religions, Religionen* 2 (1975): 55–80.

Ali, Lukman. *Unsur Adat Minangkabau dalam Sastra Indonesia, 1922–1956*. Jakarta: Balai Pustaka. 1997.

Allen, Emma R. *Analysis of Trends and Challenges in the Indonesian Labor Market*. Manila: Asian Development Bank, 2016.

Andaya, Leonard Y. "Unravelling Minangkabau Ethnicity". *Itinerario* 24, no. 2 (2000): 20–43.

Antara. "Penghuni Panti Jompo Meningkat". 23 July 2008 <http://www.antaranews.com/berita/110195/penghuni-panti-jompo-meningkat> (accessed 18 September 2016).

————. "Anggaran Kemsos Hanya Mampu Melayani 100.000 Lansia". 30 May 2012 <http://www.antarasumbar.com/berita/sosial/j/25/227415/anggaran-kemsos-hanya-mampu-layani-100-000-lansia.html> (accessed 18 September 2016).

————. "Gubernur Mengajak Beri Perhatian Pada Lansia". 20 June 2014 <http://www.antarasumbar.com/berita/provinsi/d/1/353902/gubernur-mengajak-beri-perhatian-pada-lansia.html> (accessed 21 September 2014).

Antoni, Siri. "Mengapa Orang Minang Mampu Bertahan di Perantauan?". *Antara Sulteng*, 15 June 2012 <http://www.antarasulteng.com/berita/1183/mengapa-orang-minang-mampu-bertahan-diperantauan> (accessed 2 September 2016).

Anwar, Khaidir. "Minangkabau, Background of the Main Pioneers of Modern Standard Malay in Indonesia". *Archipel* 12, no. 1 (1976): 77–93.

Arditono. "Melihat Kebahagiaan Dua Nagari di Solsel yang Bakal Nikmati Listrik". Padang Ekspres, 25 October 2015 <http://www.news.padek.co/detail/a/41327> (accessed 27 July 2016).

Arifin, Zainal. "Dualitas Praktik Perkawinan Minangkabau". *Humaniora* 21, no. 2 (2004): 150–61.

Astuti, Vitaria Wahyu. "Hubungan Dukungan Keluarga dengan Tingkat Depresi pada Lansia di Posyandu Sejahtera GBI Setia Bakti Kediri". *Jurnal Penelitian STIKES Kediri* 3, no. 2 (2012): 78–85.

Atran, Scott, Douglas L. Medin and Norbert O. Ross. "The Cultural Mind: Environmental Decision Making and Cultural Modeling Within and Across Populations". *Psychological Review* 112, no. 4 (2005): 744–76.

Badan Kependudukan dan Keluarga Berencana Nasional. "Jumlah Balita, Remaja, dan Lansia per Wilayah: Sumatera Barat". 2011a <http://aplikasi.bkkbn.go.id/mdk/MDKReports/KS/tabel102.aspx> (accessed 21 August 2016).

————. "Sejarah BKKBN". 2011b <http://www.bkkbn.go.id/ViewProfil.aspx?ProfilID=21 (accessed 19 July 2016).

Badan Pusat Statistik (BPS). *Survei Sosial dan Ekonomi Nasional (Susenas)*. Jakarta: BPS, 2009.

————. *Umur dan Jenis Kelamin Penduduk Indonesia: Hasil Sensus Penduduk 2010*. Jakarta: BPS, 2011.

————. "School Participation Rate by Province, 2003–2013". 2014a <http://www.bps.go.id/eng/tab_sub/view.php?kat=1&tabel=1&daftar=1&id_subyek=28&notab=3> (accessed 17 September 2016).

————. *Statistik Penduduk Lansia*. Jakarta: BPS, 2014b.

————. *Statistik Penduduk Lanjut Usia 2014: Hasil Survei Sosial Ekonomi Nasional*. Jakarta: BPS, 2015.

————. "Persentase Penduduk Buta Huruf Menurut Kelompok Umur, 2011–2015". *Susenas 2003–2015*. 2016 <https://www.bps.go.id/linkTableDinamis/view/id/1056> (accessed 19 July 2016).

Badan Pusat Statistik (BPS) Kota Padang. *Padang dalam Angka*. Padang: BPS, 2015.

Badan Pusat Statistik (BPS) Sumatera Barat. "Persentase Pengeluaran Penduduk Daerah Perkotaan dan Pedesaan Menurut Kabupaten /Kota dan Golongan Pengeluaran per Kapita Sebulan". 2014 <http://sumbar.bps.go.id/ linkTabelStatis/view/id/371> (accessed 18 August 2016).

———. "Indikator Sosial Budaya 2003, 2006, 2009 dan 2012". 2016a <http://sumbar. bps.go.id/linkTabelStatis/view/id/186> (accessed 31 August 2016).

———. "Jumlah Penduduk dan Laju Pertumbuhan Penduduk Menurut Kabupaten/ Kota di Provinsi Sumatera Barat, 2010, 2014, dan 2015". 2016b (http://sumbar. bps.go.id/linkTabelStatis/view/id/399 (accessed 1 September 2016).

———. "Penduduk Berumur 15 Tahun Ke Atas Menurut Golongan Umur dan Jenis Kegiatan Selama Seminggu yang Lalu, 2004–2015". 2016c <http://sumbar.bps. go.id/linkTabelStatis/view/id/72> (accessed 30 August 2016).

———. "Rata-Rata Lama Sekolah Penduduk Provinsi Sumatera Barat". 2016d <http://sumbar.bps.go.id/linkTabelStatis/view/id/378> (accessed 18 August 2016).

———. *Statistik Sosial dan Kependudukan*. Padang: BPS, 2016e.

Barendregt, Bart. "The Sound of 'Longing for Home': Redefining a Sense of Community through Minang Popular Music". *Bijdragen tot de Taal-, Land-en Volkenkunde* 158, no. 3 (2002): 411–50.

Barford, Anna, Danny Dorling, G. Davey Smith and Mary Shaw. "Life Expectancy: Women Now on Top Everywhere". *BMJ* 332 (2006): 808.

Barresi, Barbara A., Marjorie Nicholas, Lisa Tabor Connor, Loraine K. Obler and Martin L. Albert. "Semantic Degradation and Lexical Access in Age-Related Naming Failures". *Aging, Neuropsychology, and Cognition* 7, no. 3 (2000): 169–78.

Berita Satu. "Jumlah Pekerja Lanjut Usia di Indonesia Tertinggi di Asia". 15 April 2014a <http://www.beritasatu.com/ekonomi-karier/178051-jumlah-pekerja-lanjut-usia-di-indonesia-termasuk-tertinggi-di-asia.html> (accessed 15 July 2016).

———. "Orang Minang Tak Lagi Tertarik Berdagang". 20 September 2014b <http:// www.beritasatu.com/nasional/211374-orang-minang-tak-lagi-tertarik-berdagang.html> (accessed 1 September 2016).

Berita Sore. "Tegakan Adat dan Syarak Berantas Maksiat di Padang". 29 March 2016 <http://beritasore.com/2016/03/29/tegakan-adat-dan-syarak-berantas-maksiat-di-padang/> (accessed 29 August 2016).

Berkman, Lisa F. and Ichiro Kawachi, eds. *Social Epidemiology*. Oxford: Oxford University Press, 2000.

Biedenharn, Paula J. and Janice Bastlin Normoyle. "Elderly Community Residents' Reactions to the Nursing Home: An Analysis of Nursing Home-Related Beliefs". *The Gerontologist* 31, no. 1 (1991): 107–15.

Biezeveld, Renske. "The Many Roles of Adat in West Sumatra". In *The Revival of Tradition in Indonesian Politics: The Deployment of Adat from Colinialism to Indigenism*, edited by Jamie S. Davidson and David Henley, pp. 203–23. Abingdon and New York: Routledge, 2007.

Brakel, Lode Frank. "Islam and Local Traditions: Syncretic Ideas and Practices". *Indonesia and the Malay World* 32, no. 92 (2004): 5–20.

Blust, Robert. "An Overlooked Feature of Malay Historical Phonology". *Bulletin of the School of Oriental and African Studies* 45, no. 2 (1982): 284–99.

Burke, Deborah M., Donald G. MacKay and Lori E. James. "Theoretical Approaches to Language and Aging". In *Models of Cognitive Aging*, edited by Timothy J. Perfect and Elizabeth A. Maylor, pp. 204–37. Oxford: Oxford University Press, 2000.

Butler, Yuko G. and Kenji Hakuta. "Bilingualism and Second Language Acquisition". In *The Handbook of Bilingualism*, edited by Tej K. Bhatia and William C. Ritchie, pp. 114–44. Malden, MA: Blackwell, 2004.

Chatra, Emeraldy. "Minang Berbenah!". *Sumbar Satu*, 22 September 2015 <http://www.sumbarsatu.com/berita/11160-minang-berbenah> (accessed 3 September 2016).

Clarke, Peter, Friedhelm Hardy, Leslie Houlden and Stewart Sutherland, eds. *The World's Religions*. Abingdon: Routledge, 2004.

Cribb, Robert and Audrey Kahin. *Historical Dictionary of Indonesia*. Lanham, MD: Scarecrow Press, 2004.

D'Andrade, Roy G. "Cultural Meaning Systems". In *Culture Theory: Essays on Mind, Self and Emotion*, edited by Richard A. Schweder and Robert A. Levine, pp. 88–119. Cambridge: Cambridge University Press, 1984.

———. "Schemas and Motivation". In *Human Motives and Cultural Models*, edited by Roy D'Andrade and Claudia Strauss, pp. 23–44. Cambridge: Cambridge University Press, 1992.

Dave, Dhaval, Inas Rashad and Jasmina Spasojevic. *The Effects of Retirement on Physical and Mental Health Outcomes*. No. w12123. Cambridge, MA: National Bureau of Economic Research, 2006.

Day, Ruth S. "Verbal Fluency and the Language-Bound Effect". In *Individual Differences in Language Ability and Language Behavior*, edited by Charles J. Fillmore, Daniel Kempler and William S.-Y. Wang, pp. 57–84. New York, San Francisco and London: Academic Press, 1979.

de Bot, Kees and Michael Clyne. "A 16-Year Longitudinal Study of Language Attrition in Dutch Immigrants in Australia". *Journal of Multilingual & Multicultural Development* 15, no. 1 (1994): 17–28.

Detik News. "Duh! 2,8 Juta Lansia di Indonesia Terlantar". 20 September 2013 <http://news.detik.com/read/2013/09/20/213955/2365230/10/duh-28-juta-lansia-di-indonesia-terlantar> (accessed 23 September 2016).

———. "Kisah Sulit Air dan Orang-Orang Kaya". 13 June 2016 <http://x.detik.

com/detail/intermeso/20160613/Kisah-Sulit-Air-dan-Orang-orang-Kaya/ index.php> (accessed 2 September 2016).

Dewan Bahasa dan Pustaka. *Kamus Dewan*. Kuala Lumpur: DBP, 2005.

Dinas Kesehatan Kota Padang. *Profil Tahunan DKK Tahun 2009*. Padang: DKK, 2010.

Dinas Pertanian dan Perkebunan. "Tanam Sekali, Panan Berkali-Kali". 2 September 2014 <http://distanbun.enrekangkab.go.id/tanam-sekali-panen-berkali-kali/> (accessed 22 September 2016).

Djohan, Djohermansyah. "Fenomena Etnosentrisme dalam Penyelenggaraan Otonomi Daerah". In *Desentralisasi dan Otonomi Daerah: Desentralisasi, Demokratisasi dan Akuntabilitas Pemerintahan Daerah*, edited by Syamsuddin Haris, pp. 209–26. Jakarta: LIPI, 2007.

Dobbin, Christine. *Islamic Revivalism in a Changing Peasant Economy: Central Sumatra, 1784–1847*. London: Curzon Press, 1983.

Dove, Michael R. and Daniel M. Kammen. "Vernacular Models of Development: An Analysis of Indonesia under the 'New Order' ". *World Development* 29, no. 4 (2001): 619–39.

Dressler, William W. "What's Cultural about Biocultural Research?". *Ethos* 33, no. 1 (2005): 20–45.

―――― and James R. Bindon. "The Health Consequences of Cultural Consonance: Cultural Dimensions of Lifestyle, Social Support, and Arterial Blood Pressure in an African American Community". *American Anthropologist* 102, no. 2 (2000): 244–60.

――――, Mauro C. Balieiro, Rosane P. Ribeiro and José Ernesto Dos Santos. "Cultural Consonance and Arterial Blood Pressure in Urban Brazil". *Social Science and Medicine* 61, no. 3 (2005a): 527–40.

――――. Camila D. Borges, Mauro C. Balieiro and Jose Ernesto Dos Santos. "Measuring Cultural Consonance: Examples with Special Reference to Measurement Theory in Anthropology". *Field Methods* 17, no. 4 (2005b).: 331–55.

――――. Mauro C. Balieiro, Rosane P. Ribeiro and José Ernesto Dos Santos. "Cultural Consonance and Psychological Distress: Examining the Associations in Multiple Cultural Domains". *Culture, Medicine and Psychiatry* 31, no. 2 (2007): 195–224.

Economist, The. "Ten Years On: How Asia Shrugged Off Its Economic Crisis". 4 July 2007 <http://www.economist.com/node/9432495> (accessed 18 July 2016).

Edmunds, June and Bryan S. Turner. "Global Generations: Social Change in the Twentieth Century". *British Journal of Sociology* 56, no. 4 (2005): 559–77.

Ellen, Roy F. "The Trade in Spices". *Indonesia Circle* 5, no. 12 (1977): 21–25.

Ellison, Christopher G. "Religion, the Life Stress Paradigm, and the Study of Depression". In *Religion in Aging and Health: Theoretical Foundations and Methodological Frontiers*, edited by Jeffrey S. Levinson, pp. 78–124. Thousand Oaks: Sage Publications, 1994.

Elson, Robert Edward. *The Idea of Indonesia: A History*. Cambridge: Cambridge University Press, 2008.

Evers, Hans-Dieter. "The End of Urban Involution and the Cultural Construction of Urbanism in Indonesia". *Internationales Asienforum* 38, nos. 1–2 (2007): 51–65.

Fanany, Ismet and Rebecca Fanany. *The Wisdom of the Malay Proverbs*. Kuala Lumpur: Dewan Bahasa dan Pustaka, 2003.

Fanany, Rebecca. "Language and Culture as Social Determinants of Health in the Context of Urbanization". In *Urban Mobility: Textual and Spatial Urban Dynamics in Health, Culture and Society: Proceedings of the Third International Conference on Urban Mobility: Its Impacts on Socio-cultural and Health Issues*, edited by Nur Wulan, Arum Budiastuti, Deny Arnos Kwary, Rebecca Fanany and Azizan Baharuddin, pp. 88-95. Surabaya: Universitas Airlangga, 2012.

—— and Ismet Fanany. "Culture, Lifestyle and Diabetes in Indonesia". *International Journal of Health, Wellness and Society* 5, no. 4 (2015): 75–85.

——, Ismet Fanany and Rafsel Tasady. "The Experience of Old Age in West Sumatra, Indonesia: Culture Shift and Cultural Consonance in the Modern Era". *International Journal of Aging and Society* 3, no. 1 (2014): 51–59.

Fatimah, Titin and Hengky Andora. "Pola Penyelesaian Sengketa Tanah Ulayat di Sumatera Barat (Sengketa antara Masyarakat dengan Investor)". *Jurnal Ilmu Hukum* 4, no. 1 (2014): 11–28.

Foulcher, Keith. "Sumpah Pemuda: The Making and Meaning of a Symbol of Indonesian Nationhood". *Asian Studies Review* 24, no. 3 (2000): 377–410.

Ghofar, M. "BPMPD: Lembaga *Adat* Miliki Peran Kembangkan Desa". 31 October 2013 <http://www.antarakaltim.com/berita/17562/bpmpd-lembaga-*adat*-miliki-peran-kembangkan-desa> (accessed 19 September 2014).

Goodenough, Ward H. "Culture". In *Encyclopedia of Cultural Anthropology*, edited by David Levinson and Melvin Embers, pp. 291–99. New York: Henry Holt, 1996.

Goral, Mira. "First-Language Decline in Healthy Aging: Implications for Attrition in Bilingualism". *Journal of Neurolinguistics* 17, no. 1 (2004): 31–52.

——, Gary Libben, Loraine K. Obler, Gonia Jarema and Keren Ohayon. "Lexical Attrition in Younger and Older Bilingual Adults". *Clinical Linguistics & Phonetics* 22, no. 7 (2008): 509–22.

Gubrium, Jaber F. and James A. Holstein, eds. *Ways of Aging*. Malden, MA and Oxford: Blackwell Publishing, 2008.

Hakimy, Idrus Dt. Rajo Penghulu. *Pokok-Pokok Pengetahuan Adat Alam Minangkabau*. Jakarta: Remadja Karya, 1984.

Hakimy, H. Idrus Dt. Rajo Penghulu. *Rangkaian Mustika Adat Basandi Syarak di Minangkabau*. Jakarta: Remadja Karya, 1988.

——. *Pegangan Penghulu, Bundo Kanduang, dan Pidato Alua Pasambahan Adat di Minangkabau*. Jakarta: Remaja Rosdakarya, 1991.

Haluan. "Kaum Mabout Menangkan Gugatan atas UBH Cs". 28 June 2016*a* <http://
  harianhaluan.com/news/detail/56286/kaum-maboet-menangkan-gugatan-
  atas-ubh-cs> (accessed 18 August 2016).

———. "Ninik Mamak Nagari Kompak Lawan Pencaplokan Tanah Ulayat". 4 May
  2016*b* <http://harianhaluan.com/mobile/detailberita/53009/ninik-mamak-
  nagari-kompak-lawan-pencaplokan-tanah-ulayat> (accessed 18 August
  2016).

———. "Suku, Harga Mati bagi Anak Minangkabau". 29 April 2016*c* <http://
  harianhaluan.com/mobile/detailberita/52749/suku-harga-mati-bagi-anak-
  minangkabau> (accessed 2 September 2016).

Handwerker, Penn W. *Quick Ethnography: A Guide to Rapid Multi-Method Research.*
  Lanham, MD: Rowman Altamira, 2001.

Hansen, Lynne. "Language Attrition: The Fate of the Start". *Annual Review of
  Applied Linguistics* 21 (2001): 60–73.

Harimansyah, Ganjar. "Bahasa dan Nasionalisme". Badan Pengembangan
  dan Pembinaan Bahasa, 2015 <http://badanbahasa.kemdikbud.go.id/
  lamanbahasa/artikel/42> (accessed 19 July 2016).

Heider, Karl G. *Landscapes of Emotion: Mapping Three Cultures of Emotion in Indonesia.*
  Cambridge and New York: Cambridge University Press, 2006.

Hendra, M.N. "Dua Unit Panti Jompo di Sumbar Kelebihan Penghuni Lansia".
  20 June 2014 <http://www.klikpositif.com/news/read/9188/dua-unit-panti-
  jompo-di-sumbar-kelebihan-penghuni-lansia.html> (accessed 18 September
  2014).

Hermana. "Penguatan Eksistensi Panti Werdha di Tengah Pergeseran Budaya dan
  Keluarga". Kementerian Sosial Republik Indonesia, 30 June 2008 <http://www.
  kemsos.go.id/modules.php?name=News&file=article&sid=704> (accessed
  11 September 2016).

Hidayatullah. "Saudi Kritik Jamaah Haji Sakit Ingin Mati di Tanah Suci".
  21 September 2014 <http://www.hidayatullah.com/berita/info-haji-umrah/
  read/2014/09/21/29916/saudi-kritik-jamaah-haji-sakit-ingin-mati-di-tanah-
  suci.html> (accessed 14 July 2016).

Hogan, Candice L., Jutta Mata and Laura L. Carstensen. "Exercise Holds Immediate
  Benefits for Affect and Cognition in Younger and Older Adults". *Psychology
  and Aging* 28, no. 2 (2013): 587.

Holden, Clare Janaki, Rebecca Sear and Ruth Mace. "Matriliny as Daughter-Biased
  Investment". *Evolution and Human Behavior* 24, no. 2 (2003): 99–112.

Holtzappel, Coen J.G. and Martin Ramstedt, eds. *Decentralization and Regional
  Autonomy in Indonesia: Implementation and Challenges.* Singapore: Institute of
  Southeast Asian Studies, 2009.

Houben, Vincent J.H. "Southeast Asia and Islam". *Annals of the American Academy
  of Political and Social Science* 588, no. 1 (2003): 149–70.

Hugo, Graeme. "Lansia: Elderly People in Indonesia at the Turn of the Century". In *Ageing in the Asia-Pacific Region: Issues, Policies and Future Trends*, edited by David R. Phillips, pp. 299–321. New York and London: Routledge, 2000.

Hulsen, Madeleine, Kees de Bot and Bert Weltens. "Between Two Worlds: Social Networks, Language Shift, and Language Processing in Three Generations of Dutch Migrants in New Zealand". *International Journal of the Sociology of Language* 153 (2002): 27–52.

Hummert, Mary L., Teri A. Garstka, Ellen B. Ryan and Jaye L. Bonnesen. "The Role of Age Stereotypes in Interpersonal Communication". In *Handbook of Communication and Aging Research*, edited by Jon F. Nussbaum and Justine Coupland, pp. 91–114. Mahwah, NJ: Lawrence Erlbaum, 2004.

Huraini, E. and G. Surmasih. "Studi Fenomenologi: Pengalaman Interaksi Sosial Lansia Dengan Sesama Lansia Dan Pengasuh di Panti Sosial Tresna Werdha 'Sabai Nan Aluih' Sicincin Kabupaten Padang Pariaman Tahun 2012". *Jurnal Ners* 8, no. 1 (2012): 96–104.

Husna, Elfira, Evi Susanti, Yuhendri Putra and Junios Junios. "Perbedaan Tingkat Insomnia Pada Lansia Sebelum Dan Sesudah Senam Lansia Di PSTW Kasih Sayang Ibu Tahun 2015". *Jurnal Kesehatan* 6, no. 1 (2015): 1–6.

Hussain, Mohammad Akhtar, Rachel R. Huxley and Abdullah Al Mamun. "Multimorbidity Prevalence and Pattern in Indonesian Adults: An Exploratory Study Using National Survey Data". *BMJ Open* 5, no. 12 (2015): e009810.

Indrizal, Edi. "Problems of Elderly Without Children: A Case Study of the Matrilineal Minangkabau, West Sumatra". In *Ageing Without Children: European and Asian Perspectives*, edited by Phillip Kreager and Elisabeth Schröder-Butterfill, pp. 49–76. New York and Oxford: Berghahn Books, 2004.

Infoasaid. *Indonesia Media and Telecoms Landscape Guide*. London: Ifoasaid, 2012.

Inglehart, Ronald and Wayne E. Baker. "Modernization, Cultural Change, and the Persistence of Traditional Values". *American Sociological Review* 65, no. 1 (2000): 19–51.

Iwan, Ikhwan. "Suluak, Ritual Naqsabandiyah dengan Ibadah 40 Hari Tanpa Putus". *Jaring News*, 24 June 2014 <http://www.jaringnews.com/seleb/hangout/63593/Suluak-Ritual-Naqsabandiyah-dengan-Ibadah-40-Hari-Tanpa-Putus> (accessed 14 July 2016).

Jahansyahtono, Ramanda. "Bujuk Pemuda Jadi Petani dengan Modernisasi Pertanian". *Kompas*, 4 January 2016 <http://bisniskeuangan.kompas.com/read/2016/01/04/151600726/Bujuk.Pemuda.Jadi.Petani.dengan.Modernisasi.Pertanian> (accessed 2 October 2016).

Jaminan Sosial Indonesia (Jamsos). "Jumlah Lansia Cukup Signifikan Sekitar 2,8 Juta". 24 May 2012 <http://www.jamsosindonesia.com/cetak/print_externallink/3068> (accessed 18 September 2016).

Jaskyte, Kristina and William W. Dressler. "Studying Culture as an Integral

Aggregate Variable: Organizational Culture and Innovation in a Group of Nonprofit Organizations". *Field Methods* 16, no. 3 (2004): 265–84.

Jati, Wasisto Raharjo. "Dilema Ekonomi: Pasar Tradisional versus Liberalisasi Bisnis Ritel di Indonesia". *Jurusan Ekonomi Pembangunan* 4, no. 2 (2012): 223–42.

Jena, Yeremias. "Multiple Vulnerabilities of the Elderly People in Indonesia: Ethical Considerations". *Philosophy Study* 4, no. 4 (2014): 277–86.

Josselin de Jong, Jan Petrus Benjamin de. *Minangkabau and Negeri Sembilan: Sociopolitical Structure in Indonesia*. The Hague: Martinus Nijhoff, 1980.

JPNN. "Wagub Minta Perantau Gunakan Bahasa Minang". 8 February 2013 <http://www.jpnn.com/read/2013/02/08/157486/Wagub-Minta-Perantau-Gunakan-Bahasa-Minang> (accessed 2 September 2016).

———."Kemensos Teruskan Rumah Baru bagi Lansia Terlantar". 6 June 2014 <http://www.jpnn.com/index.php?mib=berita.detail&id=238672> (accessed 18 September 2016).

Juliani, Reni, Hafied Cangara and Andi Alimuddin Unde. "Komunikasi Antarbudaya Etnis Aceh dan Bugis-Makassar Melalui Asimilasi Perkawinan di Kota Makassar". *KAREBA: Jurnal Ilmu Komunikasi* 4, no. 1 (2016): 70–87.

Junus, Umar. "Some remarks on Minangkabau Social Structure: Introduction". *Bijdragen tot de Taal-, Land- en Volkenkunde* 120, no. 3 (1964): 293–326.

Kaba News. "Bahasa Minang Terancam Punah?". 1 June 2016 <http://www.kabanews.com/bahasa-minang-terancam-punah/> (accessed 2 September 2016).

Kabar Nias. "Tak Buat Perda Soal Bahasa, Kepala Daerah Langgar Konstitusi". 5 August 2015 <https://kabarnias.com/budaya/tak-buat-perda-soal-bahasa-kepala-daerah-langgar-konstitusi-2171> (accessed 19 July 2016).

Kantor Wilayah Kementerian Agama Provinsi Sumatera Barat. "Kemenag dan Baznas Serahkan Zakat Bagi Lansia". 28 June 2016 <https://sumbar.kemenag.go.id/berita/380569/kemenag-dan-baznas-serahkan-zakat-bagi-lansia> (accessed 14 July 2016).

Kartika, Dian Dewi. "Mudik Perantau Geliatkan Sektor Riil". Pemerintah Provinsi Sumatera Bara, 26 July 2013 <http://www.sumbarprov.go.id/details/news/992> (accessed 21 September 2016).

Kato, Tsuyoshi. *Matriliny and Migration: Evolving Minangkabau Traditions in Indonesia*. Ithaca, NY: Cornell University Press, 1982.

———. "Dynamics of the Frontier World in Insular Southeast Asia: An Overview". *Southeast Asian Studies* 34, no. 4 (1997): 611–21.

Keane, Webb. "Public Speaking: On Indonesian as the Language of the Nation". *Public Culture* 15, no. 3 (2003): 503–30.

Keasberry, Iris N. "Elder Care and Intergenerational Relationships in Rural Yogyakarta, Indonesia". *Ageing & Society* 21, no. 5 (2001): 641–65.

Keijzer, Merel. "Language Reversion Versus General Cognitive Decline: Towards a New Taxonomy of Language Change in Elderly Bilingual Immigrants". In *Modeling Bilingualism: From Structure to Chaos — In Honor of Kees de Bot*, edited by Monika S. Schmid and Wander Lowie, pp. 221–32. Philadelphia: John Benjamins, 2011.

Kementerian Agama. "Jemaah Haji Lansia Dapat Ajukan Percepatan Keberangkatan". 11 March 2016*a* <http://haji.kemenag.go.id/v2/content/calon-jemaah-haji-lansia-bisa-ajukan-percepatan-keberangkatan> (accessed 14 July 2016).

———. "Waiting List Jemaah Haji". 2016*b*. <http://haji.kemenag.go.id/v2/basisdata/waiting-list> (accessed 14 July 2016).

Kementerian Kesehatan Republik Indonesia. *Peta Kesehatan Indonesia 2010*. Jakarta: Kementerian Kesehatan, 2012.

———. *Gambaran Kesehatan Lanjut Usia di Indonesia*. Jakarta: Kementerian Kesehatan, 2013.

———. *Beban Penyakit, Trauma dan Faktor Risiko di Indonesia*. Jakarta: Kementerian Kesehatan, 2015.

———. *Lansia di Indonesia*. Jakarta: Kementerian Kesehatan, 2017.

Kementerian Sosial Republik Indonesia. "Penguatan Eksistensi Panti Werdha di Tengah Pergeseran Budaya dan Keluarga". 30 June 2008 <http://www.kemsos.go.id/modules.php?name=News&file=article&sid=704> (accessed 28 July 2016).

———. "Tugas Bersama Siapkan Lansia Sejahtera, Mandiri dan Produktif". 3 June 2016 <http://www.kemsos.go.id/modules.php?name=News&file=article&sid=19076> (accessed 28 July 2016).

Kemper, Susan and Jose C. Lacal. "Addressing the Communication Needs of an Aging Society". In *Technology for Adaptive Aging*, edited by Richard W. Pew and Susan B. Van Hemel, pp. 129–49. Washington, D.C.: National Academies Press, 2004.

Kemper, Susan, and Tracy L. Mitzner. "Language Production and Comprehension". In *Handbook of the Psychology of Aging*, edited by James E. Birren and K. Warner Schaie, pp. 378–98. San Diego and London: Academic Press, 2001.

Kim, Jungmeen E. and Phyllis Moen. "Retirement Transitions, Gender, and Psychological Well-Being: A Life-Course, Ecological Model". *Journals of Gerontology Series B: Psychological Sciences and Social Sciences* 57, no. 3 (2002): P212–22.

Koenig, Harold, Dana King and Verna B. Carson. *Handbook of Religion and Health*. Oxford University Press, USA, 2012.

Kompas. "Media Massa: Kembalikan Makna kepada Kata". 16 December 2009 <http://bisniskeuangan.kompas.com/read/2009/12/16/21233395/media.massa.kembalikan.makna.kepada.kata> (accessed 19 July 2016).

———. "Jejak Para Perantau". 9 September 2013 <http://travel.kompas.com/

read/2013/09/09/0746257/Jejak.Para.Perantau> (accessed 17 September 2016).

———. "Gubernur Jateng Segera Berlakukan Aturan Sehari Berbahasa Jawa". 8 September 2014*a* <http://regional.kompas.com/read/2014/09/08/20241191/Gubernur.Jateng.Segera.Berlakukan.Aturan.Sehari.Berbahasa.Jawa> (accessed 18 September 2016).

———. "Pasar Properti Padang Terhambat Status Tanah Ulayat". 10 April 2014*b* <http://properti.kompas.com/read/2014/04/10/1524470/Pasar.Properti.Padang.Terhambat.Status.Tanah.Ulayat> (accessed 18 August 2016).

Köpke, Barbara, Monika S. Schmid, Merel Keijzer and Susan Dostert, eds. *Language Attrition: Theoretical Perspectives*. Philadelphia: John Benjamins Publishing, 2007.

Krause, Neal. "Religious Meaning and Subjective Well-Being in Late Life". *Journals of Gerontology Series B: Psychological Sciences and Social Sciences* 58, no. 3 (2003): S160–70.

———. "Common Facets of Religion, Unique Facets of Religion, and Life Satisfaction among Older African Americans". *Journals of Gerontology Series B: Psychological Sciences and Social Sciences* 59, no. 2 (2004): S109–17.

———, Jersey Liang, Benjamin A. Shaw, Hidehiro Sugisawa, Hye-Kyung Kim and Yoko Sugihara. "Religion, Death of a Loved One, and Hypertension among Older Adults in Japan". *Journals of Gerontology Series B: Psychological Sciences and Social Sciences* 57, no. 2 (2002): S96–107.

Kreager, Philip and Elisabeth Schröder-Butterfill. "Gaps in the Family Networks of Older People in Three Indonesian Communities". *Journal of Cross-Cultural Gerontology* 22, no. 1 (2007): 1–25.

Krier, Jennifer. "The Marital Project: Beyond the Exchange of Men in Minangkabau Marriage". *American Anthropologist* 27, no. 4 (2000): 877–97.

Kristyaningsih, Dewi. "Hubungan Antara Dukungan Keluarga Dengan Tingkat Depresi Pada Lansia". *Jurnal Keperawatan* 1, no. 1 (2011): 21–23.

Kusumowardani, Andreany and Aniek Puspitosari. "Hubungan Antara Tingkat Depresi Lansia Dengan Interaksi Sosial Lansia di Desa Sobokerto Kecamatan Ngemplak Boyolali". *Jurnal Terpadu Ilmu Kesehatan* 3, no. 2 (2014): 184–88.

Langlois, Francis, Thien Tuong Minh Vu, Kathleen Chassé, Gilles Dupuis, Marie-Jeanne Kergoat and Louis Bherer. "Benefits of Physical Exercise Training on Cognition and Quality of Life in Frail Older Adults". *Journals of Gerontology Series B: Psychological Sciences and Social Sciences* 68, no. 3 (2013): 400–404.

Levi-Strauss, Claude. *The Elementary Structures of Kinship*. James Harle Bell, trans. Boston: Beacon Press, 1969.

Levin, Jeff and Linda M. Chatters. "Religion, Aging, and Health: Historical Perspectives, Current Trends, and Future Directions: Public Health". *Journal of Religion, Spirituality & Aging* 20, nos. 1–2 (2008): 153–72.

————, Linda M. Chatters and Robert Joseph Taylor. "Religious Factors in Health and Medical Care among Older Adults". *Southern Medical Journal* 99, no. 10 (2006): 1168–69.

Lewis, M. Paul, Gary F. Simons and Charles D. Fennig, eds. *Ethnologue: Languages of the World, Seventeenth edition*. Dallas: SIL International, 2016 <http://www.ethnologue.com/language/min>.

Lian Kwen Fee. "The Construction of Malay Identity across Nations: Malaysia, Singapore, and Indonesia". *Bijdragen tot de Taal-, Land-en Volkenkunde* 157 (2001): 861–79.

Lindsey, Timothy. *Indonesia: Law and Society*. Sydney: Federation Press, 2008.

Loeb, Edwin. "Patrilineal and Matrilineal Organization in Sumatra". *American Anthropologist* 36, no. 1 (1934): 26–56.

Mabry, J. Beth, Roseann Giarrusso and Vern L. Bengtson. "Generations, the Life Course, and Family Change". *The Blackwell Companion to the Sociology of Families*, edited by Jacqueline Scott, Judith Treas and Martin Richards, pp. 87–108. Malden, MA and Oxford, UK: Blackwell. 2004.

MacKay, Anna J., Lisa Tabor Connor, Martin L. Albert and Loraine K. Obler. "Noun and Verb Retrieval in Healthy Aging". *Journal of the International Neuropsychological Society* 8, no. 6 (2002): 764–70.

Makki, M. Ali. "Munculnya Gangguan Mental Masyarakat Lanjut Usia dan Upaya Pencegahannya". *Al-Tatwir* 2, no. 1 (2016): 83–118.

Makruf, Aadiaat. "Kantor Pegadaian Padang Dipenuhi Nasabah Menebus Barang". *Antara News*, 24 June 2016 <http://epaper.antarasumbar.com/berita/180315/kantor-pegadaian-padang-dipenuhi-nasabah-menebus-barang.html> (accessed 30 July 2016).

Marmot, Michael, Sharon Friel, Ruth Bell, Tanja AJ Houweling, Sebastian Taylor and Commission on Social Determinants of Health. "Closing the Gap in a Generation: Health Equity through Action on the Social Determinants of Health". *The Lancet* 372, no. 9650 (2008): 1661–69.

Masithoh, Anny Rosiana, Achir Yani S. Hamid and Luknis Sabri. "Pengaruh Latihan Ketrampilan Sosial terhadap Kemampuan Sosialisasi pada Lansia dengan Kesepian di Panti Wredha Semarang". *Jurnal Keperawatan Soedirman* 7, no. 2 (2012): 78–85.

Mata Rakyat. "Peringatan Hari Lansia Nasional ke19 di Provinsi Sumatera Barat". 17 June 2015 <http://matarakyatnews.com/berita-lokal/padang/peringatan-hari-lansia-nasional-ke-19-di-provinsi-sumatera-barat/> (accessed 11 September 2016).

McAuley, William J. and Rosemary Blieszner. "Selection of Long-Term Care Arrangements by Older Community Residents". *The Gerontologist* 25, no. 2 (1985): 188–93.

Minang Lamo. "Penginjil dari Ranah Minang 1927–2012". 29 August 2013

<http://minanglamo.blogspot.com.au/2013/08/penginjil-dari-ranah-minang-1927-2012.html> (accessed 21 July 2016).

Mindel, Charles H. and C. Edwin Vaughan. "A Multidimensional Approach to Religiosity and Disengagement". *Journal of Gerontology* 33, no. 1 (1978): 103–8.

Moberg, David O. "Predicaments in Researching Spirituality and Religion: A Response to Glicksman's 'Contemporary Study of Religion and Spirituality Among the Elderly'". *Journal of Religion, Spirituality & Aging* 21, no. 4 (2009): 297–309.

Montolalu, Lucy R. and Leo Suryadinata. "National Language and Nation-Building: The Case of Bahasa Indonesia". In *Language, Nation and Development in Southeast Asia*, edited by Lee Hock Guan and Leo Suryadinata, pp. 39–50. Singapore: Institute of Southeast Asian Studies, 2007.

Muhadjir. "Pengangguran Semakin Meningkat di Indonesia". *Miraj News*, 7 November 2015 <http://www.mirajnews.com/id/angka-pengangguran-semakin-meningkat-di-indonesia/89318> (accessed 30 August 2016).

Mukhlis, P., Edward Poelinggomang, Abdul Madjid Kallo, Bambang Sulistyo, Anwar Thosibo and Andi Maryam. *Sejarah Kebudayaan Sulawesi*. Jakarta: Direktorat Jenderal Kebudayaan, 1995.

Mukhlison. "Padang Miliki Perda Pelestarian Adat Istiadat Nagari". *Antara News*, 30 June 2012 <http://www.antarasumbar.com/berita/8766/padang-miliki-perda-pelestarian-adat-istiadat-nagari.html> (accessed 29 August 2016).

Mukhlisun. "Pemkab: Sengketa Tanah Ulayat Selesaikan Secara Adat". *Antara News*, 23 August 2013 <http://www.antarasumbar.com/berita/56314/pemkab-sengketa-tanah-ulayat-selesaikan-secara-adat.html> (accessed 29 July 2016).

———. "Gubernur Mengajak Beri Perhatian pada Lansia". *Antara News*, 20 June 2014 <http://sumbar.antaranews.com/berita/103081/gubernur-mengajak-beri-perhatian-pada-lansia.html> (accessed 23 September 2016).

Muktiyo, Widodo. "Globalisasi Media: Pusaran Imperialisme Budaya di Indonesia". *Jurnal Komunikasi Massa* 3, no. 2 (2010): 115–22.

Mulyana. "Pengunaan Bahasa Indonesia di Ruang Publik Rendah". *Antara*, 13 July 2016 <http://www.antarabanten.com/berita/25056/penggunaan-bahasa-indonesia-di-ruang-publik-rendah> (accessed 19 July 2016).

Munoz, Paul Michel. *Early Kingdoms of the Indonesian Archipelago and the Malay Peninsula*. Singapore: Didier Millet, 2006.

Musgrave, Simon. "Language Shift and Language Maintenance in Indonesia". In *Language, Education and Nation-Building: Assimilation and Shift in Southeast Asia*, edited by Peter Serrcombe and Ruanni Tupas, pp. 87–105. Palgrave Macmillan, UK, 2014.

Mutajali, Ali Rahman. "Begini Menteri Pertanian Gairahkan Pemuda Desa Mau Bertani". *Tribun News*, 7 October 2015 <http://www.tribunnews.com/

nasional/2015/10/07/begini-menteri-pertanian-gairahkan-pemuda-desa-mau-bertani> (accessed 2 October 2016).

My Tse, Mimi. "Nursing Home Placement: Perspectives of Community-Dwelling Older Persons". *Journal of Clinical Nursing* 16, no. 5 (2007): 911–17.

Nanda, Tri. "Di 50 Kota, 3.100 Warga Lanjut Usia Masih Terlantar". *GoSumbar*, 26 April 2016 <http://www.gosumbar.com/berita/baca/2016/04/27/di-50-kota-3100-warga-lanjut-usia-masih-terlantar#sthash.s3vVbdf8.dpbs> (accessed 12 September 2016).

Narulita, Richy. "Perbedaan Tingkat Depresi antara Lansia yang Memiliki Keluarga dengan Lansia yang Tidak Memiliki Keluarga". *Jurnal Mutiara Medika* 9, no. 2 (2016): 101–7.

Nasution, Mario Sofia. "Lebaran, 71 Kecelakaan Lalu Lintas Telah Terjadi di Sumbar". *Antara News*, 11 July 2016 <http://www.antarasumbar.com/berita/181621/lebaran-71-kecelakaan-lalu-lintas-telah-terjadi-di-sumbar.html> (accessed 31 August 2016).

Navis, A.A. *Alam Takambang Jadi Guru*. Jakarta: Gramedia, 1984.

Nesti, Meksi Rahma. "Variasi Leksikal Bahasa Minangkabau di Kabupaten Pesisir Selatan". *Arbitrer* 3, no. 1 (2016): 46–61.

Nugroho, Joko. "Pemkab Lakukan Sosialisasi Gender Lanjut Usia Cacat". Antara News, 13 June 2013 <http://sumbar.antaranews.com/berita/43931/pemkab-lakukan-sosialisasi-gender-lanjut-usia-cacat.html> (accessed 30 July 2016).

———. "200 Warga Lansia Dapat Santunan". *Antara News*, 7 January 2015 <http://sumbar.antaranews.com/berita/130510/200-warga-lansia-dapat-santunan.html> (accessed 28 July 2016).

Nusa News. "Lindungi Warganya yang Puasa, Walikota Padang Meradang dan Menentang Perda Mendagri Soal Melarang Razia". 15 June 2016 <http://www.nusanews.com/2016/06/lindungi-warganya-yang-puasa-walikota.html> (accessed 12 July 2016).

Oktaninda, Sri. *Makna Sosiologis Pergeseran Peran Ninik Mamak dalam Keluarga Minangkabau*. Jakarta: FISIP-UNEJ, 2009.

Paauw, Scott. "One Land, One Nation, One Language: An Analysis of Indonesia's National Language Policy". *University of Rochester Working Papers in the Language Sciences* 5, no. 1 (2009): 2–16.

Padang Ekspres. "Pedagang dan Parkir Masalah Klasik Pariwisata". 7 August 2015 <http://www.koran.padek.co/read/detail/33837> (accessed 20 August 2016).

Padang Media. "Dilematis, Pembangunan Terhambat karena Warga Bertahan". 8 July 2014 <http://www.padangmedia.com/1-Berita/88383-Dilematis--Pembangunan-Terhambat-Karena-Warga-Bertahan.html> (accessed 28 September 2016).

Padangtime. "Devi Kurnia: Jangan Biarkan Generasi Muda Tidak Mengenal Adat dan Budaya Minagkabau". 25 September 2015 <http://padangtime.com/read-3678--devi-kurnia-jangan-biarkan-generasi-muda-tidak-mengenal-adat-dan-budaya-minangkabau.html> (accessed 9 September 2016).

Peletz, Michael G. "The Exchange of Men in Nineteenth Century Negeri Sembilan (Malaya)". *American Ethnologist* 14, no. 3 (1987): 449–69.

———. "Comparative Perspectives on Kinship and Cultural Identity in Negeri Sembilan". *Sojourn: Journal of Social Issues in Southeast Asia* 9, no. 1 (1994): 1–53.

Pemerintah Kabupaten Banyumas. "Biro Hukum Provinsi Jateng Sosialisasikan Perda Pendidikan dan Bahasa Jawa di Banyumas". 19 June 2013 <http://www.banyumaskab.go.id/read/15697/biro-hukum-provinsi-jateng-sosialisasikan-perda-pendidikan-dan-bahasa-jawa-di-banyumas> (accessed 19 July 2016).

Pemerintah Kota Bukittinggi. "Refungsi KAN sebagai Katup Penyelamat (Safety Valve) Konflik Pertanahan di Sumbar". 2 May 2016 <http://www.bukittinggikota.go.id/index.php?file_id=47&class=news&act=read&news_id=17107> (accessed 29 July 2016).

Pemerintah Kota Padang. *RPJM Kota Padang, 2009–2014*. Padang: Pemerintah Kota Padang, 2008.

———. *Profil Kota Padang*. 2016 <http://www.padang.go.id/index.php/gambaran-umum-kota-padang> (accessed 20 August 2016).

Perpustakaan Muslim Indonesia. "Meninggal di Tanah Haram, Mati Syahid?". 2015 <http://www.perpusmuslim.com/2015/10/meninggal-di-tanah-haram-mati-syahid.html> (accessed 14 July 2016).

Perserikatan Muhammadiyah. "Beranda". 2016 <http://www.muhammadiyah.or.id/> (accessed 16 July 2016).

Phillips, Nigel. "Notes on Modern Literature in West Sumatra". *Indonesia Circle* 5, no. 12 (1977): 26–32.

Pikiran Rakyat. "Perda Bahasa Jangan Jadi Macan Ompong". 18 March 2015 <http://www.pikiran-rakyat.com/seni-budaya/2015/03/18/320359/perda-bahasa-daerah-jangan-jadi-macan-ompong> (accessed 19 July 2016).

Pratomo, Harwanto Bimo. "Di Era Soeharto, Petani Indonesia Menjadi Penyumbang Pangan Dunia". *Merdeka*, 29 April 2015 <https://www.merdeka.com/uang/di-era-soeharto-petani-indonesia-menjadi-penyumbang-pangan-dunia.html> (accessed 22 September 2016).

Prins, Jan. *Adat en Islamietische plichtenleer in Indonesië*. 's-Gravenhage/Bandoeng: W. van Hoeve, 1954.

Publika News. "Agar Adat Minang Tak Lagi Sebatas Retorika". 21 March 2012 <http://www.publikanews.com/2012/03/agar-adat-minang-tak-lagi-sebatas.html> (accessed 3 September 2016).

Purbaya. "Duh! 2,8 Juta Lansia di Indonesia Terlantar". 20 September 2013 <http://news.detik.com/read/2013/09/20/213955/2365230/10/duh-28-juta-lansia-di-indonesia-terlantar> (accessed 18 September 2014).

Puspitasari, Lia and Kenichi Ishii. "Digital Divides and Mobile Internet in Indonesia: Impact of Smartphones". *Telematics and Informatics* 33, no. 2 (2016): 472–83.

Putri, Rima Berlian and Fredia Heppy. "Hubungan Depresi dengan Kejadian Insomnia pada Lansia di Panti Sosial Tresna Werdha Kasih Sayang Ibu Batusangkar". *Jurnal Kesehatan* 5, no. 1 (2016): 82–91.

Rahmat, Mardikola Tri. "Wabup: 3.100 Lansia di Lima Puluh Kota Terlantar". *Antara News*, 27 April 2016 <http://www.antarasumbar.com/berita/175635/wabup-3100-lansia-di-limapuluh-kota-terlantar.html> (accessed 28 July 2016).

Rastogi, Vaishali, Eddy Tamboto, Dean Tong and Tunnee Sinburimsit. *Indonesia's Rising Middle-Class and Affluent Consumers: Asia's Next big Opportunity*. Boston Consulting Group, 2014 <https://www.bcgperspectives.com/content/articles/center_consumer_customer_insight_consumer_products_indonesias_rising_middle_class_affluent_consumers/> (accessed 5 March 2015).

Republic of Indonesia. *Undang-Undang Nomor 52 Tahun 2009 tentang Perkembangan Kependudukan dan Pembangunan Keluarga*. Jakarta: Republik Indonesia, 2009.

Republika. "Jamaah Haji Percaya Meninggal Saat Berhaji akan Masuk Sorga". 21 September 2014a <http://www.republika.co.id/berita/jurnal-haji/berita-jurnal-haji/14/09/21/nc8vmn-jamaah-haji-percaya-meninggal-saat-berhaji-akan-masuk-surga> (accessed 14 July 2016).

———. "Perda Bahasa Daerah di DIY Tunggu UU Kebudayaan Disahkan". 8 May 2014b <http://www.republika.co.id/berita/nasional/jawa-tengah-diy-nasional/14/05/08/n597uo-perda-bahasa-daerah-di-diy-tunggu-uu-kebudayaan-disahkan> (accessed 18 September 2016).

Riau Mandiri. "BPS: Pedesaan Sumbar Masih Rentan Kemiskinan". 20 July 2016 <http://riaumandiri.co/read/detail/37150/bps-:-pedesaan-sumbar-masih-rentan-kemiskinan.html> (accessed 28 July 2016).

Ricklefs, Merle Calvin. *A History of Modern Indonesia since c. 1200*. Basingstoke and New York: Palgrave Macmillan, 2008.

Romney, A. Kimball and Carmella C. Moore. "Toward a Theory of Culture as Shared Cognitive Structures". *Ethos* 26, no. 3 (1998): 314–37.

———, Susan C. Weller and William H. Batchelder. "Culture as Consensus: A Theory of Culture and Informant Accuracy". *American Anthropologist* 88, no. 2 (1986): 313–38.

Ryan, Ellen Bouchard, Sheree Kwong See, W. Bryan Meneer and Diane Trovato. "Age-Based Perceptions of Language Performance among Younger and Older Adults". *Communication Research* 19, no. 4 (1992): 423–43.

Sakur, Yunistianningsih, Moh. Karmin Baruadii and Sance Lamus. "Penggunaan Bahasa Buol pada Ranah Keluarga Kawin Silang di Desa Lintidu Kecamatan Paleleh Kabupaten Buol". *KIM Fakultas Sastra dan Budaya* 3, no. 2 (2015): 3–12.

Salari, Sonia. "Invisible in Aging Research Arab Americans, Middle Eastern Immigrants, and Muslims in the United States". *The Gerontologist* 42, no. 5 (2002): 580–88.

Salleh, Abdul Razak, Harry Ramza and Mohammad Alinor Abdul Karim, eds. *Diaspora, Adat dan Kekerabatan Minangkabau*. Jakarta: Kemala Indonesia, 2015.

Sari, Merita and Ni Luh. "Penggunaan Bahasa Bali dalam Keluarga Kawin Campur Bali-Jawa di Kelurahan Kerobokan Kelod, Kecamatan Kuta Utara, Kabupaten Badung". *Humanis* 15, no. 1 (2016): 64–71.

Sartini, Ni Wayan. "Perilaku Bahasa Diaspora Orang Bali di Jawa Timur: Kajian Sosiolinguistik". *Jurnal Keilmuan Bahasa, Sastra, dan Pengajarannya* 1, no. 1 (2015): 54–62.

Schmid, Monika S. "First Language Attrition". *Wiley Interdisciplinary Reviews: Cognitive Science* 4, no. 2 (2013): 117–23.

Schröder-Butterfill, Elisabeth. "Inter-Generational Family Support Provided by Older People in Indonesia". *Ageing and Society* 24, no. 4 (2004): 497–530.

—— and Ruly Marianti. "A Framework for Understanding Old-Age Vulnerabilities". *Ageing & Society* 26, no. 1 (2006): 9–35.

—— and Tengku Syawila Fithry. "Care Dependence in Old Age: Preferences, Practices and Implications in Two Indonesian Communities". *Ageing & Society* 34, no. 3 (2014): 361–87.

Searle, John R. *The Construction of Social Reality*. New York: Simon and Schuster, 1995.

Seliger, Herbert W. and Robert M. Vago. *First Language Attrition*. Cambridge: Cambridge University Press, 1991.

Sen, Krishna and David T. Hill. *Media, Culture and Politics in Indonesia*. Singapore: Equinox Publishing, 2006.

Septiningsih, Dyah Siti and Tri Na'imah. "Kesepian Pada Lanjut Usia: Studi tentang Bentuk, Faktor Pencetus dan Strategi Koping". *Jurnal Psikologi Undip* 11, no. 2 (2012): 1–9.

Setijanti, Purwanita, Johan Silas, Susetyo Firmaningtyas and Hartatik. "Eksistensi Rumah Tradisional Padang dalam Menghadapi Iklim dan Tantangan Jaman". In *Simposium Nasional RAPI IX FT UMS*, pp. 54–62. Surakarta: Universitas Muhammadiyah Surakarta, 2012.

Singgalang. "Bertekad Majukan Sumbar DPP – IKM Disosialisasikan". 29 July 2016 <http://hariansinggalang.co.id/bertekad-majukan-sumbar-dpp-ikm-disosialisasikan/> (accessed 30 July 2016).

Sinthania, Debby. "Studi Fenomenologi: Pengalaman Interaksi Sosial Lansia Dengan Sesama Lansia Dan Pengasuh Di Panti Sosial Tresna Werdha 'Sabai Nan Aluih' Sicincin Kabupaten Padang Pariaman". *Jurnal Kesehatan* 6, no. 2 (2015): 118–25.

Smith-Hefner, Nancy J. "Youth Language, Gaul Sociability, and the New Indonesian Middle Class". *Journal of Linguistic Anthropology* 17, no. 2 (2007): 184–203.

Sneddon, James Neil. "Diglossia in Indonesian". *Bijdragen tot de Taal-, Land-en Volkenkunde* 159, no. 4 (2003a): 519–49.

———. *The Indonesian Language*. Sydney: University of New South Wales, 2003b.

Soderberg, Craig D. and Kenneth S. Olson. "Indonesian". *Journal of the International Phonetic Association* 38, no. 2 (2008): 209–13.

Solo Pos. "Merindukan Perda Bahasa Jawa". 6 December 2011 <http://www.solopos.com/2011/12/06/merindukan-perda-bahasa-jawa-127399> (accessed 18 September 2016).

Sperber, Dan. "Anthropology and Psychology: Towards an Epidemiology of Representations". *Man* 20, no. 1 (1985): 73–89.

Spolsky, Bernard. *Language Policy*. Cambridge: Cambridge University Press, 2004.

Stark, Alexander. "The Matrilineal System of the Minangkabau and its Persistence Throughout History: A Structural Perspective". *Southeast Asia: A Multidisciplinary Journal* 13 (2013): 1–13.

Strauss, Claudia and Naomi Quinn. *A Cognitive Theory of Cultural Meaning*. Cambridge: Cambridge University Press, 1997.

Stuart, Mary and Michael Weinrich. "Home-and Community-Based Long-Term Care Lessons from Denmark". *The Gerontologist* 41, no. 4 (2001): 474–80.

Suara Pembaruan. "2,8 Lansia Terlantar Butuh Uluran Tangan". 29 May 2013 <http://www.suarapembaruan.com/home/28-juta-lansia-terlantar-butuh-uluran-tangan/36270> (accessed 18 September 2016).

Sudadi. "Proses Pembangunan di Papua Masih Terhambat Sengketa Tanah Adat". 6 April 2014 <http://suarapapua.org/2014/04/13/proses-pembangunan-di-papua-masih-terhambat-sengketa-tanah-adat/> (accessed 19 September 2014).

Sudha, Shreeniwas and Elizabeth J. Mutran. "Ethnicity and Eldercare Comparison of Attitudes toward Adult Care Homes and Care by Families". *Research on Aging* 21, no. 4 (1999): 570–94.

Sudradjat, Adjat. "Mensos: 126.000 Lansia Terima Bantuan pada Juni". *Antara News*, 13 April 2016 <http://www.antarasumbar.com/berita/174602/mensos-126000-lansia-terima-bantuan-pada-juni.html> (accessed 30 August 2016).

Sumarty, Betty and Nur Azizah. *Revitalisasi Peran Ninik Mamak dalam Pemerintahan Nagari*. Yogyakarta: Universitas Gadjah Mada, 2007.

Sumbar Satu. "Kapolres Agam: Kekerabatan Minang yang Masih Kuat Modal Utama Menekan Masalah Sosial". 9 February 2015 <http://www.sumbarsatu.com/berita/9516-kapolres-agam-kekerabatan-minang-yang-masih-kuat-modal-utama-menekan-masalah-sosial> (accessed 2 October 2016).

Suprapto, Hadi. "85% Pedagang Tanah Abang Asal Padang". *VivaNews*, 6 October 2009 <http://bisnis.news.viva.co.id/news/read/94714-orang_padang_kuasai_pasar_tanah_abang> (accessed 17 September 2016).

Sutrisno, Elvan Dany. "Ketua MPR dan Muhammadiyah Bahas Pengeloalaan Lansia". *Detik News*, 6 January 2016 <http://news.detik.com/berita/3112092/ketua-mpr-dan-muhammadiyah-bahas-pengelolaan-lansia> (accessed 16 July 2016).

Syukra, Anita. *Hubungan antara Religiusitas dengan Kejadian Depresi pada Lansia di Panti Sosial Tresna Werdha (PSTW) Sabai nan Aluih Sicincin Kabupaten Padang Pariaman*. Padang, West Sumatra: Universitas Andalas, 2012.

Tamrin, Tamrin. "Pemertahanan Bahasa Bugis dalam Ranah Kelkuarga di Negeri Rantau Sulawesi Tenga". *Sawerigading* 20, no. 3 (2016): 403–12.

Tas' ady, Rafsel, Ismet Fanany and Rebecca Fanany. "Sickness Ruins the Complexion, Breeding Disappears without Gold: Culture and the Interpretation of Illness among the Minangkabau of West Sumatra, Indonesia". *International Journal of Health, Wellness and Society* 2, no. 4 (2012): 31–41.

Taufik, Irfan. "Warnet Tutup dari Buka Puasa Sampai Tarawih". *Antara News*, 22 June 2015 <http://www.antarasumbar.com/berita/150830/warnet-diminta-tutup-dari-buka-puasa-sampai-tarawih.html> (accessed 12 July 2016).

Teeuw, Andries. "The History of the Malay Language". *Bijdragen tot de Taal-, Land- en Volkenkunde* 2de Afl (1959): 138–56.

———. "The Impact of Balai Pustaka on Modern Indonesian Literature". *Bulletin of the School of Oriental and African Studies* 35, no. 1 (1972): 111–27.

Tempo. "Di Padang, Fauzi Bowo Puji Perantau Minang". 6 September 2012 <https://m.tempo.co/read/news/2012/09/06/230427758/di-padang-fauzi-bowo-puji-perantau-minang> (accessed 1 September 2016).

———. "Mitos dan Fakter Gerhana Matahari Total di Indonesia". 22 January 2016 <https://m.tempo.co/read/news/2016/01/22/095738452/mitos-dan-fakta-gerhana-matahari-total-di-indonesia> (accessed 12 July 2016).

Thornton, Robert and Leah L. Light. "Language Comprehension and Production in Normal Aging". In *Handbook of the Psychology of Aging*, edited by K. Warner Schaie and Sherry L. Willis, pp. 261–88. New York, San Francisco and London: Academic Press, 2006.

Uker, Damres and Rebecca Fanany. "The Traditional Decision-Making Process of Berkaul in Tanjung Emas, West Sumatra: Its Nature and Significance". *Sojourn: Journal of Social Issues in Southeast Asia* 26, no. 1 (2011): 1–15.

United National Population Fund. "UNFPA Award Laureates". 2014 <http://www.unfpa.org/public/home/about/popaward/pid/4641> (accessed 18 July 2016).

United Nations. *World Mortality Report 2009*. New York: United Nations, Population Division, 2011.

Vago, Robert M. "Paradigmatic Regularity in First Language Attrition". In *First Language Attrition*, edited by Herbert W. Seliger and Robert M. Vago, pp. 241–52. Cambridge: Cambridge University Press, 1991.

Van Eeuwijk, Peter. "Urban Elderly with Chronic Illness: Local Understandings and Emerging Discrepancies in North Sulawesi, Indonesia". *Anthropology & Medicine* 10, no. 3 (2003): 325–41.

Vaswani, Karishma. "Indonesia's Love Affair with Social Media". *BBC News Asia*, 16 February 2012 <http://www.bbc.co.uk/news/world-asia-17054056> (accessed 20 August 2016).

Viva News. "Lebaran, Lansia di Panti Jompo Berharap Dijenguk Keluarga". 7 July 2016 <http://www.viva.co.id/video/read/57441-lebaran-lansia-di-panti-jompo-berharap-dijenguk-keluarga> (accessed 12 September 2016).

von Benda-Beckmann, Franz and Keebet von Benda-Beckmann. *Political and Legal Transformations of an Indonesian Polity: The Nagari from Colonisation to Decentralisation*. Cambridge: Cambridge University Press, 2013.

Waters, Gloria S. and David Caplan. "Age, Working Memory, and On-Line Syntactic Processing in Sentence Comprehension". *Psychology and Aging* 16, no. 1 (2001): 128–44.

Wheaton, Blair. "Models for the Stress-Buffering Functions of Coping Resources". *Journal of Health and Social Behavior* 26, no. 4 (1985): 352–64.

Widodo, Supriyanto. "Pemertahanan Bahasa Ibu: Studi Kasus Bahasa Jawa di Papua". *Kibas Cendrawasih: Jurnal Kebahasaan dan Kesastraan* 10, no. 2 (2016): 103–8.

Widyanto, Untung. "Masyarakat Adat Usulkan Indigenisasi Pembangunan". Tempo Online, 6 September 2012 <http://www.tempo.co/read/news/2012/09/06/078427922/Masyarakat-Adat-Usulkan-Indigenisasi-Pembangunan> (accessed 19 September 2014).

Wilkinson, Richard G. and Michael Gideon Marmot. *Social Determinants of Health: The Solid Facts*. Copenhagen: World Health Organization, 2003.

Wingfield, Arthur and Elizabeth A.L. Stine-Morrow. "Language and Speech". In *The Handbook of Aging and Cognition*, edited by Fergus I. M. Craik and Timothy A. Salthouse, pp. 359–415. New York: Lawrence Erlbaum Associates, 2000.

World Bank. "December 2017 Indonesia Economic Quarterly: Decentralization that Delivers". World Bank Databank, 2017 <http://www.worldbank.org/en/country/indonesia/publication/indonesia-economic-quarterly-december-2017> (accessed 11 March 2018).

———. "Fertility Rates, Total". World Bank Databank, 2018 <https://data.worldbank.org/indicator/SP.DYN.TFRT.IN> (accessed 11 March 2018).

World Health Organization. *WHO Country Cooperation Strategy, 2007–2011*. Geneva: WHO, 2008.

———, ed. *Global Health Risks: Mortality and Burden of Disease Attributable to Selected Major Risks*. Geneva: WHO, 2009.

———. "Global Health Observatory". 2013 <http://apps.who.int/gho/data/node.main.3?lang=en> (accessed 18 July 2016).

————. "Indonesia Country Profile". 2014 <http://www.who.int/countries/idn/en/> (accessed 18 July 2016).

Yayasan Stroke Indonesia. "Indonesia Tempati Urutan Pertama di Dunia dalam Jumlah Terbanyak Penderita Stroke". 2012 <http://www.yastroki.or.id/read.php?id=341> (accessed 31 August 2016).

Yeni, Fitra. "Hubungan Emosi Positif dengan Kepuasan Hidup Pada Lanjut Usia (LANSIA) di Kota Padang Provinsi Sumatera Barat". *Jurnal Ners* 9, no. 1 (2016): 10–21.

Zulfihendri, Jimy. "Analisis Fonologi Bahasa Minangkabau di Kanagarian Silongo Kabupaten Sijunjung". *Hantaran* 4, no. 2 (2015): 1–23.

INDEX

ABOUT THE AUTHORS

Rebecca Fanany has a PhD in Public Health from University of Tasmania. She is currently in the School of Health, Medical and Applied Sciences at Central Queensland University in Melbourne, Australia. Her research centres on the impact of language and culture on health and illness, with a focus on cultural consonance and the conceptualization of health. She has many years of experience in Asia and Indonesia where she has several long-term research relationships and collaborations and has worked with WHO and UNESCAP in the region. She is the author of several books and numerous articles and publications. Her textbook, *Health as a Social Experience*, is an introduction to the social determinants of health that is used at both the undergraduate and postgraduate levels. The present work is the result of several years of research in West Sumatra and other parts of Indonesia and reflects ongoing study of health and social change.

Ismet Fanany is a sociolinguist with a PhD from Cornell University. He is currently Professor of Language and Society in the School of Humanities and Social Sciences at Deakin University in Melbourne. His interests relate to the experience of ageing and social change in modern Indonesia, in particular the interaction between local and national culture with an emphasis on language and language issues. He has worked with universities and other institutions across Indonesia and is a well-known writer and social commentator. In addition to a range of scholarly works on topics such as disaster reconstruction, ageing in Indonesia, and the development of the Indonesian language, he is the author of many short stories and two novels and has a strong interest in modern Indonesian society in the global context. The research presented in this book represents an integration of these elements in an interdisciplinary approach to ageing in a traditional society in a modern nation.

www.ingramcontent.com/pod-product-compliance
Lightning Source LLC
Chambersburg PA
CBHW060146280326
41932CB00012B/1653